Festival, Culture, and Identity in Lübeck

Festival, Culture, and Identity in Lübeck

Nordic Days, 1920–1960

Erika L. Briesacher

LEXINGTON BOOKS
Lanham • Boulder • New York • London

Published by Lexington Books
An imprint of The Rowman & Littlefield Publishing Group, Inc.
4501 Forbes Boulevard, Suite 200, Lanham, Maryland 20706
www.rowman.com

86-90 Paul Street, London EC2A 4NE

British Library Cataloguing in Publication Information Available

Library of Congress Cataloging-in-Publication Data Is Available

ISBN: 978-1-4985-8501-9 (cloth : alk. paper)
ISBN: 978-1-4985-8502-6 (electronic)

♾™ The paper used in this publication meets the minimum requirements of American National Standard for Information Sciences—Permanence of Paper for Printed Library Materials, ANSI/NISO Z39.48-1992.

For Team Mongoose—you've always been the reason.

Contents

Acknowledgments

Acknowledgments are always the hardest to write, at least for me. I want to ensure I name and amplify everyone who helped me along the way, who challenged and shaped my thinking, and who are "my people" in a variety of ways. This project, in some form or another, has stretched across nearly seventeen years, many degrees (not only just mine), three institutions in three different states, moves, and a pandemic. I've benefited from fantastic family and friends, teachers, colleagues, students, archivists, librarians, and institutions. To try and name all of them is likely impossible, but I would be remiss if I didn't try to name as many as I can.

First, many, many thanks to Eric Kuntzman, my ever-patient editor at Lexington Books, along with Rachel Kirkland, Alexandra Rallo, Kasey Beduhn, and Brian Hill, as well as the blind reviewer who gave me incredibly valuable notes. This project continually stretched longer than I intended or wanted it to, interrupted as it was by the novel coronavirus. In any case, I could not have brought it to fruition without you all. Special thanks to Varsha Venkatasubramanian, who skillfully and thoughtfully indexed the book. In the same vein, I want to thank the Graduate Student Senate at Kent State University and Academic Affairs at Worcester State University, both of which provided important funds for foundational research. Archivists and staff at the Hansestadt Archiv Lübeck, the Altonaer Museum in Hamburg, the Kiel Stadtarchiv, the Kent State University Library, the Newberry Library, the University of North Carolina-Wilmington special collections, the University of North Carolina-Chapel Hill library, and the University Museum at Southern Illinois University Edwardsville. This project would not exist without the varied, diverse, and dynamic collections at each institution. Special thanks as well to the library staff at Worcester State University, who tracked down all manner of resources for me.

Beyond editors and institutions, I have been guided and shaped by numerous teachers and mentors. First, I thank my doctoral adviser, Richard Steigmann-Gall, who has provided suggestions and support, from my dissertation to my manuscript; even though my first instinct is to go to the theory, I'm more mindful of the evidence as well. Additional necessary thanks to my doctoral committee—Shelley Baranowski, Rebecca Pulju, Stephen Harp, and David Purcell—whose comments, courses, ideas, and questions throughout the first iteration of this project informed the entire process. I would be remiss if I didn't mention important mentors from my MA program, especially Laura Milsk Fowler, Christienne Hinz, and Leigh Anne Eubanks, who all shaped my approach to history and research in profound ways. Thanks to Jared Poley; as an editor and mentor, you've been invaluable.

More than anything, I've been incredibly lucky to have fantastic colleagues. Beginning in graduate school and continuing in my career at Worcester State, I'm thankful to be able to talk shop, challenge and interrogate ideas and concepts, and laugh (and rant) a lot. I consider you more than just colleagues. So, in no particular order (and as complete a list as I think I have), thank you to Tanya Mears, Alison Okuda, Dionna Richardson, Elizabeth Siler, Amber Vayo, Charlotte Haller, Bob Smith, Tona Hangen, Tom Conroy, Josh Koenig, Colleen Sullivan, Jeremy Andreatta, Maddy Campbell, Monika Flaschka, Jessica Leveto, Matt Phillips, Jeff O'Leary, Greg Jones, Mike Hill, Carrie Ray Hill, Kate Stewart, Sarah O'Keeffe, Denise Jenison, Rachel Boaz, Ursula Dalinghaus, Mike Baker, Steve Corvi, and many others. Special thanks for the editing genius (of the proposal as well as the manuscript) to Dr. Lisa A. Kramer—it's a much better product because of you. To my students, both graduate and undergraduate, who have become my colleagues, I appreciate the trust you put in me and the work we do; special mention to Michelle Henault, Ann Lane, Brian Volk, Christopher Ives, Shawn Driscoll, Matthew Vajda, Tim Jarvis, Augusto "Goose" Diaz, Mo Maloney, Dan Cook, and Karen Potter. Your provocative and thoughtful questions, the comments on drafts, and everything else mean more than you know.

Lastly, family and friends. This has been a long journey, and it hasn't always been easy. To my siblings and their families, siblings-in-law and their family, my mother-in-law, and my Mom, thank you for braving months at a time with me and transatlantic ship travel, constantly hearing about this project whether I was excited or frustrated. I don't say it enough, but I appreciate every minute of it (even when we missed the train . . . a few times). To aunts, uncles, and cousins, thank you for putting up with my chatter when it wasn't always clear what I was talking about. To the Honorary family, especially Shannon Hines, Zach Goebelt, Jeremy Coffman, Efrén Hernández, Michele Zimmerman, Dionna Richardson and Omar Alayyubi, Jeff and Kate Stumpo, Lisa Kramer and Nathan Lee, Paul and Patty Butenhoff (Paul's many draft readings!), and many more, thank you so much for your support. To new friends Svea and Jürgen Feldhoff in Lübeck and Helga and Arno Müller in QM2/Hamburg/Travemünde, I thank you for the depth of knowledge and friendship you freely gave us. To my dad and my father-in-law, neither of whom saw any part of this project, thank you for being part of it anyway.

And finally, to Alex, Kael, Tobin, and Annika, thank you. I'm not quite sure how to put into words how very necessary you have been, how much you sacrificed for research trips, and how much you've cheered me on. I couldn't do it without you.

Introduction

Arriving in Lübeck's main train station, a modern building with shops, a McDonald's, and a travel bureau housed in a contained historic façade, belies the geographic and metaphorical sprawl of the city itself. Home to four platforms and ten tracks, the Lübeck station (*Hauptbahnhof*, or Hbf) lacks the overwhelming enormity of the Hamburg main station only 50 kilometers away. Its history of back-and-forth upkeep, decline, and restoration embodies the history of Lübeck itself. In many ways contingent upon surrounding environs or in-the-moment necessities, the Lübeck station is an understated welcome to a city made up of diverse districts and neighborhoods, stretching from a rural interior to the Baltic Sea and over to the border with Mecklenburg-Vorpommern—the former border with East Germany. The thoroughfare that leads to the main westerly road to the central district—the historic *Innenstadt*—takes one across the Trave Canal and faces immediately the medieval-gate-turned-museum, the Holstentor. Lining the canal set behind the Holstentor are the blocks of buildings topped by quintessential northern-European stepped facades. Iconic as the Holstentor and architectural skyline is to the city of Lübeck (the Holstentor is a representative structure of Lübeck throughout Germany and the rest of Europe), the red brick structure welcomes citizens and guests alike, itself also an embodiment of the long history of a town and its people. Guarding against invaders during the Hanseatic era, ravaged during the occupation, and repurposed during and after the Third Reich, the Holstentor as much as the main train station provides an initial introduction to the complexities that make up the city of Lübeck, its history, and its people.

My first trip to Lübeck in the summer of 2010 did not have this initial introduction. Arriving via auto after a days-long voyage on ship and train, I entered the city on the A1 hardly paying attention to my surroundings outside of fellow drivers. I only sought my apartment, the proper place to deposit my rental car, and food. I remember so little of this first entry into Lübeck, and it's almost disappointing. When I returned in 2015 for a second research trip, though, I was able to experience Lübeck by rail and the Holstentor. Seeing the city this way, and realizing how those buildings fit together and present themselves in context allows the spaces and places of the city to become texts all their own, understood in a variety of ways depending on the reader's background, previous experience, and location in time and space. That June, I had the good fortune to attend the annual Lübeck *Volksfest* parade with new local friends who were eager to show off their homes. We met at the *Alten Zolln*, billed as the oldest tavern in the city, to watch the lengthy parade and partake in food, drink, and conversation. It was another eye-opening experience, this time from inside the central district and shaped by the narrative of people versed in informal, prosaic knowledge of Lübeck's history, stories, and myth.

This parade and the accompanying town festival simultaneously served as a testament to heritage as well as a look toward the future, demonstrating how culture, identity, politics, and economy are intermingled in the life of a city and its people. The day with our friends stretched into the evening, as we walked the streets of the *Innenstadt*, hearing about the lore of the buildings and city as well as stories about their own lived experiences. The carnival just across the Trave Canal could have been situated in my native Wisconsin, but for the language, the kitsch, and the atmosphere. After eating a fantastic burger at a local restaurant, we said our goodbyes and I felt like I *knew* and appreciated the city better than I ever had before. My participation in the *Volksfest* events and shared experience with Lübecker friends echoed the process by which people construct, communicate, and perform their world and their place in it.

This book is about a city: a city through the eyes of outsiders and locals, a city of inclusion and exclusion, a city on shifting borders and in governments that sought to use it and its people in a multitude of ways. This book is also about the people of Lübeck and the way(s) they saw and presented themselves, to each other and to visitors, in the construction and constant renegotiation of what their city and by extension their lives and experiences meant in changing historical and cultural contexts. The objects and events they produced give us the sense that, more than just the influence of structural forces like a turbulent economy or the realities of politics, people in Lübeck made choices to affect the direction they would go and the ways in which they would perform and present their city. Studying midsized towns like Lübeck remind us that populations outside major metropolitan areas face equally contentious social, economic, and political pressures, often without the attention or resources of larger cities. Part of the reason Lübeck is so important is that it was *not* a major economic or political hub after World War I. Its reputation rested on its Hanseatic tradition and its cultural contributions to the region and the nation.

At the same time, though, this book is about more than the city itself. Rather, this book uses a particular place—Lübeck—as a way to uncover "how we think about local history, about context and complexity, about the growth of community and the perpetuation of memory."[1] People frame (extra)ordinary times in personal and connective ways, and these ways are often guided by institutions' attempts to shape how everyday people think about themselves and their community. To that end, this helps bring another central theme of this study into focus: the importance of everyday economic concerns, in individual and collective decision-making. Lübeck provides a vital and dynamic example where finance, culture, and identity combined and evolved to help shape twentieth-century Germany. Lübeck's population had to define itself in new contexts—a democratic Germany in new international systems in the 1920s and the 1950s, wildly dramatic economic circumstances, an authoritarian racist regime—and its leaders chose to do so through cultural festivals and continual efforts to ensure the city's vitality and sustenance. It built on an already emergent community of collectors and cultural tourists who took advantage of the economic climate and turned currency into a collectible.[2]

For Germany, in particular, World War I forced an intense political change from authoritarian monarchy to liberal democracy. Not only did Germans navigate deprivation at home, riots and mutiny, and the abdication of the Kaiser, they had to cobble together a functional government while awaiting peace terms. For its part, the goals of the leaders of the Weimar Republic were sharply different from those of Imperial Germany or, indeed, any conception of a German nation-state up until the twentieth century. Consensus building underscored the Weimar Constitution, at least according to dominant parties' platforms. Gone was the Prussian tiered voting structure; gone was the official dominance of the *Junker* class in politics. Also gone was the swagger that accompanied the Wilhelmine war machine, replaced with a severely decentered sense of identity. And just as quickly, extremists on both the left and right sought to destroy the fledgling republic.

In this postwar context, the city of Lübeck began planning a ten-day festival, *Nordische Woche* [Nordic Week], designed to call attention to the city, its heritage, and its interconnectedness with its Scandinavian neighbors. The resulting event echoed beyond the 1921 festival, adapted to the needs of the Nazis in 1938 and again in the postwar Federal Republic over several years in the 1950s. Because of this, the theme of festival, which centers financial, social, and cultural discourses and motivations, is a third central narrative of this book. As Jonathan Sperber has observed, "Always an arena of mass participation in public life, festivals have been, since 1789, intimately connected with the revolutionary process. The parades, banners, posters, decorations, temporary statuary, songs and speeches . . . create a rich and varied field of symbols, ideal for semiotic investigation."[3]

More than a local affair, *Nordische Woche* had the trappings of an international-regional fair, smaller than world's fairs, which became a common site of calculated sociocultural constructions of national identity for exhibitors and attendees alike in the late nineteenth and early twentieth centuries. These fairs also presented economic and political opportunities for planners and elite supporters. Lübeck's *Nordische Woche* cemented new frames of discourse and redefined old interpretations and symbols within the framework of the Weimar Republic. Wooing visitors and an audience to *Nordische Woche* with the promise of collectible notes and a trade show, Lübeck defined not only its own identity but also what German identity on the Baltic Sea would and could look like. It also foreshadowed the ways German identity excluded whole communities and allowed for ideological in-groups to frame and execute genocide with mass support.

Tying the lenses of place, economic concerns, and festival together is the overarching theme of how German national identity after two world wars re-emerged and was rehabilitated, and how regions and municipalities fit into these national narratives. How did the locality of Lübeck invent both itself and the German nation in the wake of global war? Additionally, how did Germans negotiate the very real tensions between local, regional, and national identity in an international context? How, in particular, did Lübeckers construct, express, and reconstruct these identities, living as they did in the shadows of bigger and more affluent metropolises and on shifting borders? The answer to many of these questions started with economic answers, grounded in real anxiety over both individual and collective survival. The pursuit of fiscal and even social stability provided rhetorical justification and even cover to increasingly myopic and destructive policies and ideology. This was especially true after World War I and, later, the onset of the global Great Depression, allowing many Lübeckers to wrap deep-seated racialist attitudes in economic and nationalist language.

Scholars have persistently analyzed how nationalism functioned in Germany, highlighting how regions and localities negotiated a national context, in part because of how relatively late Germany unified.[4] Additionally, the existence of *two* Germanys after World War II complicates how nationalism is typically understood, keeping German nationalism a major topic of study. This book sheds light on the roles of regionalism and internationalism in German nationalism, particularly as national identity was rebuilt after the world wars. In addition, my analytical foci demonstrate the fragmented and multivalent nature of German culture, one that was susceptible to the blandishments of the Nazi appeal, yet sought to attain a stable, more cohesive structure. This expands upon previous perceptive and insightful investigations by analyzing how Lübeckers and other northwestern Germans, present on historic borderlands with Denmark, the Baltic, and the "East," discussed and constructed their German national identity. The centrality of the national question in twentieth-century Germany—the location of borders, the ways that Germans connected to each other, the primacy of language in spite of varied regional *Plattdeutsch* (so-called "low German") dialects—contextualizes the decisions made by a variety of German governments during war and peace framed as economic and social survival.

BACKGROUND AND CONTEXTS

The era after World War I ushered in a new normal for Germans, and Lübeckers in particular. Persistent economic instability, diplomatic isolation, and social dislocation plagued the beginning of the Weimar Republic. Though there were attempts to strengthen and highlight nationalist rhetoric and policy, the historic regionalism of Germany flourished and the legitimacy of the government was ostensibly in the people's hands. The constitution was an invention of "the German people [*Volk*], united . . . and inspired by the determination to renew and establish its realm of freedom and justice."[5] While the preamble explicitly put "the people" in charge, it opened up many questions about how to do that. The sense that this was a stark divergence from past political structures contributes to the tendency to analyze German history as a series of stops and starts, lurching from conflict to conflict instigating dramatic change. It was true there were some major differences, but there were continuities as well, as this study will demonstrate.

Europe, too, confronted how the war had changed it socially, culturally, and politically.[6] The emergence of the League of Nations was evidence of formalizing spaces for European-led international diplomacy and a sense of a globally connected world. Social, political, and economic rules were in flux and had to be rewritten utilizing new voices such as women and the working class, even as traditional elites clung to power. Similar trends emerged in other nations around the world, but Germany provides a dynamic case study to elucidate how those factors and actors interacted on many simultaneous levels. Konrad Jarausch and Michael Geyer made the point that "the Weimar Republic finally offered the Catholic, democratic, and socialist skeptics of Bismarckian unification a chance to reconstruct a shrunken Germany in a more progressive image . . . [and] sought to reconcile conflicting views on the shape of national community by stressing 'the political freedom and responsibility, the ethical dignity of democracy.'"[7] Inherent in the challenges facing Weimar Germany were questions about economic practices, political expression, and sociocultural manifestations of identity that would allow Germans to coalesce around a unified, coherent national identity.

The Weimar Republic, brought into existence contemporaneously with the signing of the Treaty of Versailles, represented a sociopolitical experiment fraught with steps and missteps, triumph and destruction. Against this backdrop, German citizens set about the work of rebuilding their cultural norms, expectations, and attitudes, perhaps mindful that the national master narrative was being rewritten. The Weimar Republic has also fascinated and confounded historians, who often consider the period a product of war and, at times, merely a precedent to Hitler. Still, the Weimar Republic has been called "an idea seeking to become reality."[8]

The search for the essence of the Weimar period and its connections to other periods have launched insightful and dynamic studies ranging from politics to theater and everything in between.[9] Because of this, as I will demonstrate, *Nordische Woche* as public performance sought to draw on cultural foundations of identity, particularly mythology, architecture, music, art, and economic structures. It also resulted in the foundation of the *Nordische Gesellschaft* (Nordic Society, hereafter NG) during the festival. This group claimed to emphasize common roots between Germans and "Nordics" and promote cultural expression, because of the historic and ongoing relationship with close-by Scandinavia.[10] Most important was the expression of identity in an international context, building on notions of geopolitics that incorporated race, nationality, culture, and political boundaries.[11]

It has been argued that world's fairs were "controlled portrayals" of a city's (and, by extension, a nation's) values, "conscious universal representations of what was thought to be progress and modernity, and they were thus both the métier and the ideal rendition of the modern city. Such exhibitions aimed to be object lessons about those beliefs, and often, indeed, their vestiges became the symbols of modern cities."[12] This focus on festivals carried on into the Third Reich and the later Federal Republic of Germany, prompting a second *Nordische Woche* in Hamburg in 1938 and three *Nordische Tage* (Nordic Days) events in 1953, 1954, and 1956. All of these festivals had potentially similar goals, though the cultural context (the interwar period versus the Nazi regime versus the West German state during the Cold War) differed. The way the festivals were connected to each other, however, differed, especially in the wake of World War II. *Nordische Woche* 1938 was essentially excised from collective memory, quarantined from the 1950s as something different and even deviant than the others. This allowed the planners of *Nordische Tage* to embrace the language of "rehabilitation" of Nordic identity in Germany, rather than having to grapple with some of its outcomes.

This is especially prescient in borderlands such as Schleswig-Holstein, where identity was constantly negotiated because the meanings and contexts of national borders changed throughout the early modern and modern periods, at various times being Danish, Prussian, German, or even independent. Building on a common "Nordic" foundation that encompassed the varied national polities, the *NG* increasingly gravitated toward racialist theories and philosophies over the 1920s, and it was later absorbed by Alfred Rosenberg's *Außenpolitisches Amt* [Office of Foreign Affairs] by September 1933. The elements that attracted Rosenberg to the *NG*, especially its activity in formulating racially based ideology, is evident even as early as 1921. While Lübeck's *Nordische Woche* contained ambiguous references to *Volk* and its meanings (particularly in Rudolf Kjellen's sense of *Geopolitik*), the NG became associated with leading racial theorists and race-based academic studies.

The NG claimed that its "work . . . would be free from economic and cultural ideas carried too far."[13] However, by the late 1930s, the NG was deeply involved in the production of the journal *Rasse*, engaging in propagandistic activities in Scandinavia, and putting on the second *Nordische Woche* in Hamburg in 1938, attended by Nazi officials as elite as Heinrich Himmler. Under Nazi control, the NG provided some access to Scandinavia via established contacts and networks. The connection between the Nazi party and the *NG* after 1933 has been highlighted by several scholars, but further analysis of the organization over the course of its lifespan is warranted, especially at the local and middle levels of administration.[14] More than anything, the NG's official rallies [*Reichstagung*] and its journal *Der Norden* reinforced the utility of political theater to make sense of the sprawling, often redundant and internally competitive Nazi bureaucracy. The cultural imprint Lübeck had, despite the decline in national prominence, was evident in the fact that Britain's Royal Air Force (RAF) began large-scale bombing raids on German cities of little strategic significance in an effort to shatter German morale with Lübeck in March 1942.[15] The NG was forced to move to Travemünde, producing much less by late 1944 than it had been as the German war effort collapsed; the capitulation in May 1945 meant that Germans had to confront complicity in and evidence of the Holocaust, denazification, and occupation.

The end of the war brought British occupation and an uncertainty about the fate of the German state. From 1945 until 1949, Lübeck, like other German cities, existed in limbo without a sovereign state and continuing military occupation. Once the Federal Republic of Germany (colloquially West Germany) was established out of merged British, French, and American occupation zones, Lübeckers grappled with being the northern terminus of the border with the German Democratic Republic (East Germany)—or what was persistently and often derogatorily called the "Soviet Zone" just outside Lübeck's city limits. Still considered a minor city, Lübeck wilted in the shadow of Hamburg, Bremen, and Kiel in British and American perceptions of importance and necessity even as the city navigated an influx of tens of thousands of refugees from the East. The subsequent sense that Lübeck was cut off from postwar recovery forced citizens to advocate for themselves in their new capital city, Bonn, and internationally—through the tried-and-true method of regional festival in pursuit of rehabilitation: *Nordische Tage* (Nordic Days).[16] The choices they made impacted the economy, the legacies of war and defeat, and the complexities of an identity that was indelibly tied up in the execution of the Holocaust.

INTERPRETIVE FRAMEWORKS

By 1960, Lübeck was, and remains, an "everyday" city, one that was outside modern-day and economic political power circles; for this reason, Lübeck and other cities like it are important historical foci. The period between 1920 and 1960 marks out spaces of comparison and contrast relating to cultural, social, and political work that historical actors have done, without splintering the history of twentieth-century Europe into blocks of time interrupted by catastrophe or focusing only on the emergence or renegotiation of broad ideologies such as nationalism, Marxism, and fascism.[17] Overall, the themes of festival, identity, inclusion, and exclusion, and the intersections of economy, objects, and behavior consistently appear across this period, clarified by five theoretical trajectories that intertwine to help explain the complexities of this work and the approaches I take in this book. This is not to overly complicate the analysis; rather, using these theorists frame the whys and ways individuals engage with the social world around them.

First and foremost, the study of public life and identity formation is the study of everyday life. The pioneer of this approach was Michel de Certeau, in his work *The Practice of Everyday Life*.[18] Referred to in German as *Alltagsgeschichte*, the study of everyday life allows historians and readers to reconsider already-familiar sources, such as political documents or legal history, in a different way. The challenge associated with this type of history is unpacking the attitudes of individuals in social context, many of whom left no explicit record of their feelings. At the same time, though, individual "everyday" people left clues to their perceptions and ideas in a variety of ways, from popular discourse in letters to newspaper editors to voting with their feet and attending (or not attending) events and functions to their purchasing patterns, what they collected, and opinion polls. These sources indicate the interplay between "strategies and tactics," which de Certeau explained as the ways in which individuals and structures (such as governments or institutions) encounter and navigate everyday life. On the one hand are the "strategies" produced by institutions such as city government—for example the city council in Lübeck—in planning and promoting spectacle, festival, or even law; on the other hand are the "tactics" individuals utilize to consume mass culture and make it personal to them and their lives (such as, for example, Lübeck citizens attending *Nordische Woche* or the three *Nordische Tage*).[19] These behaviors can be analyzed against extraordinary events, tumultuous periods, or stretches of relative calm, highlighting the ways people and institutions adapt to changeable conditions.

De Certeau's work builds on that of Pierre Bourdieu, who analyzed the ways individuals portray their identities and social positions through the display of objects. If de Certeau helps analyze actions, Bourdieu targets taste and objects in social settings, particularly through the concept of "cultural capital." Elaborating on the Marxian category of class, Bourdieu, in his work *Distinction: A Social Critique on the Judgment of Taste*, complicates how people order themselves in society and how they demonstrate their "place."[20] One example is how individuals decorate their homes, especially what they choose to display and what they collect in the context of their purchasing power or according to social mores. At the same time, though, Bourdieu remarked on how status can be ascertained in ways not solely tied to income or monetary wealth. Bourdieu explained the different axes that affect social behavior and patterns in cultural terms, which also demonstrate that elements such as politics or the economy are, at their core, cultural constructions. The degree to which historical actors participate in or benefit from their production owe a great deal to understanding and mobilizing culture in the moment, as well as how that culture shifts or evolves. As Bourdieu argued, "Consumption is, in this case, a stage in a process of communication, that is, as act of deciphering, decoding, which presupposes practical or explicit mastery of a cipher or code."[21] Put another way, one must understand the cultural language before one can belong, and this is not contingent only on purchasing power.[22]

All of this indicates that historical actors are social beings, analyzed contextually and in consideration of the norms and attitudes that framed their world. Emile Durkheim witnessed many of the events of World War I and its resolution, crafting his ideas about society, social facts, and social actors during the 1900s and 1910s when much of Western Europe was transformed. His analysis of society formed the basis for sociology as a field, and his ideas about *anomie* (the condition(s) of normlessness) certainly apply to and even echo events and patterns present in German history.[23] With this in mind, I analyze how economics, politics, and culture intersected, combined, competed, and complemented each other to impact human activity in society. Durkheim's ideas contribute a sociological perspective about events that were fundamentally social, whether it reveals massive social change, ruthless reaction, or even a commitment to status-quo politics of chaos, fear, and uncertainty.

Bridging from Durkheim's analysis of society are two perspectives that seek to explain, at least partially, how individuals categorize themselves and others, grouping the people around them in relation to themselves. While related to Bourdieu's analysis of social status and taste, the theories of Gordon Allport and Benedict Anderson help explain how in-groups, defined in a variety of ways ranging from ethnicity and race to "nation," operate in social settings.[24] This happens in a couple of different ways. Gordon Allport's work on prejudice and social categorization is an important analysis of 1920s Germany and continued to apply well after World War II. Clearly, an exclusive racial nation did not magically appear on the night of January 30, 1933, when Adolf Hitler assumed the office of the German chancellor. Nor, at the same time, was race as explicitly articulated as a dominant element of mainstream German nationalism or identity during the 1920s as it was during the 1930s and after, though it was often implicitly understood. Allport's social psychological work regarding individuals' notions of social belonging frames the narrative that emerged in Germany during the 1920s and was inspired by the widespread acceptance of racialized, exclusive identity. He also helps explain the reactions against members of out-groups, the malleable boundaries between and around social groups, and "the fact that scapegoats of different breeds are so often harnessed together shows that it is the *totality* of prejudice that is important rather than specific accusations against single groups."[25]

At the national level, Benedict Anderson expanded beyond in-groups formed along racial, ethnic, or kinship lines, though those elements are still important constructions. Anderson's work underpins my analysis of German nationalism and the formation of national identity. It provides a more structural—or at least a more wide-ranging—example of identity writ large. Most importantly, Anderson contributes the concept of an "imagined community," a nationalism that binds citizens together using shared language, heritage (or, rather, collective myth-making), and narrative in a context where all members could not possibly know each other.[26] This arguably applies to Allport's analysis of the formation of in- and out-groups as well. In Germany, which was traditionally regional rather than national, Anderson's notion of an imagined community resonates effectively, as continually shifting ideas of what comprised "Germanness" and "greater Germany" depended on exigent political, social, and diplomatic factors. Anderson's ideas about how national feeling and nationalist rhetoric spread are important when considering public discourse about events and activities such as local festivals that had national implications. Applied to issues related to political attitudes and behavior to common activities such as keeping souvenirs from an event, these concepts deepen our understanding of the social and individual forces at work in Germany, and indeed elsewhere, in the twentieth century and beyond.

ORGANIZATION AND STRUCTURE

Because this study involves a detailed examination of local culture, the printing and production of objects and monetary systems, the planning and execution of *Nordische Woche* and *Nordische Tage*, and the establishment of the *NG*, this book draws on material—letters, newspaper clippings, and the correspondence of influential city leaders—from city archives of Lübeck and Kiel. Additionally, material related to communities and collectors come from the *Altonaer Museum für Kunst und Kulturgeschichte*, historic sites and museums in Lübeck and Travemünde, and public spaces in northwestern Germany.

In this chapter, I have largely laid out the analytical frameworks that guide the rest of the chapters; the theoretical concepts introduced here will be explained further in the rest of the book. In chapter 1, I explain the immediate post–World War I period beginning in 1919 in Lübeck, highlighting social, political, and cultural challenges to the establishment of the Weimar Republic. The economic circumstances in Germany—especially spiraling hyperinflation, followed by a short period of stability—provides the skeleton for understanding the complexities of the period. In this chapter, the debates about whether or not to attempt a regionally international festival focused first and foremost on the material benefits such an event could bring Lübeck. Secondary to the discussion—though often paired with the economic or financial argument(s)—was the desire to make Lübeck "important" again, to highlight what Lübeck contributed to a postwar German nation despite a long period of decline and the perceptions of it as a periphery to modern progress. After a year of public discussion, in municipal meetings as much as in the media of the day, attention shifted to how to title and focus the event. Eventually landing on "*Nordische Woche*" rather than other suggestions, the festival inherently sought to connect Lübeck to its Scandinavian ("Nordic") neighbors, foster goodwill in the wake of World War I, and, more importantly, bring in monetary resources to a city passed over in favor of larger urban centers and regions that produced resources prioritized resources.

Chapter 2 focuses on how *Nordische Woche* played out. Planned largely by leaders in city government and the business community (especially the Chamber of Commerce), the events were decidedly public, courting local and visiting populations alike. Using primary evidence from sources as diverse as archival material from planning committees, correspondence between town and business leaders, and material objects from the festival events, this chapter argues that *Nordische Woche* was intentional and important. Additionally, focusing on points of interest in the city center demonstrates how the district simultaneously served a series of venues and exhibits in their own right. While personal accounts about the festival remain elusive, evidence from newspaper columns and letters, reports to the city council, and material artifacts such as the commemorative *Festschrift* and other exhibition material reveal a well-attended festival that reached beyond the borders of Germany and suggest the roots of a German identity later exploited by the Nazis. Acting as a valuable and successful investment, *Nordische Woche* was a high point for some Lübeckers before the depths of hyperinflation and the political-economic recalibration of the middle 1920s.

Chapter 3 deals with the emergence of the *NG* in Lübeck, dedicated to "continuing the work" begun during *Nordische Woche* up through 1938. While some of this was about maintaining or creating Lübeck's place in an international, regional, and national setting, it was also about expanding on an identity-based concept introduced during the festival itself: that Lübeck's history was Nordic, and this history was important, interesting, and multifaceted. Growing to a membership that opened a permanent home on Breitestraße in the heart of Lübeck's *Innenstadt* to establishing trips across Scandinavia (especially after the currency reform in 1924), the NG represented a constituency who believed their activities were cultural work. The NG also provided a platform to mainstream fringe ideas about the centrality and supremacy of Nordic peoples not only in Lübeck's history but that of the entire Baltic region and, indeed, the rest of Germany. The increasing acceptance of racialized identity—of so-called "Nordics" as well as that weaponized against Jews and other marginalized groups—permeated the society so much that by 1926 it was a main vehicle for right-wing hypernationalist rhetoric and aided its integration across cultural, economic, and social sectors. It is a case study for how the Nazis seeped into the very fabric of German society, building on existing, long-held prejudices and the fertile ground of cultural identities in a period of economic and material catastrophe.

Chapter 4 takes up the Lübeck's wartime experience between 1938 (with the acceleration of persecution of Jews during Kristallnacht) and 1947. In this chapter, I discuss the resurrection of *Nordische Woche* as a Nazi ideological fair in 1938. Moved to Hamburg, the major north German epicenter of trade and international linkages, this *Nordische Woche* lacked the local connections that motivated the event in the first place. This time, it was a means to exhibit the evolution of a coordinated racist national community, situated two weeks after the Munich Conference and two weeks before *Kristallnacht*. Though *Nordische Woche* 1938 detached from the local origins of its predecessor, the continued activities of the NG was an example of a regional organization that integrated into the larger whole. By the time World War II began, Lübeck was still on the periphery, though now a physical and potentially ideological gateway to Scandinavia. Outside of the messaging of the NG, the way seemed physically distant in Lübeck, at least to its "Aryan" population. Though Lübeck Jews suffered extreme circumstances and relatively early deportation, the war only fully engulfed

Lübeckers' imaginations after the RAF raid of March 28–29, 1942. Forming the foundation for local memory of the war, the long-lasting destruction of the city center and parts of outlying neighborhoods dominated accounts of wartime, eclipsed only by the influx of refugees and relocated concentration-camp and enslaved victims of the Nazi regime in the waning days of the Third Reich. The end of the war initiated occupation and a complete meltdown of any functional government or society, prompting a legal and moral reckoning for the crimes of the Third Reich. In all of this, the dominant narrative coming out of the war was of the suffering of the innocents (especially after the bombing) and silence about the experience of Lübeck's Jews even as the Allied prosecuted the International Military Tribunal at Nuremberg.

Chapter 5 traces ongoing tensions between the Soviets and the Western allies (triggering events such as the Berlin Blockade and Airlift), which established the tenor and tone of the postwar period. It also framed the challenges that cities and regions would encounter as the Cold War took hold and calcified, dominating European relations and diplomacy. Establishing two German states—the western state allied with NATO and the eastern state incorporated into the Soviet bloc—further complicated matters as Germans sought rehabilitation, redemption, and normalization after the devastation of World War II and the Nazis' crimes. The existence of multiple policies regarding denazification and the future function of Germany helped expose the ideological fractures of the tenuous wartime alliance, and this manifested in the lived experiences of Germans under occupation. For Lübeck, the largest city directly on the border of competing occupation zones—and later competing German states—this challenge meant disruption to local and regional trade as well as a shift in the frame of understanding of who Lübeckers were. This was especially true as Lübeckers experienced a stabilized West German state on the border with East Germany, as economic and industrial rejuvenation unevenly improved circumstances across the country. Lübeckers in particular and most of Schleswig-Holstein in general felt left out of the "economic miracle" and ignored in favor of other cities and regions; to combat this, city leaders hatched a plan to stage a new regional festival: *Nordische Tage*. The 1950s' festivals, first held in 1953 and last held in 1956, drew directly on the *Nordische Woche* of 1921, claiming an injection of much-needed capital, tourism, and attention in a mechanizing, interconnected world. Plans for *Nordische Tage* events into the 1960s never materialized, but the festivals that did occur demonstrate the ways Lübeckers navigated postwar and Cold War realities.

Chapter 6, the conclusion, refocuses on the concepts that underpin the book as a whole, musing on collective memory, the role of identity, and precisely how the past is mobilized to construct meaning in the present. Rather than raising new points or representing evidence, the conclusion serves more as a reflection on the reasons for writing this book.

NOTES

1. Carol Kammen, *On Doing Local History*, Third Edition (Lanham, MD: Rowman & Littlefield, 2014), xiv.

2. Erika Briesacher, "A Narrative in Notgeld: Collecting, Emergency Money, and National Identity in Weimar Germany," in *Money in the German-Speaking Lands,* ed. Mary Lindemann and Jared Poley (New York: Berghahn Books, 2017), 203–218.

3. Jonathan Sperber, "Festivals of National Unity in the German Revolution of 1848–1849," *Past and Present,* No. 136 (Aug. 1992), 116. While Sperber's study focused on 1848 and 1849, his analysis of festival culture can be extended to any time period of social and economic change. Indeed, the use of planned mass spectacle was used consistently by the Nazis and other cultural groups.

4. Excluding theories of nationalism, a plethora of studies focusing on conceptions and perceptions of German nationalism have been undertaken, especially considering the concept of *Heimat.* The following represent the most relevant studies that informed this dissertation: Celia Applegate, *A Nation of Provincials: The German Idea of Heimat* (Berkeley: University of California Press, 1990); Elizabeth Boa and Rachel Palfreyman, *Heimat: A German Dream: Regional Loyalties and National Identity in German Culture* (Oxford: Oxford University Press, 2000); Rogers Brubaker, *Citizenship and Nationhood in France and Germany* (Cambridge, MA: Harvard University Press, 1992); Alon Confino, *The Nation as a Local Metaphor: Württemberg, Imperial Germany, and National Memory, 1871–1918* (Chapel Hill: University of North Carolina Press, 1997); Geoff Eley and Jan Palmowski, eds., *Citizenship and National Identity in Twentieth-Century Germany* (Stanford: Stanford University Press, 2008); Mary Fulbrook and Martin Swales, eds., *Representing the German Nation: History and Identity in Twentieth-Century Germany* (Manchester: Manchester University Press, 2000); Abigail Green, *Fatherlands: State-Building and Nationhood in Nineteenth-Century Germany* (Cambridge: Cambridge University Press, 2001); Mark Hewitson, *Nationalism in Germany, 1848–1866: Revolutionary Nation* (New York: Palgrave MacMillan, 2010); Hagen Schulze, *The Course of German Nationalism: From Frederick the Great to Bismarck, 1763–1867* (Cambridge: Cambridge University Press, 1991).

5. "Weimar Constitution," in Anton Kaes et al., *The Weimar Republic Sourcebook* (Berkeley: University of California Press, 1995), 46.

6. Some groundbreaking works on the changes associated with World War I are Modris Eksteins, *Rites of Spring: The Great War and Birth of the Modern Age* (New York: Houghten Mifflin & Company, 1989); Paul Fussell, *The Great War and Modern Memory* (Oxford: Oxford University Press, 2000); Margaret MacMillan, *Paris 1919: Six Months that Changed the World* (New York: Random House, 2001); Nicholas J. Saunders, ed., *Matters of Conflict: Material Culture, Memory, and the First World War* (London: Routledge, 2004); Jay Winter, ed., *The Legacy*

of the Great War: Ninety Years On (Columbia, MO: University of Missouri Press, 2009); Jay Winter, *Sites of Memory, Sites of Mourning: The Great War in European Cultural History* (Cambridge: Cambridge University Press, 1998); and Robert Wohl, *The Generation of 1914* (Cambridge, MA: Harvard University Press, 1979). Regarding the impact of and changes brought on by World War II, see Tony Judt, *Postwar: A History of Europe since 1945* (New York: Penguin, 2005); Keith Lowe, *Savage Continent: Europe in the Aftermath of World War II* (New York: St. Martin's Press, 2012); Ian Buruma, *Year Zero: A History of 1945* (New York: Penguin, 2013); Ian Kershaw, *To Hell and Back: Europe 1914–1949* (New York: Penguin, 2016); and Ian Kershaw, *The Global Age: Europe, 1950–2017* (New York: Penguin, 2018)

7. Konrad H. Jarausch and Michael Geyer, *Shattered Past: Reconstructing German Histories* (Princeton: Princeton University Press, 2003), 232–233.

8. Peter Gay, *Weimar Culture: The Outsider as Insider* (New York: Harper & Row Publishers, 1968), 1. See also Peter Gordon and John P. McCormick, eds., *Weimar Thought: A Contested Legacy* (Princeton: Princeton University Press, 2013) and Hans Mommsen, *The Rise and Fall of Weimar Democracy* (Chapel Hill: University of North Carolina Press, 1998).

9. Notably Anton Kaes, *Shell Shock Cinema: Weimar Culture and the Wounds of War* (Princeton: Princeton University Press, 2009); Janet Ward, *Weimar Surfaces: Urban Visual Culture in 1920s Germany* (Berkeley: University of California Press, 2001); Eric D. Weitz, *Weimar Germany: Promise and Tragedy* (Princeton: Princeton University Press, 2007); Bernd Widdig, *Culture and Inflation in Weimar Germany* (Berkeley: University of California Press, 2001); and Jonathan Zatlin's *The Currency of Socialism: Money and Political Culture in East Germany*, provide a bridge between earlier studies of German culture and the current project.

10. Commemorating material produced during *Nordische Woche* 1921 did not mention the *Nordische Gesellschaft*, but professional men who had been active in the planning of *Nordische Woche* were present on the first board of directors, and historians generally link the two, especially Hans-Jürgen Lutzhöft, *Der Nordische Gedanke in Deutschland, 1920–1940,* Kieler Historischen Studien (Stuttgart: Ernst Klett Verlag, 1971), 55. This contention also exists in Hans-Adolf Jacobsen, *Nationalsozialistische Außenpolitik, 1933–1938* (Frankfurt am Main: Alfred Metzner Verlag, 1968), 484 and Hans-Dietrich Loock, *Quisling, Rosenberg, und Terboven: Zur Vorgeschichte und Geschichte der Nationalsozialistischen Revolution in Norwegen* (Stuttgart: Deutsche Verlags-Anstalt, 1970), 165. Further evidence for their connection comes from the *Nordische Gesellschaft* file in the *Deutsch Kongress-Zentrale* [DKZ] collection, Hoover Institute, Stanford, CA: Box 227, Folder *Nordische Woche* 1938.

11. The study of geopolitics, especially as framed by Friedrich Ratzel and Rudolf Kjellen, conceived of a culturally determined space. Several scholars noted how geopolitics was incorporated as a major element in nationalist thought, as well as Hitler's conception of *Lebensraum* in the 1930s and 1940s. See especially Charles Kruszewski, "International Affairs: Germany's *Lebensraum*," *The American Political Science Review*, Vol. 34, No. 5 (Oct. 1940), 964–975; George Kiss, "Political Geography into Geopolitics: Recent Trends in Germany," *Geographical Review,* Vol. 32,

No. 4 (Oct. 1942), 632–645; Woodruff D. Smith, "Friedrich Ratzel and the Origins of *Lebensraum*," *German Studies Review*, Vol. 3, No. 1 (Feb. 1980), 51–68; and Ola Tunander, "Swedish-German Geopolitics for a New Century: Rudolf Kjellen's 'The State as a Living Organism,'" *Review of International Studies*, Vol. 27, No. 3 (July 2001), 451–463. The latter article, in particular, emphasizes that Kjellen's conception of geopolitics was not inherently racist or Nazi, but that the ideas were easily adapted to those ideologies.

12. Mauricio Tenorio-Trillo, *Mexico at the World's Fairs: Crafting a Modern Nation* (Berkeley: University of California Press, 1996), 2. Tenorio-Trillo analyzed Mexico's activities at world's fairs before and after the 1910 Revolution, making the connection between trauma, the international sphere, and the act of building (or renegotiating) national identity, arguing that "world's fairs emerged out of—and embodied—nationalistic interests," both constructive and instructive (8). See also Robert W. Rydell, *All the World's a Fair: Visions of Empire at American International Expositions, 1876–1916* (Chicago: University of Chicago Press, 1987); Paul Greenhagh, *Ephemeral Vistas: A History of the Expositions Universelles, Great Exhibitions, and World's Fairs, 1851–1939* (Manchester: University of Manchester Press, 1988); Shanny Peer, *France on Display: Peasants, Provincials, and Folklore in the 1937 Paris World's Fair* (Albany: State University of New York Press, 1998); and Marco Duranti, "Utopia, Nostalgia and World War at the 1939–40 New York World's Fair," *Journal of Contemporary History*, Vol. 41, No. 4 (Oct. 2006), 663–683.

13. Jacobsen, *Außenpolitik*, 484.

14. Joachim Joesten, "The Nazis in Scandinavia," *Foreign Affairs*, Vol. 15, No. 4 (July 1937), 720–728; Geoffrey Field, "Nordic Racism," *Journal of the History of Ideas*, Vol. 38, No. 3 (Jul.–Sept. 1977), 523–544; Birgitta Almgren et al., "Alfred Rosenberg und die Nordische Gesellschaft," *NORDEUROPAforum: Zeitschrift für Politik, Wirtschaft und Kultur,* 18 Jahrgang (Feb. 2008), 7–51. Joesten also had several books and articles on the subject of Scandinavia and the Nazis, particularly in terms of social and cultural infiltration via the Nordische Gesellschaft after 1933.

15. Prompting what has been called the "Baedeker Raids" after the popular German travel guides, the bombing of Lübeck on March 28, 1942 began and back-and-forth cycle of bombing and reprisal between the Luftwaffe and the RAF. The impact of widespread bombing—of militarily strategic and cultural/civilian targets alike—has been demonstrated by A. C. Grayling, *Among the Dead Cities: The History and Moral Legacy of the WWII Bombing of Civilians in Germany and Japan* (New York: Walker & Co./Bloomsbury, 2007).

16. Unlike the original *Noridsche Woche*, *Nordische Tage* was held in 1953, 1954, and 1956; there were plans for another *Nordische Tage* sometime in 1957, 1958, or 1960, but the event never occurred ostensibly due to rising costs and diminished returns. This period will be discussed more fully in Chapter 6.

17. Some examples include Ivan T. Berend, *History Derailed: Central and Eastern Europe in the Long Nineteenth Century* (Berkeley: University of California Press, 2003); David Blackbourn, *History of Germany, 1780–1918: The Long Nineteenth Century* (Malden, MA: Blackwell Publishing, 2003); Mark Mazower, *Dark Continent: Europe's Twentieth Century* (New York: Vintage Books, 1998); Maarten

Van Ginderachter and Marnix Beyen, eds., *Nationhood from Below: Europe in the Long Nineteenth Century* (London: Palgrave Macmillan, 2012); Robert O. Paxton and Julie Hessler, *Europe in the Twentieth Century* (Boston: Wadsworth, 2005);and Richard Vinen, *A History in Fragments: Europe in the Twentieth Century* (London: Da Capo Press, 2002), among others. Mazower and Paxton are both commonly used in undergraduate classrooms as textbooks and contribute to a large body of literature that attempt to distill complex and challenging contexts into digestible histories.

18. Michel de Certeau, *The Practice of Everyday Life*, trans. Steven Rendall (Berkeley: University of California Press, 1984).

19. De Certeau further explains how space, particularly *urban* space, factors into strategies, tactics, and practice in individuals' lives, even interrogating perspective granted by urban structures such as skyscrapers to the layout of the street-level grid. He argues that the "city," itself a definable (though not static) concept, is itself a place where practices are framed through discourse, ideology, and object. See in particular Chapter VII, "Walking in the City," in *The Practice of Everday Life*, 91–110.

20. Pierre Bourdieu, *Distinction: A Social Critique of the Judgment of Taste*, translated by Richard Nice (Cambridge: Harvard University Press, 1984).

21. Ibid., 2.

22. This connects explicitly to de Certeau's statement that individuals are consumers, particularly of the productions the structure strategically makes. How individuals consume that structure can be, according to Bourdieu, ascertained by the objects they display or social trends.

23. Durkheim highlighted the concept of anomie in his landmark study *Suicide*, first published in 1897. See Emile Durkheim, *Suicide: A Study in Sociology*, Reissue Edition, translated by John A. Spaulding (New York: Free Press, 1997). He had also considered the concept in his doctoral dissertation *The Division of Labor in Society*, translated by W. D. Halls (New York: Free Press, 1997). For scholarly analysis of Durkheim's life and work, see Dominick LaCapra, *Emile Durkheim: Sociologist and Philosopher*, Critical Studies in the Humanities, Revised Edition (Ithaca: Cornell University Press, 2001).

24. Indeed, Bourdieu provides the opportunity to interrogate the fissures, fractures, and intersections of a variety of status markers in relation to race, ethnicity, and national identity, especially in terms of class identities. If anything, the overlay of Bourdieu's ideas complicates those of Allport and Anderson, revealing a matrix of privileges and barriers.

25. Gordon W. Allport, *The Nature of Prejudice*, 25th Anniversary Edition (Cambridge, MA: Perseus Books, 1979), 69. Emphasis original.

26. Benedict Anderson, *Imagined Communities: Reflections on the Origins and Spread of Nationalism* (London: Verso, 1991).

Chapter 1

Finance, Festivals, and the Aftermath of the Great War

"When the Hansa League was founded six hundred years ago, Germany was in as deplorable a state as it is today," wrote op-ed author Wilhelm Möller in August 1920.[1] The article ran in both the *Eisenbahn-Zeitung* and the *Lübecker General-Anzeiger*, describing a scene where intrepid merchants took over leadership of both the trading league and the city of Lübeck itself, managing land and sea travel, importing food, and raising the general standard of living. This story of resurrection from a state of decline mirrored prevailing attitudes in Lübeck, that in 1920 had neither the Hanseatic League nor its accompanying stature to counternarratives of pessimism and inferiority. Möller continued,

> Nobody doubts that we need something similar today. . . . Lübeck has been working on the design of its industrial and transport facilities for decades before the war, so that the re-establishment and strengthening of its connections with foreign countries are entirely in line with its previous goals.[2]

The tone of Möller's op-ed reflected the pervasive sense that Lübeck needed a rebirth and needed to claim a space in Germany that compared to that of the largest cities and most important centers of trade, culture, and finance. The centrality of the Hanseatic identity in Lübeck (present even today) has been simultaneously mobilized as a glorious former past that needed to be recaptured as well as a durable legacy enshrined on the Rathaus that borders the central *Marktplatz*, a space to gather, to market, and to politick. The square remains central to the central district, and the survival of the structure and the so-called shield wall, dating to the 1300s, indicate how the past remains present in many ways. Inherent in all the nostalgia for the Hanseatic past was the focus on business and the economy, first and foremost; recalling an independent city run by merchants who populated the city council grounded economic activities and ends as foregone conclusions. Everything else—society, culture, politics—followed.

Möller urged Lübeckers to mount what he called a "Hanseatic Day" to create the conditions for businesses to network, for business leaders to trade ideas, and for companies to solve multinational traffic and economic problems together. "All of these measures and work," he claimed, "would resolve the current standstill, direct traffic back on the right track and prevent artificial disaster."[3] He warned, though, that this couldn't be expressly a top-down affair, nor could the people wait for the national government to rescue them. Möller proved to be prescient in that the festival, which came to be known as *Nordische Woche*, proved to be more than business and networking. The public also had to negotiate cultural messages and extrapolate the meaning associated with the component events. However, the pursuit of economic ends and the injection of capital into Lübeck and the surrounding region was hard to ignore. Business leaders headed the committees, and they explicitly articulated their goals in media outlets and public fora.

The way that message was dissected and digested was far from uniform based upon personal circumstances, experience, and identity. Festival planning took place out in the open, true, but the logistical and practical decisions ultimately fell to local leaders, partially because they held the keys to the coffers. Many of these council members were also leaders in local commerce and industry, demonstrating the symbiotic relationship between trade and governance. The slate of committees was established in order to organize all of the competing aspects of the festival and targeted local businesses in order to ensure their support as well as financial contributions. While the various committee meetings were advertised in local papers and held in the *Rathaus*, it is unclear (and not recorded) how many citizens attended. The implication of such a move was that members of the public could contact specific committee members in order to facilitate the planning process or at least provide input. Overall, festivals and tradeshows were a recognized way to affect the economy as well as culture, and the development of *Nordische Woche* in Lübeck was no exception.

This chapter highlights, in particular, festival planning, especially considering the goals and debates that were considered the most important behind the scenes. *Nordische Woche* evolved over two years, led by business community, devoted committees, and a lot of public discussions. The planning process highlighted physical and metaphorical connections to Lübeck's immediate neighbors, with a large dose of Hanseatic history and collective memory. Debates raged over what constituted a "successful" celebration, but more than anything it was quantified as a positive return on investment: a profit. Many focused on the economic facets and potential profits attendees would bring. Others argued that success was less tangible, that attention to and acknowledgment of the city as an important contributor to the new German state was necessary to ensure Lübeck's continued survival. However success was framed, there was an underlying tone of insecurity and the attitude that Lübeck was an underdog that needed to shed its "little Lübeck" status.[4]

TO HOLD OR NOT TO HOLD—THE EARLY STAGES OF PLANNING

As early as December 1919, the discussion was underway among city leaders about the possibility of hosting a tradeshow with the intent of drawing in financial and tourism resources. At that time, however, the Lübeck *Handelskammer* [Chamber of Commerce] rejected the plan in spite of public discourse.[5] The rejection of the plan did not stem from lack of interest. Rather, an ongoing struggle between competing national organizations—the existing Standing Exhibition Committee for German Industry and a proposed Reich Exhibition Office. On one hand, this represented competing ideas for how a holistic *national* approach to tradeshows and fairs should be organized. On the other hand, cities like Lübeck were caught between power struggles connected to "the trade show industry," including debates over labeling Leipzig, Frankfurt, and Hamburg as permanent "exhibition cities [*Messestädten*]."[6] In many ways, this represented a tactic by interest groups to guide the behaviors of member organizations; it also had the potential to funnel resources to selected entities to the detriment of others.

Those "others" had to devise strategies to ensure they were able to share in the tradeshow landscape. The initial rejection of a tradeshow in Lübeck was met by approval of the Standing Exhibition Committee, and its representative further remarked that "the question of the future of the German trade fair industry will probably be clarified at a Reich trade fair conference to be called by us, as has already been indicated in some other circulars."[7] Festival planners were up against the argument that a proliferation of festivals would, essentially, create audience fatigue and unnecessary competition for visitors' leisure budget, especially when one considers the potential for events in other countries, regions, and cities.[8] It is important, however, to note that these fears came from outside the city. Lübeckers viewed the so-called "splintering [*Zersplitterung*]" effect argument against regional festivals mobilized by national industrial associations as an attempt to maintain prominence over Lübeck and Schleswig-Holstein more broadly.[9] Domestic as well as international locations competed for audiences, exhibitors, and Marks, and critics argued that the limitations presented by the postwar economy meant that resources and materials needed to be conserved. To that end, fairs such as those most often held in Leipzig "should be avoided" following the protocol and agreements between competing exhibition cities.[10] Arguments to this effect were advocated by the Standing Exhibition Commission for German Industry more as a way to ensure its own authority, well before any official steps had been taken by the city council in Lübeck to begin planning something in earnest.

The timing of such a discussion is interesting, especially considering the challenges facing Germany at the time. World War I had been over for little more than a year, and widespread trepidation over political chaos persisted in the wake of the Paris Peace Conference and localized uprisings across Europe. The ongoing Russian Revolution/civil war exacerbated political tensions and concerns, as well, as it did across the continent. Local economic pressures were at the forefront of city leaders' minds, though, and these concerns dominated public discourse. This raised the stakes in Lübeck, where businessmen and municipal leaders wanted to avoid losing face and a sizeable investment as well as local political power. The view that Lübeck would be overlooked by national organizations and even the central government was only reinforced by interlocking national and international debates.

Financial investment—or the lack of it—was equated to an overt judgment of a city or region's worth or value to the nation. Arguments for hosting festivals highlighted the benefits that building exhibition halls and gathering spaces had, whether the location was Hamburg, Lübeck, or Frankfurt.[11] The *Hamburgische Export-Zeitung* pointed out, rather condescendingly, that even such a small city as Lübeck was attempting to mobilize resources and funds to host a festival or tradeshow, so of course Hamburg should do the same. The implication, of course, was that Hamburg was obviously more significant, and the rhetoric surrounding the tradeshow debate highlighted how municipalities and regions jockeyed for attention, attendees, and currency. It also underscored how inequitable cities' positions were in relation to each other. Hamburg had assumed the mantle of Germany's most important port after unification, and its influence across central and western Europe grew along with global trade.

Lübeck's persistence in the face of institutional dismissal emphasized the desire to be considered a destination, a serious city, rather than a backwater culturally and/or geographically distant from national centers such as Frankfurt, Berlin, Leipzig, and Munich—and how much was possibly up for grabs. The general assumption, especially expressed by organizations headquartered or centered in Berlin, was that Lübeck wished to model its potential festival on the Leipzig fairs, which had enjoyed continent-wide attention for centuries.[12] To that end, a letter sent in June 1920 to the city senate by the French Economic Mission [*Französische Wissenschaftsmission*] requested foreknowledge of any trade show to be held in Lübeck, possibly because it was much closer. In reply, the senate stated that there were no plans to hold a festival that year.[13] Rumor dominated discourse, though, and it sometimes had the effect of planting ideas in planners' heads. Suggestions of some sort of event, advocated for in newspapers across the region, exploded into a full-on debate about possible profits as well as the risk that Lübeck would step on Leipzig's toes. Nothing had even been definitively planned, and even the mention of holding a festival brought out strong feelings from stakeholders in Lübeck and outside of it, just as it had the year before.

It was in late summer 1920 that festival proponents such as Wilhelm Möller intensified their efforts, remarking that the city found itself a "mediator between Eastern and Western Europe, the Nordic countries and Central Europe" due in part to the construction of the Elbe-Trave-Canal as well as its history as a center of early modern trade with international partners.[14] Business and trade networks led to cultural bridges and tangible connections, across which people and ideas traveled. In this way, Möller argued, nation-building (or, in this case, rebuilding) could not be limited to governmental interaction but required that "all heads and hands must be active" in the process.[15] The links between culture, economics, and nation were stressed, especially in editorials, to persuade politicians and the people about the mutually constitutive importance of festival and the solutions it had created.

By late 1920, Lübeck's commercial and municipal leaders began planning, in earnest, an event that they felt would aid in achieving closure from World War I as well as challenge the restrictions and constrictions Germany faced in the 1920s.[16] Examples of this were common in the press. In an editorial from October 13, 1920, the *Eisenbahn-Zeitung* argued that a festival in Lübeck (as well as other locations) was beneficial politically. It would make "clear to other nations the potential global calamity if Germany were condemned to misery" as well as provide internationally "an image of the German spirit, in trade and commerce, technology and art in spite of the lost war, despite the revolution and despite the oppressive Conditions of Versailles under which the German people live."[17] A festival in Lübeck, according to the *Eisenbahn-Zeitung*, could have an ameliorative effect on the city in particular and on Germany as a whole. What better way to move past the metaphorical destruction of the war than have Germany be a functional member of the European community? While not exactly rehabilitative, Germany's ability to rebuild and participate in the interconnected global economy was a step in the right direction.

It is important to note that the considerations were first for Lübeck and its surrounding areas and then for Germany as a whole. Extending formal and informal branches to the Scandinavian countries drew on a particular reading of shared—or at least similar—histories dating to the Hanseatic League, and attempted inroads with countries that had remained neutral in World War

I.[18] Centering Lübeck in the overtures toward the international community detached foreign relationships from formal diplomatic channels as well as national baggage from the war (despite the fact Germany had violated Belgium's neutrality in 1914). Shoring up or even resuscitating relationships with the north presented the best option for Germany after the Treaty of Versailles, and Lübeck was best situated to take advantage of it, even more so than its hulking neighbor to the west, Hamburg.

At the same time, though, commentators expressed suspicion as well as a large dose of skepticism and caution about both the plans and the promises of a festival in Lübeck. In the *Hamburgischer Correspondent* from October 20, 1920, for example, "R.M." remarked rather sardonically that "in the Lübeck press, propaganda was made for a Hanseatic Day [*Hanseatentag*] from which one expected golden mountains to appear," pointing out that theory and practice were two different things.[19] The fact that in October the language of "Hanseatic Day" persisted, echoing Möller's op-ed that summer, seemed to target the mythos of the Hanse and challenge any positive expectations of what the festival could bring. There was certainly cynicism that city leaders would promise far more than they could deliver. Even festival supporters alluded to a "reluctant social democracy [*widerstrebende Sozialdemokratie*]" that complicated both the planning process and the debates that surrounded it.[20] The complex tapestry of national and regional political parties and interest groups, as well as the sheer number of them, made even the best intentions impossible to achieve.

FORMULATING THE FESTIVAL

The central question in the press shifted after October 1920 from "Should there be a festival in Lübeck?" to "How should the festival in Lübeck look?" This is not to imply that all debate about the wisdom of holding a festival disappeared, but by and large commentators and observers turned to the festival's scope. The shift in the principal question in the media made it seem like decisions had been made, and it contravened the attempts of the Standing Exhibition Committee to control the tradeshow landscape. This part of the strategy had paid off. Clearly, there were complementary and competing interests from all sectors of society. Local labor groups and industrial firms wanted to be certain of a tradeshow atmosphere, where their products and services were front and center. Community leaders, on the other hand, focused on broader and more general economic issues as well as related political and social necessities. In the midst of it all was public opinion, for such a multifaceted festival required time, planning, and most of all money, prioritizing budgets and taxes away from other things. In addition, it was ostensibly these citizens who would form a large percentage of attendees, though planners, even in the initial stages, desired an international audience.

Utilizing other festivals both as a model and a starting point for competition, planners, and the public alike debated how best to organize and promote a festival. As previously mentioned, the *Eisenbahn-Zeitung* clearly took interest in the event, releasing a series of editorials advocating for swift action in Lübeck, even going so far as to complain that Kiel was already planning festivals for 1921 despite having just completed its "Autumn Week for Art and Science [*Herbstwoche für Kunst und Wissenschaft*]."[21] No doubt there was money for the railroads on the table in the short term, moving attendees and goods. At the same time, though, the *Eisenbahn-Zeitung* was published in conjunction with the *Lübecker Neueste Nachrichten*, aligned with liberal-center politics. It was originally published by the local writer (and patron of Thomas Mann) Ida Boy-Ed's family, and Boy-Ed's involvement in mounting *Nordische Woche* likely contributed to the paper's support. Politics aside, providing efficient service would only benefit railroad companies in the long run as well, especially if a local festival was a company's or consumer's first experience with the city. Solid infrastructure leading to further investments in the region would only serve to grow future infrastructure, a boon for Lübeck's future.

Perhaps representing the first challenge was what to name the festival, even when planning was in hypothetical terms. Throughout 1920, writers interchangeably referred to Lübeck's possible festival as Hanseatic Day [*Hanseatentag*], a tradeshow [*Mustermesse*], and Scandinavian Week [*Skandinavische Woche*]. Though the exact parameters of the festival including the name were undetermined, what *was* clear was the festival was meant to position Lübeck internationally, even as a sense of local identity had to be addressed. Additionally, a middle level of identity—national—was an implicit undercurrent tying together the local and the international. The "imagined communities" populating and including Lübeck were very much a focus, especially the shared histories that would be mobilized and promoted as central to Lübeckers. This also had the effect of implicitly excluding those who did not belong.

Many discussions about the nascent planning for the festival began with allusions to exhibitions in other cities, particularly Kiel (the aforementioned *Herbstwoche* and a concurrent *Nordische Messe* tradeshow) and Hamburg, which was preparing for the tentatively named *Übersee-Woche* (later called *Kultur- und Sport Woche*) held in August 1921. In both cases, the festivals in Kiel and Hamburg celebrated the respective city's uniqueness in the German context as well as in international life. Kiel's *Herbstwoche* centered on the time of year, though it did also include a competing *Nordische Messe* tradeshow, adopting the northerly gaze framed by Lübeck. Hamburg's festival started out focusing on the Baltic region, though it ostensibly became about the culture and sport. Commentary on the festival planning focused on Lübeck's traditional international role on the Baltic Sea, implying that Lübeck could improve on Kiel's idea as no other city could.[22] Indeed, Kiel's adoption of "Nordic" terminology seemed to bear out the resonance or at least the possibilities associated with emphasizing northern ties, and the tacit acceptance of similar language demonstrated an attempt to define a fluid Nordic or Baltic community. Even the definition of what constituted "Scandinavia" was ambiguous at best; Finland was at times identified separately from Norway, Sweden, and Denmark, while at others was grouped together with them; Iceland was absent entirely.[23]

Official steps to recognize a festival in Lübeck and its scope were begun in November 1920 with a request put into the Chamber of Commerce and the city Senate Commission for Commerce and Shipping; even here the decision to host the festival was debated, alluding to the ongoing discussion in the media.[24] This represents an important step, one of action and not of talk. It positioned the festival as a Senate-sanctioned, city-wide event, rather than one mounted cultural or trade organizations and simply located in the city. By November 29, the Chamber of Commerce reported that city Senator Dr. Georg Kalkbrenner and Senate President Eschenburg would meet to begin planning a "culture and business" week, set for summer 1921.[25] Several individuals quickly associated themselves with planning and became the faces of the event. Kalkbrenner, in particular, led the effort in securing financing as the chair of trade and shipping as well as the tax authority.[26] His ubiquity in communications and media statements reinforced the financial aspects of hosting the event. Ernst Boie, head of a local manufacturing firm located in the *Innenstadt* and president of the Chamber of Commerce, visibly advocated and fundraised among industrial firms. Ida Boy-Ed, described by the *New York Times* as one of the foremost German literary figures, adopted the role of sole woman and honorary cultural "ambassador" associated with planning the festival.[27] She also served as a channel to Thomas Mann, serving as his host when he visited Lübeck and his constant correspondent and defender throughout the early twentieth century. Jan Grosse, Senate Syndikus, rounded out the field of individuals who were heavily invested in seeing a successful festival take place in 1921.[28]

Despite continuing criticism from organizations such as the Standing Exhibition Commission for German Industry that Lübeck was splitting national audiences and resources, plans continued for a festival that would present **the** Lübeck city leaders wanted to promote nationally and internationally. The possibility that Lübeck would mount this festival on a recurring basis seemed a foremost concern of the Standing Exhibition Commission, resulting in a missive from the Chamber of Commerce trying to clarify the plan, pointing out that a date had not even been picked yet.[29] The concern about festival proliferation mirrored the very real problems confronting the German state in the form of unregulated *Notgeld.* Though these two topics were not analyzed together, the arguments that the Standing Exhibition Committee was making about the detrimental effects of too many local festivals could just as easily have been about the persistent, largely unregulated currencies. The very reason that Lübeck planners wanted to stimulate the local economy—the inability of the national government to cover all debts and stem inflation in a unified way across the country—ensured continued atomization of localities and geographic regions. Of necessity, insular and locally driven actions meant the situation would continue and even worsen, despite the strategies enacted by organizations with a national scope.

While business and industry were clearly driving considerations for festival planners, heavily romanticized cultural messaging was important, too. In some ways, the exhibitions, tradeshow, and commerce provided opportunities to commodify nebulous or imagined readings of early modern history, particularly in relation to Lübeck's connections to Scandinavia. And though the character of the festival asserted uniqueness in the German context, it was not the only regional festival to highlight these geographic or historical connections. The festival provided an opportunity to frame the imagined community of the Baltic, built for centuries and drawing on a history in common. That is not to say Scandinavian commentators or observers viewed that history in the same way, but festival planners saw it as a way to take control of the discourse and place Lübeck squarely in the middle. For this reason, planners followed the development of the *Übersee-Woche* in Hamburg with interest. The Chamber of Commerce's archive chronicling the debates surrounding and execution of what became known as *Nordische Woche* included clippings and information about the Hamburg exposition. In particular, the financial aspects of putting on such an exhibition—an expensive proposition and one that carried a degree of risk—worried planners in Lübeck. Despite the nostalgia for the Hanseatic League, Lübeck could hardly marshal necessary support by reminding investors of its *former* glory. The need to invite visitors who could financially support the venture seemed of utmost importance. In the case of Hamburg's exhibition, foreigners—particularly Americans—were highly sought as sympathetic visitors with money to spend.[30]

By December 1920, the Chamber of Commerce and the Lübeck city senate had voted unanimously to hold the festival, choosing to commission a "free committee" to plan the event under the guidance of the senate. On December 6, the name *Nordische Woche* was finally settled in order to promote a regionally inclusive environment and perhaps even attract curious attendees from nearby cities with their own festivals. The Chamber of Commerce argued that earlier suggestions for the festival name, especially "Baltic Week," represented a preference for visitors from those countries.[31] "Nordic Week" was a much more ambiguous term, as it could mean northern nations, a cultural identity, or a Scandinavian locus, adaptable according to need. It also meant visitors from well outside of northern Europe could also find ways to connect to the themes, events, and performances. In order to recruit volunteers to make planning go as smoothly as possible, Senator Kalkbrenner circulated a call to serve on the committee to plan an event to "rally the German drive for reconstruction . . . and maintenance of the economic and cultural relations with the Nordic countries."[32] From this call, committees were established to deal with the various aspects of the events: theater and concert itineraries, an accommodations committee dealing with matters related to lodging for the duration of the week, and public relations. The bureaucratic organization and separate incorporation of the festival lent credence to the idea that *Nordische Woche* could recur, as the official structures would already be in place.[33]

Local leaders quickly began conducting meetings and issuing invitations to serve on committees. While public opinion and a multitude of newspaper editorials over the previous year had been instrumental in bringing the matter of *Nordische Woche* before the Chamber of Commerce and the Lübeck city senate, the majority of committee spots were filled by business leaders and well-known community leaders. Senator Kalkbrenner sent, for example, a personal letter to Ida Boy-Ed asking for her cooperation and participation on the committee organizing lectures, in part because of her existing connections within the literary world and with Thomas Mann in particular.[34] Business played the dominant role, though. Firms leaped at the chance to have a hand in the proceedings or official contracts with the city, such as Hermann Buck of Buck and Willmann Conveyance [*Spedition*]. In a letter to Dr. Kalkbrenner, Buck referenced the benefits to be felt by hometown companies rather than those in other cities, especially in the transportation of goods and people to and from Lübeck.[35] Local leaders wanted to foster their relationships with international and regional dignitaries outside of the context of national interests. The pursuit of material gains to Lübeck in particular were the foundation upon which all this networking would be carried out. Lübeckers had to take care of Lübeck, and planners linked the goal of the city's survival and prosperity to the success of the festival.

FESTIVAL PLANNING IN CULTURAL CONTEXT

The decision to host a festival with a broad interest base was no small undertaking. The initial plan, as advertised regionally, was to host *Nordische Woche* in June 1921, the height of the festival season. This could capitalize on other nearby festivals, especially those that were more established; they could reinforce each other, advertising another (regional) tourist experience. At the same time, they could also attempt to compete and draw attendees *away* from those events in favor of their own. Whatever the motivation, business leaders sought to take advantage of what they could. Economic realities had to be considered, and a short planning time could have been a way to hold down costs and get a jump on other festivals that were already scheduled for the late summer. Memos about the cost and potential profit of hosting *Nordische Woche* were circulated as a way to court advertisers and donations. As a whole, the business community pledged a contribution of 50,000 Marks to guarantee an initial operating budget.[36] What this meant for matching city funds remained to be seen.

Nordische Woche promised "a resurgence of German-Scandinavian economic and cultural relations."[37] To meet these lofty promises, the planning committee had to sell Lübeck to potential attendees as a prime place to hold an international festival despite not being the urban center Berlin, Frankfurt, or Hamburg was. It was an independent imperial city that had variably existed in and separately from French-, Danish-, and Prussian-controlled territory and in many ways typified debates over nationality and its connection to the land and physical space. Lübeck's proximity to the Danish border—which had shifted due to the 1920 plebiscite mandated by the Treaty of Versailles, ostensibly based on Woodrow Wilson's "Fourteen Points"—contextualized local conversations about the complexities of identity and claims to territory as well as the meanings of borders and borderlands.[38]

The focus on trade and established networks between Lübeck/northwestern Germany and Scandinavian countries *including* Denmark prioritized economic connections and contextualized border disputes as a breakdown in historic business relationships. This was more concrete, in theory, than engaging in political and nationalist discourses. Planners insisted that *Nordische Woche* was to be "non-partisan [*parteiloser*]," overtly adhering to no one political perspective.[39] Germany's borderlands played an essential role in navigating economic, diplomatic, and cultural relationships with surrounding nations even as the borders themselves changed. In Lübeck, this was demonstrated by its well-established ferry service to Finland, Sweden, and eastward toward Latvia across the Baltic. Fish and shipping, too, originated in the borough of Travemünde, serving as Lübeck's most identifiable internationally oriented industries. The certain goal, though, was to build on those networks and expand Lübeck's economic footprint, one that could pay back the contributions of area organizations and individuals with a profit in the end. Area hotels and restaurants were counting on large foreign or out-of-town crowds, and the Accommodation Committee [*Wohnungsausschuss*] sought additional lodging houses in the immediate region as overflow alternatives.[40]

Nordische Woche was also promised as a vehicle for the establishment of related cultural and social organizations, providing opportunities for cross-marketing and venues for sports tourism. Some of the first events to be considered were lectures by notable literary and academic personalities, such as Rudolf Kjellen of Uppsala and hometown figure Thomas Mann, reflecting Ida Boy-Ed's input.[41] This brought a note of gravitas to the proceedings as well as widened potential attendees to school groups. Beyond these more esoteric offerings, sports competitions and organizational tournaments were considered an easy sell and spanned social strata. One example was the creation of the *Lübecker Regatta-Verein*, which moved quickly to join the national regatta racing body and host a race in conjunction with *Nordische Woche*. Representatives even went to Berlin to be sanctioned for the proposed youth regatta, heralded as the first of its kind in Germany, which was accepted.[42] This made it possible to draw together competitors from across Germany, further diversifying potential audience while also entering a sports network that promised events beyond one festival in June.

By February, the plan for a June *Nordische Woche* fell apart, in part blamed on the realities of the early 1920s, namely the "harsh demands of the Entente on Germany," the economic crisis confronting the region in general, and the difficulty in fundraising on short notice.[43] By the middle of the month, a new date—the first week in September—circulated in official memoranda, planning meetings, and marketing. Senator Dimpker of the Central Planning Committee pointed out several issues that necessitated moving the festival to the fall, such as difficulty in securing students' passports, economic depression in Germany and Finland, and the fact that most people would have finalized their summer holiday plans already.[44] Moreover, he added, "ultimately, this event is supplying a business card for Lübeck as a major trading center."[45] It would do no good to go forward with planning when the target audiences of the festival were uncertain to attend or the events appeared disorganized. Dimpker's point reinforced the reality of international environs, especially leftover hostility and distrust toward Germany in the wake of the war. Coupled with economic distress domestically as well as regionally, planners needed more time to sell the event.

The sweeping scope of *Nordische Woche* became clear once talks were underway to move the festival to early September. In some ways, the added time increased advertising potential (and possibly more visitors), but it also increased budgetary requests.[46] The change in schedule, while practical in some respects, put some events such as the Regatta in jeopardy. In a letter to Dr. Kalkbrenner, the *Lübecker Regatta-Verein* maintained that it had to go forward with the June date but assured him that it would utilize the event as an advance promotion for *Nordische Woche*.[47] Materially, *Nordische Woche* planners could not count on money from the *Regatta-Verein* in the planning. Funding would have to be drawn from other sponsors or from municipal coffers. On the other hand, continuing the association between the Regatta and *Nordische Woche* essentially meant the event unofficially spanned the entire summer season, bookending other, even more established events. *Nordische Woche* ultimately landed between three other regional festivals: *Kultur- und Sportwoche* in Hamburg (August 12–24, 1921) and the concurrent *Kieler Herbstwoche für Kunst und Wissenschaft* and *Nordische Messe* tradeshow (September 16–18, 1921).

Though cultural and social organizations served as fundamental (and easily salable) components of festival planning, the fishing, manufacturing, and shipping sectors of Lübeck industry sought to maintain a major focus in planning and advance advertising. By incorporating the specific *local* industrial scene, planners were able to provide a framework for the tradeshow or economic aspect of *Nordische Woche*, eschewing a general exhibition of industry for a more focused event highlighting Lübeck's export industry and how it related to international and other German examples.[48] One major example was the focus on Lübeck's marzipan industry, recognized for its quality by the 1800s and represented by dominant firms like Niederegger, Carstens, and Lubeca Marzipan; Lübecker marzipan today is categorized under the European Union's "protected geographical indication," which provides quality controls and safeguards regional specialties.[49] Lübeck was presented as not only a place of history but also a possibility with a scrappy, persistent populace who fought for the survival of their city. In this way, planners explicitly conceived of the festival in layered terms, with the local identity (in this case, Lübeck's economic, industrial, and business life) considered on its own merits, in reference to the *national* context, and then to a broader international scope. *Nordische Woche*, and by extension Lübeck's industry and culture, became an export in its own right.

Again, the parameters of the festival demarcated by its title meant that the international scope was somewhat limited, with special emphasis placed on relationships between Lübeck and traditional trading partners near or on the Baltic Sea in an effort to "rally the German drive for reconstruction and maintenance of economic and cultural relations with the Nordic countries."[50] The Central Planning Committee reached out to organizations designed to foster international relations, such as the German-Finnish Association [*Deutsch-Finnländische Vereinigung*], as well as embassies and other cultural institutions with a presence in Lübeck. Overtures were also extended to Scandinavian organizations and universities with the hope that they would contribute to the event, and the festival was presented as a unique moment where various German institutions, not just those based in Lübeck, could contact brethren industries based internationally.[51] The planning notes centered on chambers of commerce in Scandinavian towns as a way to bring together a multitude of industries and organizations.[52]

NOTGELD AND *NORDISCHE WOCHE*

Another major way event planners sought to capitalize on international linkages was to produce *Notgeld* for the festival, and reflections on the cultural and social environs of the period were part of the discussion regarding its issue. *Notgeld* originally appeared at the outset of World War I as a stop-gap measure to buy the government time to transition to a wartime economy. It really entered Germans' everyday lives and their economic lexicon from 1916 to 1917, issued not only by the *Reichsbank* but also by state-level governments, city governments, and individual firms. As could be expected, the system was difficult if not impossible to regulate, and the persistence of *Notgeld* after the war embodied the ongoing economic instability of the postwar period.[53] *Notgeld*, itself, was analyzed in different categories, especially distinguishing between larger-denomination circulated bills and smaller mostly uncirculated bills issued in series (*Serienscheine*). Though both types of *Notgeld* were viewed as collectible, comparable to stamps or coins, *Serienscheine* was derided, especially by the expert Dr. Arnold Keller, as unserious and lacking the gravitas "real" collectors would want.

Still, collectors did want *Notgeld*, collectible series included, and this was an existing network planners wanted to tap in advance of *Nordische Woche*. A letter from a representative of the Bankhaus Fritz Kiemstedt to Ernst Boie, the head of the Central Planning Committee, indicated that 500,000 Marks worth of *Notgeld* should be printed for the festival; most importantly, though, the letter argued that 400,000 of those *Scheine* were to be distributed throughout Germany and internationally where "I have it in mind that this money will disappear off the street as quickly as possible and end in collectors' albums."[54] The Kiemstedt bankhouse estimated the cost of printing the *Notgeld* to be approximately 25,000 Marks, far less than the face value of the notes. Shipping costs, as well, would remain low while promoting the festival and marketable to collectors for purchase which would enrich the festival's available financial resources, especially in terms of foreign currency. While not intended as circulating, it was to be "good" for the duration of the festival, not only mimicking circulating *Notgeld* but also "bringing the term '*Nordische Woche*' into circulation as well as *Notgeld*-like bills."[55]

By 1921, *Notgeld* was controversial and planners discussed issuing *Notgeld* confidentially, though it was later advertised in the collectors' circular *Das Notgeld* for sale or trade.[56] The view that small bills and currency in general were subject to shortage resulted in regular correspondence to localities, municipalities, firms, and private lenders regarding the issue of *Notgeld*. For example, form letters periodically requested copies of the *Scheine* that was issued as an attempt to keep track of a system that defied orderly regulation.[57] While the *Reichsbank* in Berlin attempted to stem spiraling inflation by at least cataloguing *Notgeld* issues, it required a degree of self-policing at the local level and in the private sector. This proved to be an inadequate measure against increasing economic normlessness (or, as Emile Durkheim discussed in his work, *anomie*), reflecting the perception of governmental—and therefore political—impotence. In a very real way, *Notgeld* privileged the tactics devised by localities, individual firms, and even individual people versus the economic strategies the national government attempted. In the short term, this situation meant that Germans could stave off unemployment *and* rising prices, but it wasn't sustainable over time.

Debates over *Notgeld* targeted this very issue: that it was an unsustainable, clunky system and its issuance was actually counterproductive to postwar economic rebuilding. In fact, in June 1921, a letter from German Finance Ministry indicated the concern that *Notgeld* had become a way to mobilize revenue rather than to rectify shortages of small bills.[58] The way that planners discussed using the notes, variably as advertisements, items of interest to collectors, and the like, bears out that concern. The capital set aside to print and distribute *Nordische Woche Notgeld* was couched as an investment, one that could be recouped overseas in the hands of collectors. It could also bring foreign currencies into Lübeck, which were more stable and marshaled more long-term purchasing power. It did nothing to shore up the value of the Mark, though, and the decentralized nature of the system meant that it was nearly impossible for the central bank to control access and influx of foreign exchange despite the ongoing efforts of the Reichsbank to assert authority over the printing and use of *Notgeld.*

Even the press entered the discussion. The *Lübeckische General-Anzeiger* printed a notice insisting that unauthorized issues of *Notgeld* could be subject to an increasing fine.[59] In the same vein, the *Lübecker Neuesten Nachrichten* published a brief on "the end of *Notgeld*," reporting that the government was relying on municipalities to restrict it in order to stabilize the currency.[60] This, again, pointed to the volatility as well as the impermanence of a system like *Notgeld.* For a monetary system built on "emergency" (i.e., temporary) necessity, the fact that *Notgeld* persisted, encouraged especially by international and domestic collectors, highlights the difficulty the Weimar Republic faced in securing its economic future in a unified way.

Despite its transient nature, the reality was that *Notgeld* was a culturally resonant resource, particularly for bringing attention to *Nordische Woche.* Other contemporaneous *Notgeld* issues promoted locations in Lübeck such as the *Schiffersgesellschaft* (the iconic restaurant, heralded as the best in Lübeck), though the number of issues were far fewer than those commemorating *Nordische Woche.*[61] Festival planners sought to saturate the market with *Nordische Woche* notes as opposed to those that only focused on the locality and coordinated imagery across materials, such as the official letterhead and circulars. For example, Alfred Mahlau created a poster to advertise *Nordische Woche* that had widespread exposure and, by April 1921, was adopted as the official logo and branding of the celebration.[62] Similarly to the art found on *Notgeld*, Mahlau's poster featured stark colors that illustrated Lübeck's role in Germany—ships moored on a pile dolphin, complete with streamers and a caption in modernist font. The poster became identified with the event, demonstrating how material culture both affected and reflected society at a given time. More importantly, it was produced by a local artist who was integrated into the fabric of the culture.[63]

Overall, local concerns framed public debates over both Lübeck's economic position in 1920s Germany and the best way to foster its vitality in the future. Though there was public discourse and even input, the decisions for its production were framed by city and business leaders. The decision to call Lübeck's festival "*Nordische Woche*" revealed planners' aspirations as much as it did about the networks already available to them. Embedded in the commercial and financial goals that centered Lübeck more than an emergent national context were less tangible navigations of local and national identity, setting the foundation for active constructions of in-groups and out-groups. The strategies festival planners employed to frame outward-facing Lübecker culture and identity were designed to structure the ways participants and observers alike consumed festival events. Even the discussions, printed in newspapers and in town-hall meetings were outlined in official ways even when they revealed clashes between municipal leaders and national organizations. The language that was used, the ways questions were asked, and the way feedback was collected all pointed to an event that had top-down orientation, even if its success depended on every day people's participation.

NOTES

1. Wilhelm Möller, "Ein Hansetag in Lübeck," *Eisenbahn-Zeitung*, 10 August 1920. HAL, HK 275.
2. Ibid.
3. Ibid.
4. Though the phrase "little Lübeck" itself does not necessarily show up in archival texts, even modern-day descriptions on travel blogs and the like adopt the view of a diminutive town or quaint little travel spot. Accounts contemporary to *Nordische Woche* tend to incorporate language that situates Lübeck as more contained, less important, and overlooked in contrast to other urban areas.
5. Letter from Burley of *Ständige Austellungskommission für die Deutsche Industrie* (6 December 1919). HAL, Handelskammer [HK] 275: Nordische Woche in Lübeck—Allgemeines.

6. "Ständige Ausstellungskommission oder Reichsmesseamt?," *Ständige Ausstellungskommission für die Deutsche Industrie,* 10 Dec. 1919, 1. HAL, HK 275.

7. Letter from Burley of *Ständige Austellungskommission für die Deutsche Industrie* (18 December 1919). HAL, HK 275.

8. Indeed, a circular from December 1919 published by the *Ständige Ausstellungskommission für die Deutsche Industrie* reprinted an article from the *Deutsche Allgemeines Zeitung* by Reichswirtschaftsminister Schmidt, basically arguing for compartmentalized tradeshows (e.g., Hamburg as a location for European economic exhibitions versus London as a general location for shows focused on European trade). HAL, HK 275.

9. "Die Berliner Handelskammer gegen die Zersplitterung der Messen," *Industrie- und Handels-Zeitung*, 26 March 1920. HAL, HK 275.

10. "Reichswirtschaftsminister Schmidt über Messefragen," HAL, HK 275. Herr Schmidt pointed out that tradeshow fragmentation or overlap could negatively affect nations "not as negatively affected by the war as we are," citing Switzerland and Sweden as specific examples. This points to a larger debate about the most effective way to undertake tradeshows generally, not just in Germany, and it informed the specific debate about whether or not to hold an exhibition of any kind in Lübeck.

11. "Was andere Städte können. Neue Messegebäude," *Hamburgische Export-Zeitung*, 21 April 1920. HAL, HK 275.

12. Letter to Magistrat der Hansestadt Lübeck from Französische Wissenschaftsmission Berlin, 28 June 1920. HAL, HK 275.

13. Memo from Lübeck Handelskammer to Senate, 9 July 1920. HAL, HK 275.

14. Möller, "Ein Hansetag in Lübeck," HAL, HK 275.

15. Ibid.

16. Abram Enns, *Kunst und Bürgertum*, 46.

17. "Zur Anregung eines Hansetages," *Eisenbahn-Zeitung*, 13 October 1920. HAL, HK 275.

18. This same point is made in Matthias Loeber, *Völkische Bewegung zwischen Weser und Ems: Richard von Hoff und die Nordische Gesellschaft in Bremen und Nordwestdeutschland* (Frankfurt am Main: Peter Lang, 2016), especially in his discussion related to *Nordische Woche* and the establishment of the *Nordische Gesellschaft.*

19. R.M., "Ein Lübecker Hanseatentag? Hamburg macht Schule," *Hamburgischer Correspondent*, 20 October 1920. HAL, HK 275.

20. "Wo bleibt Lübeck?" *Eisenbahn-Zeitung*, 14 October 1920. HAL, HK 275.

21. Ibid. The tone of the editorial is evident in the title, implying that Lübeck risked being left behind if other cities, in this case Kiel, continued to put on festivals and tradeshows unchallenged.

22. "Eine skandinavische Woche in Lübeck," *Lübeckische-Blatter*, 31 October 1920. HAL, HK 275.

23. "Verehrter Schumacher!" n.d. HAL, HK 275. Interestingly, there were no references to Iceland in the planning or execution of *Nordische Woche* in 1921.

24. Auszug aus dem Protokoll der Senatskommission für Handel und Schiffahrt, 16 November 1920. HAL, HK 275.

25. Handelskammer, 29 November 1920. HAL, HK 275.

26. Gerhard Schneider, "Georg Kalkbrenner," in *Lübecker Lebensläufe aus neun Jahrhunderten*, ed. Alken Bruns (Neumünster: Wachholtz Verlag, 1993), 197.

27. "Ida Boy-Ed Speaks for German Women: The Fatherland Now Stands for Home, She Says in 'The Soldier Mother,'" *New York Times*, 11 April 1915. Boy-Ed was viewed as an early women's activist in Germany, residing for much of her life in Lübeck and maintaining a defiant independence.

28. Grosse proved to be important as a local leader and a legal consultant; his records from this period later served as the foundation of archival recontruction that happened after Lübeck was bombed and the headquarters of the *Nordische Gesellschaft* was destroyed. Abram Enns argued that the involvement of Kalkbrenner, Boie, and Grosse demonstrate a "romanticized" mission for *Nordische Woche*, and this has been recently reiterated by Matthias Loeber.

29. Letter to Das Ausstellungs- und Messe-Amt der Deutschen Industrie from president of Lübeck Handelskammer, 8 January 1921. HAL, HK 275.

30. "Das Ausland und die Uebersee-Woche," *Hamburgischer Correspondent*, 9 November 1920. HAL, HK 275.

31. Zum Protokollauszug vom 16. November 1920 (Nr. 15831). HAL, HK 275.

32. "Nordische Woche in Lübeck," 10 January 1921. HAL, HK 275.

33. "Mitglieder des Präsidiums des Hauptausschusses und der Unterausschüsse zur Verbereitung der nordischen Woche." HAL, HK 275.

34. Letter from Senator Kalkbrenner to Ida Boy-Ed, 21 January 1921. HAL, 1.2 Neues Senats-Akten [NSA] 2462: Nordische Woche 1921, 1921–1923.

35. Letter from Buck and Willmann to Dr. Kalkbrenner, 13 January 1921. HAL: 1.2 NSA 2462. In particular, Buck referenced Hamburg, Riga, and Helsinki, all cities that had relationships with Lübeck through transportation systems.

36. "Aktenvermerk" from Dr. Keibel, 26 January 1921. HAL, HK 275.

37. Enns, *Kunst und Bürgertum*, 46.

38. The issues surrounding the 1920 plebiscite and its fallout is complex, reaching back centuries and complicated by modern diplomatic, military, and social concerns (such as the Second Schleswig War of 1864). For further reading, see J. Laurence Hare, *Excavating Nations: Archaeology, Museums, and the German-Danish Border* (Toronto: University of Toronto Press, 2015) and Peter Thaler's "A Tale of Three Communities: National Identification in the German-Danish Borderlands," *Scandinavian Journal of History*, Vol. 32, No. 2 (Jun 2007): 141–166 and *Of Mind and Matter: The Duality of National Identity in the German-Danish Borderlands* (West Lafayette, IN: Purdue University Press, 2009).

39. "Nordische Woche in Lübeck: Ein Ruf zu einmütiger Arbeit!" *Lübeckische Anzeiger*, 20 January 1921. HAL, HK 275.

40. "Niederschrift über die Versammlung des Wohnungsausschusses," 4 February 1921. HAL, HK 275. In particular, the committee wanted to house visitors in the nearby resort towns of Travemünde and Schwartau; Travemünde is today considered part of the greater Lübeck port area, set immediately on the Baltic Sea.

41. "Versammlung des Hauptausschusses der 'Nordischen Woche' am *Dienstag, dem 1 Februar 1921*," HAL, HK 275. Emphasis original.

42. Letter from Lübecker Regatta-Verein to Dr. Kalkbrenner, 4 March 1921. HAL, 1.2 NSA 2462.

43. "Niederschrift über die Besprechung betreffend *Verlegung des Zeitpunktes* der *Nordischen Woche*," 10 February 1921. HAL, HK 275. Interestingly, further examination of these minutes reveal a debate about whether the primary focus of the festival would be cultural or economic.

44. "Sitzung des *Hauptausschusses der 'Nordischen Woche'* 11 February 1921," 2. HAL, HK 275.

45. Ibid.

46. Here again we see a bit of competitive spirit, as the second annual Autumn Week in Kiel was scheduled for mid-September, announced in mid-February. Considering the fact that the steering committee was observing how Kiel and Hamburg planned their respective festivals, it is incredibly interesting that *Nordische Woche* ended up being held between the Hamburg and Kiel festivals.

47. Letter from Lübecker Regatta-Verein to Dr. Kalkbrenner, 4 March 1921. HAL, 1.2 NSA 2462.

48. "Niederschrift über die Industriellen-Besprechung," 28 February 1921, 2. HAL, HK 275. The meeting took place, as many of the economic or industrial committee meetings did, in the *Schiffersgesellschaft* building, the traditional center of the shipping and fishing guild. Today, it is recognized as the best restaurant in Lübeck, with local fare its emphasis, as well as a meeting place for local and international members of the *Schiffersgesellschaft.*

49. For explanation of the history in marzipan in Lübeck, see Antjekathrin Graßmann, *Das Neue Lübeck-Lexicon: Die Hansestadt von A bis Z* (Lübeck: Schmidt & Romhild, 2011), especially the entries for "marzipan" and "Niederegger." For discussion about the official designations protecting traditional regional food products, see the European Commission's page: https://ec.europa.eu/info/food-farming-fisheries/food-safety-and-quality/certification/quality-labels_en.

50. "Nordische Woche in Lübeck," *Hamburgischer Correspondent*, 10 February 1921. HAL, HK 275.

51. "Mitteilung," 1 April 1921 (Nachrichtenamt correspondence). HAL, HK 275. Even the Board of German Industry and Commerce [*Hauptausschuss des deutschen Industrie- und Handelstages*] acknowledged this by scheduling a meeting to be run at the festival to take advantage of the gathering of international business leaders and industries.

52. "Niederschrift der Versammlung des *Ausschusses der 'Nordische Woche' für wirtschaftliche Tagungen*" 18 February 1921, 2. HAL, HK 275.

53. Detailed and thorough discussions of postwar economic conditions and *Notgeld* in general appear in both Gerald Feldman, *The Great Disorder Politics, Economics, and Society in the German Inflation, 1914–1924* (New York: Oxford University Press, 1993) and Bernd Widdig, *Culture and Inflation in Weimar Germany* (Berkeley: University of California Press, 2001). Additionally, for a pointed discussion about the connections between *Notgeld* and national cultural meanings see Briesacher, "A Narrative in *Notgeld*."

54. Letter to Ernst Boie from Bankhaus Fritz Kiemstedt, 10 March 1921. HAL, HK 275.

55. Letter to the Polizeiamt from Dr. Kalkbrenner, 22 August 1921. HAL, Polizeiamt [PA] 3769: Ausgabe v. Notgeld, 1915–1925.

56. *Das Notgeld*, 1 September 1921 (Nr. 13), p. 415. In the list of *Notgeld,* issues from *Nordische Woche*'s competitors from Hamburg and Kiel were also listed; *Notgeld* printed exclusively for festivals were common and were aimed directly at collectors.

57. Memo from Reichsbankstelle to Senatskanzlei Lübeck, 2 October 1920. HAL, PA 3769. This example is representative of missives sent between the end of World War I and well into the 1920s prior to the introduction of the *Rentenmark* in 1924 by Hjalmar Schacht.

58. Memo from Reichsminister der Finanzen, 3 June 1921. HAL, PA 3769.

59. "Unbezechtigte Notgeldausgabe," *Lübeckische General-Anzeiger*, 26 July 1921. HAL, PA 3769.

60. "Das Ende des Notgeldes," *Lübecker Neueste Nachrichten*, 22 August 1921. HAL, PA 3769.

61. Memo from Neumann, *Haupt-Polizeiwachtmeister,* 26 October 1921. HAL, PA 3769. The disparity in issues was striking; as compared with 100,000 *Nordische Woche* notes, only 5,000 notes depicting the *Schiffersgesellschaft* were produced at this time.

62. Enns, *Kunst und Bürgertum*, 47. This poster was also featured on one of the issues of *Notgeld* for the event, which served as currency.

63. Mahlau later gained fame for designing the corporate logo for Niederegger, the world-famous marzipan confectionary based in Lübeck, as well as stained-glass windows for St. Mary's after World War II.

Chapter 2

Celebration, Culture, and Commerce

Nordische Woche *1921*

The Lübecker Regatta scheduled for June 18–19, 1921, was to serve as the philosophical beginning to the festival season in Lübeck and the advance event for *Nordische Woche*. Twenty-eight clubs, including two from Denmark and one from Finland, entered 512 rowers and 108 boats; if not for the stormy conditions and rocky seas on the Breitling, a widening of the Trave River in the eastern Lübeck neighborhood of Schlutup, the Regatta may have been the preamble it was intended to be.[1] And yet, it demonstrated interest and placed Lübeck on the holiday schedule. The registrations justified the approximately 646,000 planners had spent up to that point, and it made the prospect of spending several 100,000 Marks more palatable to the city council, even in deepening economic uncertainty.[2] The process to that point—the planning, the debate in the press and in public opinion, and the actual mobilization of resources—had taken nearly two years, and the cooperation between the public and private sectors was extremely important.

The festival represented a financial risk, but enough emphasis was put on cultural and diplomatic benefits to help offset the investment. The months between the canceled regatta and *Nordische Woche* events provided ample advertising and public-relations time, moving the council and the various subcommittees beyond the planning stage and into execution. Philosophical or discursive questions were still considered in popular media, but planners largely considered the festival sold to Lübeckers and turned their attention elsewhere. Committee leaders inventoried the businesses that would be approached to further contribute, support, advertise, and provide showcases for the tradeshow portion of the festival, bolstered by promised local and regional revenues and reinforced by the (still confidential) commemorative *Notgeld*. That being said, though, a wary collective eye watched the expenditures go up, pinning hopes for a successful week on the issues of *Notgeld* and advance ticket sales to specific performances and sport.[3]

This chapter details how economic and political concerns implicitly and explicitly played a guiding role in mounting *Nordische Woche*, embodied in the material produced as collectible advertisements, including advance programs and the more substantial *Festschrift*. The use of these promotional materials harnessed the mass market and what Benedict Anderson termed print capitalism to help identify and even define the contours of an imagined community centered in Lübeck. Most important to this imagined community was one built on an in-group that focused on particular readings of geographically tethered history and culture, especially one that centered Lübeck's particular past.

The incorporation of specific local places as exhibition space where the festival played out in public—museums, the central *Marktplatz*, restaurants throughout the city, the *Fußball* pitch—framed the ways in which festivalgoers consumed the events and were meant to navigate their place in the world, in terms of local as well as national identity. Pulling all of this together was the driving motivation for mounting *Nordische Woche* in the first place: to ensure economic survival in a national context that did not seem to prioritize Lübeck or even the Baltic coast as integral, productive places. The narratives that accompanied *Nordische Woche* demonstrated the tactics municipal leaders employed in negotiating postwar German relations while also mobilizing strategies within which festival-goers made their decisions.

THE LEAD-UP TO *NORDISCHE WOCHE*

The week leading up to the official beginning of *Nordische Woche* encapsulated the complexities as well as the potential of the festival. First, the murder of Matthias Erzberger, the minister of finance, at the hands of the "Organisation Consul," a right-wing paramilitary group mobilized by Hermann Ehrhardt and made up of ex-*Freikorps* members connected to the Kapp Putsch, threatened national stability—and arguably international participation in *Nordische Woche*. A flurry of official communiques regarding the black, white, and red flag, which was associated with both Imperial Germany and right-wing organizations, led to public discussions about the potential political messaging displaying that flag at festival events. Days earlier, Ida Boy-Ed had written an op-ed in the *Leipziger Illustrierte*, insisting that *Nordische Woche* was adopting a nonpartisan posture, even before Erzberger's murder, clearly responding to discomfort with even the appearance of political affinity. According to Boy-Ed, and other city leaders who pointed to her op-ed, the prevalence of the "schwartz-weiß-rot" flag was an expression of Lübecker's entrenched connections to its merchant and marine past, not some wink and nod to right-wing activists.[4]

Whether or not Boy-Ed convinced anyone of the "nonpartisan" spirit of either the flag or the festival is debatable. The *Lübecker Volksbote*, which claimed to be a voice of the working class in the city, reported on Boy-Ed's column in what could be interpreted as either snark or ambivalence. Regardless, in the wake of Erzberger's death, Berlin ordered all black-white-and-red flags be removed on August 29 in favor of the Republic's black, red, and yellow flag, if only to prevent international misunderstandings or to keep the peace.[5] The success or failure of *Nordische Woche* was connected to the ability to maintain calm in the wake of Erzberger's death, and organizers feared any messaging that challenged the perspective that Germany was a stable trading partner or ally despite *previous* "political and military collapse" could derail the whole enterprise.[6]

Against this backdrop, the *Lübecker Volksbote* reported the winners of the Handiwork Competition [*Handarbeiten Wettbewerb*] on August 29 too, signaling the first results of *Nordische Woche* events. The competition, which drew participants from across the country, promised several cash prizes, with a top prize of 500 Marks.[7] Competitors were to submit their work between August 15 and 20 in a range of categories of handcrafts, from weaving to embroidery, lace to cross-stitch. A jury of representatives from the German Women's Clothing and Culture Association [*Verein für deutsche Frauenkleidung und Frauenkultur*] as well as the director of Lübeck museums Dr. Carl Georg Heise decided the winners and put together an exhibition of them in the St. Annen-Museum. Most of the winners were women, starting with the first-prize winner, Anna Wewer of Altona-Elbe, who won the top prize with her black, yellow, and white woven teapot warmer; other winners included Eva Marcus of Bremen, who won two prizes for embroidery projects, and Mrs. E. Kaldenbach of Lübeck, for a child's coat with a hat and muff.[8]

What is incredibly interesting is the fact that the jury, in communicating its decisions, highlighted that beauty and artistry can be found even in humble objects that focus on everyday function. For every category, the explanations justifying the level of skill necessary to create each object—regardless of how small or seemingly simplistic—rendered these objects worthy of display alongside religious and sacred art in the St. Annen-Museum for a full four weeks.[9] The emphasis was on originality, excluding works that appeared to employ established or circulated patterns, down to even the motifs and designs each crafter used. This event explicitly targeted the working class, and especially *women*, in ways that other events did not. It also demonstrated how important participation was to the success of *Nordische Woche*, incorporating as many different types of events, audiences, and locations around the city as possible—all while drawing people from across the region. After all, if crowds did not come, there would be no return on investment.

In addition to German visitors, foreign tourists, dignitaries, and student groups attended events, some stretching the duration of the festival. Most of the countries considered "Scandinavian" or "Nordic" by Germans, particularly Denmark, Norway, and Sweden, had maintained neutrality during World War I, and so there was a statement to be made by reinforcing postwar connections with them.[10] The way "Nordic" was constructed by Lübeck's planners, though, included Finland and sometimes Iceland. Finland could be considered a border region in northern Europe, linguistically distinct from the other "Scandinavian" countries as well as in terms of its history vis-à-vis Russia, but it was also connected to continental Europe through shipping and Baltic trade routes.

In this way, *Nordische Woche* was a vehicle to define "Nordic" identity and geography in ways it perhaps had not been before; expanding "Nordic" identity to include Finland could then also include Lübeckers. Finnish groups responded, expanding upon a footprint already in place locally through trade groups and other collaborative organizations, sending students on study-abroad trips utilizing Lübeck's ferry port. Traveling aboard the *Poseidon*, thirty-four Finnish students left Helsinki on August 30 to begin a ten-day trip which included musical performances, lectures, and a "Finland Day."[11] Lübeck was home to several exchange societies focused on language, student groups, and the business community, such as the *Deutsch-Finnländischen Vereinigung*.[12] Another example was the *Deutsch-Dänisch Fehmarnbahn-Komitee*, which concentrated on continuing or expanding access to the island of Fahmarn in the Baltic Sea. The island had been under the control of both Denmark and Germany, representing another borderland that could be incorporated in the wider "Nordic" community highlighted by *Nordische Woche*, especially after the plebiscite.[13] Embassy staff and foreign dignitaries, such as the Norwegian emissary in Dresden, were another type of foreign participant who contributed to the diverse attendee lists, even if their invitations were pro forma and ceremonial.[14] All of these examples demonstrate the intersection of interests that *Nordische Woche* organizers appealed to, and their strategies (as well as the 300,000-Mark advertising budget) were successful enough to actually draw in some visitors.[15]

Those visitors inherently brought economic assets with them, and Lübeck's business community wanted to court trading partners and cultivate them as return visitors. At the same time, the lure of reaching out to Scandinavians had cultural import as well, focusing on how lectures, concerts, and most importantly sporting events would foster and strengthen the relationship between Germany and the immediate region beyond business or diplomatic sectors.[16] In a letter to Dr. Jan Grosse, a major figure in the staging of *Nordische Woche* and a leader of the community, the festival was referred to as "joint" or "cooperative preparation," highlighting the discourse of mutually beneficial outcomes, especially for Finnish groups who advertised back to their German hosts.[17]

STAGING SPACES

The German and foreign tourists were provided a city-wide landscape in which to attend lectures, buy merchandise, and take in performances, especially in the community venues throughout the *Innenstadt* that make up the city's "Seven Spires." Running parallel and to the east of Breitestraße, the pedestrian-street spine of the central district, is Königstraße, beginning at the thirteenth-century Heiligen-Geist-Hospital and running southward. Shops, restaurants, and churches line the streets, including the museum church *Katharinenkirche* at the corner of Königstraße and Glockengrießerstraße. The façade of *Katharinenkirche* today is dark and Gothic, with statues dating from the late 1920s protected from the birds and the elements by wire cages; passers-by are protected, as well, from brick and mortar. The medieval church connected to the *Katharnineum*, the gymnasium school known for educating some of Lübeck's oldest families, has long served more as a gathering and exhibition space rather than a sacred place of worship for the city.

It was as much a showpiece as a pavilion, having hosted exhibitions and events throughout the nineteenth century, especially artistic displays and as meeting space for interest groups. Great care had been taken to preserve its late-medieval character and vaulted spaces with important connections to specific Lübeck families and the region more broadly. The space showcased iconic Lübeck architecture in the basement *Unterchor*, Emil Nolde's religiously themed artistic works of the early 1900s on the main floor, and displayed founding documents associated with the city itself in the *Oberchor* for the duration of *Nordische Woche*.[18] As with other exhibition spaces, *Katharinenkirche*'s part in *Nordische Woche* events tied several narratives together in order to reinforce the multifaceted approach the planners wanted.

The Nolde exhibition was an interesting case study in terms of the hopes and realities surrounding *Nordische Woche*. A Schleswig native, Nolde experimented with a variety of themes, styles, and movements, including *Die Brücke* in 1906 and the Berlin Secession in 1911. He painted subject matter ranging from religion to flowers in a style that categorized him as one of the first Expressionists—and he harbored antisemitic views, at least philosophically supporting the Danish section of the Nazi Party by the late 1920s.[19] The collection exhibited during *Nordische Woche* proudly displayed *Maria Aegyptica* and other contemporary pieces juxtaposed against the setting; later discussions of the exhibit posited that *Katharinenkirche*'s environs elicited a most "vibrant effect."[20] Some of Nolde's work formed the basis of the new

Behnhaus museum's collections, in an ongoing effort to connect Lübeck's present with its past.[21]

The complexities of Nolde's art and the man himself reveal much about the moment of September 1921, when postwar tensions collided with attempts to normalize international relations and contour national identity. There were tremors beneath the surface of the events and in the background, ripples that later seemed to foreshadow the susceptibility of an identity focused on the region and a narrative that assigned a particular people to it. One only had to look at the Erzberger assassination and the threat of political extremism to see that. *Nordische Woche* exhibitions and events contributed to the ongoing definition of what—and who—constituted "Nordic" culture. Present-day discourse about how to remember Emil Nolde, his art, and his politics focuses on the complexities, and a similar approach wraps around the history and memory of *Nordische Woche* as well.[22]

Other exhibitions such as the historical display sponsored by the city archives and the city library focused on the institutions themselves, their roles within the community and the region, and the history of Lübeck in general.[23] This subtly acknowledged the intersection of culture, economics, and festival planning, making all parts of the festival, including the message, interconnected with the logistics of its execution and *public*. In addition, by presenting the history of Lübeck from its Hanseatic era forward to the modern period, one can again see how important it was to postwar Germans to get beyond the immediate past in international relations.

Interestingly, the desire to promote not only Lübeck but Germany in the best possible light led to controversy regarding invited guests and speakers. One speaker was viewed as "too Communist" or inappropriate to give introductions for northern guests, demonstrating that the public viewed the international stage promoted by *Nordische Woche* planners as political and important to the overall perception of Germany by foreigners.[24] In some ways, it centered on the business-oriented and financial aspirations underlying even cultural events; everything, it seemed, was an advertisement.

Nordische Woche, metaphorically and in reality, wove together layers of society. While logistical and financial demands continued to be of concern, the festival itself embodied optimism. Attempting to rectify cultural, economic, and political discord with one all-encompassing festival was a tall order, necessitating events that touched on many parts of everyday life. Put another way, it was incredibly difficult to be everything to everyone, while formulating and emphasizing a cohesive national and cultural identity. Ultimately, the planners effectively were able to sell the festival as a dynamic event with lasting impact filtered through the language and assertion of a particular identity. This was achieved not only through the active participation of festivalgoers but also by the production of cultural artifacts meant to reinforce the narrative, sometimes explicitly. These objects, in their own right, tell another part of the story of *Nordische Woche*, establishing a framework upon which Lübeck, Germany, and an emerging "Nordic" identity coalesced.

ADS AND PRICING

The dominant collectible souvenirs related to *Nordische Woche* that have survived were *Notgeld* and other printed ephemera such as exhibition guides and the sizeable *Festschrift*. These were designed to give explicitly explain the contexts of component events of the festival, especially its ideological and even academic foundations. They also functioned as programs, listing itineraries, artworks and objects on display, and logistical information. The actual process of creating and putting together these booklets was both delegated and centralized. Initial authority was delegated to Carl Georg Heise, the director of museums, by the central planning committee.[25] Heise further collaborated with city librarian Willy Pieth, producing the exhibition guide to historical documents in *Katharinenkirche* and emphasizing the community role the city library played alongside its other cultural institutions.[26] These guides were savable as souvenirs or archivable in their own right as institutional evidence of exhibition. Additional printed material was solicited from foreign participants, promoted as marketing material for participating locations and, less overtly, as a way to highlight external connections from Lübeck outward. The commemorative element of these textual productions lent materiality to the objects, one that is often not attributed to printed texts. However, because of the way these pamphlets were constructed and distributed, the intentional approaches to mass-producing them, and because of their collectability—especially the fact they likely would have been displayed rather than read for content—allows us to think about these textual documents through the lens of material culture.[27]

Requests for advance copies of the program had poured in throughout August, as well as general inquiries about prices to rent booth space, the reasons for the festival, and logistical information. This usually took the form of postcards addressed directly to the *Nordische Woche* main offices at city hall, necessitating telephone conversations with the Lübeck-based printer to fulfill orders from larger groups, such as the *Luther-Gesellschaft* of Wittenberg, which ordered 500 copies of the schedule.[28] This communication demonstrated the interest as well as the concerns of attendees, who made decisions regarding their participation based upon a variety of factors, whether it was cost, timing of events, or taste. What drove these individual decisions is less clear than the slate of options attendees had; the responses to individual inquiries are also unknown.

Perhaps the most ubiquitous source connected with commemorating *Nordische Woche* was *Notgeld.* Building on the existing networks of collectors, as well as international interest in acquiring new issues, the notes were printed to reflect the participants and encapsulate what made *Nordische Woche* unique in a field of local festivals, even those with a similar name or essence. Even in the 2020s, one hundred years later, *Notgeld* from the *Nordische Woche* tradeshow proliferates in online auctions, antique shops, and sites dedicated to collecting *Notgeld.* In many ways, this highlights the dominant economic aims of the festival as well as the available means to advertise and commemorate the events. It also places *Nordische Woche* within the existing framework of commercial exhibitions that were discussed in Chapter 2. The tradeshow *Notgeld* series depicted each Scandinavian flag and mimicked regular currency for the duration of the festival (especially where the commercial booths were set up) as a collectible set.

An alternate series of notes, the so-called *Stadtkasse* series, presented iconic images of Lübeck with captions, such as the *Holstentor* and *Rathaus*, buildings that were recognizable as Lübeck landmarks and that were important sites for *Nordische Woche* activities. On one hand, this imagery is consistent with the overall locally oriented discourse surrounding *Nordsiche Woche*; on the other hand, it was evidence of an increasingly frequent practice of stamping over or adding marks to already existing notes (known as an overprint, or *Aufdruck*), cutting down on printing costs and connecting the *Stadtkasse* series to *Nordische Woche* events. Most often, such overlays or imprints altered the value of notes, very common even for regulated *Reichsbank* notes after 1922 as hyperinflation spiraled out of control. It is interesting that, in this case, a small circular *Nordische Woche* overprint was included; not all issues available to collectors today include the overprint.

The best way to understand how *Nordische Woche* was ultimately presented, especially in light of the ongoing public discourse, is by analyzing the *Festschrift* edited by Heinz Mahn and the booklets detailing the individual exhibitions at sites across the city. The *Festschrift* served as the main guide to *Nordische* Woche, including advertisements, essays, daily schedules, and resources for attendees. It was meant to be widely available and relatively inexpensive (despite its overall price tag of 83,700 Marks for the entire run), bound in stiff cardstock rather than cloth or traditional hardcover binding.[29] Shorter versions including only the schedule of events were both sent out and advertised in newspapers across the country, allowing attendees to map out their trip and order tickets to performances or sporting events.

More than anything, the *Festschrift* promoted regional sponsors with two sections of advertising, front and back. The advertisements offer a unique glimpse into 1921 Lübeck, as well as what would be of interest to festivalgoers and the nation generally. While the advertisements were aimed at a general audience, three distinct types existed and literally reflected Anderson's notion of print capitalism. These types reflected the different layers of identity evident in *Nordische Woche*—local, regional/national, and international. Advertisements that centered Lübeck, for example, highlighted the industries most connected with the city: marzipan, seafaring and fishing, and manufacturing. Marzipan, which even today is recognized as a Lübeck delicacy, featured prominently with spaces in the second advertising section for Niederegger and Carstens in particular.[30] To highlight Lübeck's role as "king" of marzipan, an advertisement for Lübecker Marzipan took up an entire page at the beginning of the second marketing section.[31]

Other images used for the local layer of identity featured manufacturing and industry, such as B. Glogner and Company presenting a factory worker with the words "Steel and Iron [*Stahl und Eisen*]" in bold.[32] This image emphasized not only Lübeck's own manufacturing landscape but also explicitly linked it with the western industrial regions such as the Ruhr Valley, contentious in 1921 because of its demilitarized status and proximity to wartime enemies. Further reinforcing Lübeck's industrial character were the ads for Ernst Boie's manufacturing firm, located in the inner-city district; it had the added benefit of boosting business for the leading proponent of *Nordische Woche* and head of the Chamber of Commerce.[33] Advertisements highlighting regional and national industries and objects of interest were also prominently featured, often with reference to Lübeck's local representatives.

The role of the sea and fisheries occupied a great deal of space in both advertising sections. One example was the *Nordische Mischenenbau Lübeck*, which marketed its industrial, efficient, "fully automatic" business activities to fish markets; it also referenced the Research Institute for the Fishing Industry on the page, highlighting necessary research and development efforts in competitive globalizing markets.[34] This reinforced the closeness of Lübeck to the Baltic Sea and how it impacted so much of everyday life, even in subtle ways, and served to frame daily fishing reports in local papers and trade communications. It must be noted, though, that the emphasis on the sea was not just for practical or industrial use. Leisure featured prominently as well. Lübeck's *Schiffersgesellschaft*, heralded as one of the best restaurants serving local fare, occupied the historic sailor's guild building on the western end of Breitestraße across from St. Jakobi, the "sailors' cathedral."[35] St. Jakobi also served as a gathering point of pilgrims traveling across northern Europe and from Scandinavia to Santiago de Compostela, following the Way of St. James. Though this facet of St. Jakobi was likely less known at the time (the pilgrimage routes in northern Germany fell into disuse after the Reformation), its connection to sailors and travelers linked religious, cultural, and occupational histories.

Outside of the *Innenstadt* and the surrounding neighborhoods, advertisements heralded Lübeck's physical and metaphorical connections beyond itself. Advertisements and promotions for Travemünde, Lübeck's popular holiday district on the Baltic Sea, emphasized travel aboard the Lübeck-Travemünde rail line, day trips, and the beach in an attempt to reach wealthy vacationers as well as those of the working class. An advertisement featuring a scuba-mask maker highlighted the role the sea played in regional life, extending even to leisure; it also resembled the gasmasks so necessary in the trenches of World War I.[36] The presence of objects even subtly recalling World War I pointed to national insecurities of the time even as they were ostensibly fixed on growth. Walter Redelstorff advertised safes manufactured by Panzer AG, headquartered in Berlin and associated with heavy wartime machinery and tanks.[37] Because of the terms of the Treaty of Versailles (which banned the manufacture of weapons of war), Panzer AG adapted its technology to legal and timely concerns. Not surprisingly, bank advertisements, all with Lübeck offices, took up much room in the *Festschrift* commercial pages.

The final layer of identity that can be discerned through the pages of advertising was international in scope. While Lübeck's role was again central, the linkages to the outside world, especially through trade and transport, were promoted as indelible to regional viability. Some of the businesses highlighted were importers, focusing on consumer goods. H. Drefelt, a purveyor of cigars and pipes, advertised not only Havana cigars but a series of "Lübeck Honor" cigars at varying price points, including the "*Schiffersgesellschaft*," the finest quality.[38] Obviously, this appealed to a specific sector of society—one that had disposable income to afford such luxury—but this definitely highlighted the role consumption played in putting on *Nordische Woche*. It also spoke to locals in ways it wouldn't have to foreign and out-of-town visitors. The most economic benefit would be in luring the more affluent into participation in the events and shopping. Ads for expensive consumer goods, such as Benz automobiles (and the Continental brand tires that went with them)[39] and specialty clothing[40] appeared alongside more mundane objects like milk cans.[41] Consumables were further reinforced by firms and companies who both advertised in the *Festschrift* and had a stand in one of the exhibit halls. Many of these industries focused on consumer goods as an example of craftsmanship, such as furniture, photography, and pianos, to name a few.

The last set of advertisements that demonstrated Lübeck's international linkages were shipping or drayage companies. One such company was Carl Lassen Shipping, highlighted because of its destinations in Scandinavia and elsewhere in Germany. Headquartered in Wasa-haus (and located on a street where several organizations related to German-Finnish relations were), Lassen's business advertised drayage to most Scandinavian countries and several Hanseatic cities. The advertisement itself was the outline of a traditional

Lübeck building with a stepped profile; each level contained the names of common destinations.[42] As mentioned before, the ferry lines across the Baltic Sea were already familiar to travelers from Scandinavia and Eastern Europe; the goal was to get them to stop. Travel was becoming more accessible, seen in the expansion of railroads and automobiles, and ferry crossings were no exception. In the second section of advertising in the *Festschrift*, several companies highlighted the frequency with which they transported people and goods to Scandinavian countries, especially Finland, Norway, and Sweden.[43]

The amount of advertising in the *Festschrift* demonstrated how fully the business and industrial community supported the events and activities of *Nordische Woche* and the reasons for that support. Just as in today's events, such sponsorship made an undertaking of this magnitude feasible, and it sought to strengthen bonds that had been tested by the war and Germany's ongoing economic insecurity. It is for this reason that the economic issues—the tradeshow, the financial goals and necessities, and the element of consumption—surrounding *Nordische Woche* cannot be understated. It was precisely the support of the commercial sector that made the other parts of *Nordische Woche* possible, especially in the form of honoraria for essays and lectures in commemorative programs and newspapers. The more academic or scholarly elements of the *Festschrift* and *Nordische Woche* events made the festival more than a business venture or money grab—though that had inspired the whole thing to begin with.

Equally important was driving home the point that this was a festival *Lübeck* put on, from the top levels of city government and influential men in the community to the everyday people who had to promote their hometown as an international festival destination. Indeed, it was Lübeckers who would create the impression that visitors would carry with them, extending not only to the city but perhaps the nation as well. For this reason, one of the first sections of the *Festschrift* detailed the government buildings (such as the *Rathaus*), churches (especially *Marienkirche*), and the *Stadttheater* that played host to specific exhibitions.[44] It is evident Lübeck city government, apart from the central planning committee, sanctioned the activities of *Nordische Woche*, due to the locations used for festival events and because of who served. The honorary chairman listed for the planning committee was "Our Magnificent Mayor Dr. Neumann."[45] In addition, royal envoys from Sweden, Denmark, and Norway (in addition to the official envoy of Finland) were listed as honorary committee members.[46] This may have been a point of courtesy, but their inclusion denoted an acceptance of the way the event was framed. There was potential upside for Scandinavian governments, as well.

The *Festschrift* included a list of "Nordic" consulates in Lübeck (Denmark, Finland, Norway, and Sweden), the head Consul, phone numbers, and addresses.[47] This encouraged an ongoing relationship with Scandinavian destinations, especially in light of the informational booklet produced by Turku, Finland's chamber of commerce (which will be discussed later on in this chapter). Festivalgoers could follow up their *Nordische Woche* experience with a trip to one or more of the profiled nations, in order to explore common roots on their own or through an organized trip. At the same time, this inclusion encouraged active participation from Norway, Denmark, Sweden, and Finland, as visitors from the respective countries would gain a relationship based upon tourism, potentially leading to economic and cultural inroads into Germany. Practical issues, such as living quarters and transportation were also addressed in the *Festschrift*, as routes to and from Lübeck from other parts of Germany, the "East," Sweden, and Denmark were included in a special *Nordische Woche* insert.[48] All of this logistical and practical information, important in orienting visitors to the city, appeared immediately in the first advertising section but before the body of essays, in order to prevent this basic information from getting lost in analysis.

This focus on travel again targeted a very specific sector of society, those who could afford to even entertain the notion of travel, regardless of scope or scale. The range of advertisements and booking information made it clear, though, that audiences were anticipated from across socioeconomic strata, demonstrated by the tiered pricing schedule for performances, sporting events, and exhibitions. Popular (though not particularly "Nordic") performances, such as Strauss's *Fledermaus*, Mozart's *Zauberflöte*, and Wagner's *Siegfried* saw detailed pricing; attempts were made to provide group rates as well, if only to inspire families or audiences traveling together to take in the performances.[49] Additionally, the possibility of "bundling" a set of performances or events brought with it the benefit of exposing audiences to multiple things. The same practice was applied to entrance fees or tickets for exhibitions, especially a series of exhibitions in one location (e.g., the three distinct exhibitions at *Katharinenkirche* and the like).[50]

NORDISCHE WOCHE IN TEXT

The non-advertising elements of the *Festschrift* included essays, some of which were excerpted in newspaper articles and mirrored or complemented lecture events. These served to intellectually and explicitly contextualize *Nordische Woche*, providing a frame of reference for festivalgoers who may not have been familiar with the preplanning public discourse leading up to opening day. The newspaper versions of essays and op-ed pieces provided by planners and participants were "teasers" for the event itself, potentially sparking interest in a particular subject to get them in the door. It also allowed participants to "scrapbook" the events from preexisting subscriptions, making the messaging more widely accessible: that Lübeck's identity was indelibly and historically wrapped up in the "Nordic" world through trade, cultural transmission, and diplomacy. This was expanded out to situate Lübeck within the *German* context, then allowing German identity to reposition itself vis-à-vis Scandinavian countries. The essays and lectures printed in the *Festschriften* and other programs afforded participants an academic element to the festival, preventing the events from being viewed merely as an exercise in banal popular culture or business exchange. There were histories here, and each essayist or speaker provided legitimacy for *Nordische Woche* in a variety of ways, which were documented in the *Festschrift.*

From the outset, the essays connected with *Nordische Woche* were meant for publication in a variety of outlets, including newspapers, journals, and several commemorative booklets. The solicitations for scholarly lectures were sent to professors and academics, offering honoraria for their work, which, in postwar Germany, appeared to reprioritize intellectual work.[51] In fact, one author highlighted the stress of producing the wished-for essay at a time when "every morsel of bread has become more expensive again."[52] The involvement in *Nordische Woche* had economic potential for the academic and scholarly participants, as they could funnel their efforts into multiple sources while promoting themselves as speakers at a time when resources were slight.

Some letters and memos asked for essays to be pared down for publication in newspapers or the popular press, as "the least expensive length to accommodate newspapers is approximately 3 typewritten pages."[53] Again, overall costs had to be considered as with any undertaking, and the ability to publish in the popular press was considered extremely important as a way to expand readership and influence. In this way, planners introduced academic or intellectual treatments of Nordic-German relations, Lübeck's history, and the import of *Nordische Woche* while keeping the general reading public in mind. These newspaper-bound essays provided a digest of the talks that were happening, adding a teaching element to the artistic, musical, and theatrical exhibitions; some of these excerpts or abridgments appeared alongside the talk itself. Drafts of essays to be included in the general *Festschrift* had been circulated among the central planning committee beforehand.[54] This element in particular showcases how planners framed the experiences for attendees, and it was within these broad structures festivalgoers navigated and consumed concepts and events.

Already known international experts contributed written work, either in newspapers or the booklets, to lend an air of authority and solemnity to the proceedings; at times this accompanied their physical presence. This, of course, meant that honoraria for already established scholars could be relatively high, something that had the potential to drive up the overall cost of publication. One example of such a solicitation was aimed at Adolph Goldschmidt, determined to be the foremost scholar on Lübeck painting and sculpture, due to his doctoral work as well as his teaching position in Sweden. Though he had not seemed inclined to participate, planners felt that he could be "persuaded" in a letter-writing campaign.[55] Ultimately, Goldschmidt submitted an essay on fifteenth-century Lübecker religious art and its export to Sweden and Finland for the *Festschrift*, though he was not physically present to lecture at the event.[56]

The first section of the essays dealt with the "Nordic" world (excluding Iceland), discussing topics such as medieval shipbuilding, the Danish school system, and Finland's struggle against Russia in reference to "old" Lübeck. These essays reinforced or articulated the contours and definitions of Nordic heritage in regards to art, trades, and craftsmanship, in much the same way advertisements focused on these things. Scandinavian contributors lent an air of scholarly cooperation, providing their expertise in analyses of the global impact of the northern nations from outside Germany. The first essay in particular associated Scandinavian maritime trade and Lübeck, tracing a narrative back to the Middle Ages and the establishment of Lübeck by Heinrich the Lion.[57] This essay pointed to the rise and decline of Lübeck and other Hanseatic cities as nation-states such as England, Holland, and Sweden began to coalesce, and it argued that Lübeck was again rebounding as a trading partner internationally on behalf of Germany.[58] This rebuilding recalled the golden age or "days of glory [*Blütezeit*]" Lübeck claimed as the seat of the Hanseatic League. The emphasis on the Hanse reveals the entrenched independence Lübeckers asserted, almost arguing that the city had to rely on itself and implies that Berlin would do little in support of either the region or the city after World War I.

The next three essays built on these opening themes by highlighting exactly how successful Lübeck had been artistically and commercially in the days of the Hanseatic League. Adding to this was Gustav Pauli's discussion of *Marienkirche*, one of the iconic cathedrals of Lübeck's historic inner city.[59] The other essays tackled themes more topically, such as Lübeck's role and culture in Germany or the role of St. George of Sweden as a central figure in art. These articles echoed the artistic exhibitions mounted throughout Lübeck, while also opening the door to comparisons with other cities. Lübeck's central memorial to Heinrich the Lion was (and still is) located near the central cathedral (the *Dom*), just as the famous statue of Roland is located in the central *Marktplatz* in Bremen. The "city of seven spires" imagery depicted on the cover of the *Festschrift* (which was the Alfred Mahlau poster) connected the motifs of religion and architecture to industry by featuring masts of ships, seven of which were printed in reflective gold. The essay "Lübeck's Industry" served to reinforce this connection, detailing the city's Hanseatic history on the Baltic.[60] Lübeck's claim to Baltic regionalism was evident here, particularly in reference to larger metropolitan centers and regions such as Berlin, Prussia, and Hamburg that existed outside the boundaries of how Lübeck municipal officials defined "their" region in an almost defensive way. This was evident in the inclusion of an article about "Lübeck's Diplomatic Situation," actively locating Lübeck within international relations.[61] It decisively built and expanded upon the festival discourse discussed in the last chapter, where German cities sought to promote themselves as international destinations, at times in competition with each other.

Some articles were more philosophical, grounded in a particular reading of history and archaeology. One example was "The Spiritual Function of the Present," by philosopher and 1908 Nobel Prize winner for Literature Rudolf Eucken, which discussed who built culture and what it consisted of in 1921.[62] This construction was to take place using artifacts and stories from the past, such as an explanation of how old Nordics built ships, traveled, and spread their culture throughout the world. Similarly, Swedish archaeologist Oskar Montelius included drawings of old or medieval boats to demonstrate how seafaring and shipbuilding improved over time through innovation. His "Figure 2" depicted a bare-bones skiff, able to hold people but not very sophisticated in design.[63] "Figure 4," however, contained a steering mechanism and had aesthetic qualities.[64] By setting up comparisons between old and new methods, the reader could form a foundation of knowledge for present-day shipbuilding, particularly the craftsmanship and modernity of it. In order to get at these roots, the article claimed, archaeological study could demonstrate how far "the Scandinavian-German North" had come in their art.[65]

There were some essays that contained seeds of racialist rhetoric and a move toward ethnic nationalism, especially the nation bound together by race. Ernst Lampén, a Finnish language teacher and writer from Helsinki, discussed how Finland came to be and how the Finnish people described themselves.[66] His main example dealt with the fact that "Finland" was a Swedish word, contrasting with the name "Suomi," which natives used for their homeland.[67] Interestingly, in his discussion of linguistic appropriation, he stated that the German word "Hansa," used to describe the economic cooperative Hanseatic League (very appropriate considering the fact Lübeck's consistent identification as a Hanseatic city) was appropriated in the Finnish language as "kansa," or *Volk*. Lampén consistently used the term to denote ownership of land and nationality, in many ways resonating with contemporary political philosophies seeking to categorize nationalism and national character.[68]

The use of the word *Volk* appeared in other essays as well. Rudolf Kjellén, who coined the phrase and concept of "geopolitics," discussed the concept of the *Volk* at length (and with a much more racialist bent), claiming that the Swedish *Volk* were "under different influences and have moved in a different direction" than the German *Volk* had.[69] He went on to elaborate that "a strong, mutual influence in the direction of Pan-Germanism exists. Never before has race and contact been so intimately intertwined with each other as in this time, the time of the greatest political disunity."[70] Toward the end of the essay, Kjellén invoked the phrase "blood is thicker than water," linking directly the concept of blood, race, and the *Volk*.

Kjellén acknowledged that German and Swedish *Völker* were not the *same* (which laid the foundations for various brethren ethnicities in racial theory) but shared enough common characteristics and values to achieve a common goal (allowing for the intellectual foundations of an overarching umbrella identity).[71] These essays reveal the undercurrents of exclusionary frames of reference in terms of identity. *Nordische Woche* drew together people who were depicted as sharing common or at least complementary history and/or heritage; there were people on the peripheries who were *not* included in this history, even if they were not explicitly targeted. Situated against the political assassination and the mobilization of the far-right in terms of ethnonationalism, the inclusion of these articles could have been a wink and a nod to activists who sought to coalesce racial allies. These essays were the closest planners came to saying that part out loud.

Other publications were produced alongside the *Festschrift* that, while not tied to particular exhibitions or *Nordische Woche* events, still took advantage of the festival audience. The volume *Lübische Forschungen* [Lübeck Research] appeared for the centennial of the Society for Lübeck History and Archaeology [*Verein für Lübeckische Geschichte und Altertumskunde*] in 1921. The book contained stand-alone essays expressly dealing with local history, focusing on topics such as Lübeck's *Marktplatz* and its importance to the city.[72] In this volume, there were no introductory or concluding essays to tie the component parts together or to connect them to festival events, instead producing a diverse compendium. Like the other collectible books, the lengthy volume was bound in soft-cover woven paper as opposed to a hardcover binding. It made the book more affordable to both produce and purchase.

While most printed materials were produced by Lübeck city government or organizations within the city, there were a few submissions from outside Germany. One major example was the city of Turku, Finland (also called Åbo), which was the terminus of a ferry line originating in Lübeck/Travemünde. Turku was a known entity to many Lübeckers because of the convenience of the ferry, and the descriptive yearbook-type booklet produced by the Turku Chamber of Commerce was simultaneously aimed at German festival-goers and Lübeck business interests.[73] This particular booklet was unique, because it represented Turku's overtures to the Lübeck hosts, two cities that pursued financial and cultural connections outside traditional diplomatic avenues.

Turku's booklet included industrial and commercial statistics, including an itemized breakdown of the city's income and outgoing expenses.[74] It also emphasized the similarities between Turku and Lübeck, including photographs of the harbor, ships, and other industry, such as John Barker's cotton mill.[75] The second half of Turku's industrial report focused on metal and metalworking, including skyrocketing prices for raw iron between 1913 and 1920.[76] This allusion to high prices due to the war and its aftermath implies that Turku, perhaps more than other neighboring cities, had common ground with Lübeck. Turku's history as a former capital city of Finland, founded in the thirteenth century and the site of at least two devastating fires, rhymed with Lübecker narratives of decline and an almost scrappy commitment to a more sustainable future. It also acknowledged a postwar period that was challenging for much of Europe, and that it would require cooperation through trade and tourism to generate recovery.

Culturally, Turku's booklet focused on more than just industrial outputs; it also detailed education and the similarities between German and Finnish schooling systems. Lübeck tried to present itself as multicultural in the sense that "Nordic" populations, especially Danish, mixed with ethnic Germans and had schools. In much the same way, the booklet presented statistics about Finnish and Swedish students in elementary and trade-school classes.[77] Turku highlighted its cultural establishments, such as its "especially noteworthy antiquity museum," *Åbo Schloss*.[78] Rounding out the description of Turku's "cultural life" were paragraphs about theater, music, publishing, other museums, and architecture. The rest of the booklet described Turku's physical landmarks, especially the harbor, culminating in a list of publications sponsored by the chamber of commerce between 1919 and 1921 led readers to other officially sanctioned information about the city and Finland in general.[79] The focus on industrial-port life would have been legible to Lübeckers as harbor life, fishing, and shipping constituted much of Lübeck's identity and industrial activity.

NORDISCHE WOCHE IN WORD AND DEED

Speeches and lectures were included in the schedule of events, at times expanding on *Festschrift* essays and at others providing space for other voices. Many of the lecturers, such as Rudolf Kjellén, were established in their fields and even advanced in age; Kjellén requested a ground-floor lecture hall early in the week, as he could not "climb steps very well" and had to return to Uppsala to give exams.[80] Thomas Mann's appearance at *Nordische Woche*, serving as a well-regarded product of Lübeck and championed by Ida Boy-Ed locally, balanced some of the senior lecturers. Mann's novel

Buddenbrooks had been published in 1901, in which he described the decline of a merchant family in Lübeck. *Nordische Woche* occurred three years before the publication of *The Magic Mountain* and eight before he was awarded the Nobel Prize in Literature, but he steadily wrote essays and short stories in this period, mostly living in Munich and touring abroad. He came to Lübeck to debut of his essay "Goethe and Tolstoy" first as a lecture, reprinted in full in the *Deutsche Rundschau,* and later published in 1925 as an expanded, stand-alone essay.[81] A piece of literary critique and commentary, "Goethe and Tolstoy," has been described as "one of the most important essays written in the German language in this century."[82] This is demonstrative of how *Nordische Woche*, and a specific lecture event during it, impacted the wider world well after festivities ended, even if the connection to the festival itself receded from memory.

Mann, in his notes and manuscripts, seemed to be drawn to reevaluate the role of writers in society and how they differed in national context—in this case, Russia (in the process of becoming the Soviet Union in 1921) and Germany. The invitation to *Nordische Woche*, given the scope and stated goals of the planners, made complete sense on many levels. Mann represented an intersection of internationalism, culture, and local pride, and precipitated Mann's actual work of writing. Most importantly, his patron Ida Boy-Ed served as the link between Mann and festival planners, and it is likely that her request impacted his ultimate participation.[83] In fact, Mann was the prototype of the desired attendee, one who would attend *Nordische Woche* events and then conveniently tour the surrounding area.[84] In addition to this lecture, Mann's essay "Freedom and Refinement" (*Freiheit und Vornehmheit*) was published in the *Festschrift*, which asked the question: "What is the 'common' [*Gemeine*]?"[85] In his further discussion of freedom, Mann's printed essay discussed similar source literature that his lecture did, assuming the audience was widely read and understood the debates about rationalism, freedom, and emotion.

In the same vein, plays and operas presented in the *Stadttheater* were a major part of *Nordische Woche* festivities, particularly in the evening. Most of the performances were German (broadly understood) and Scandinavian classics, such as several performances of Ibsen plays, operas by Mozart and Wagner, and symphony performances of works by Sibelius and Grieg. Beethoven's *Fidelio* opened it all, followed by a welcome party in the *Ratskeller*. Seat groups were priced on a sliding scale, with some performances free to the public while others (especially *Meistersinger* by Wagner and *Fledermaus* by Strauss) were priced higher.[86] The pricing structure of these performances demonstrated how some works were valued more than others or at least were enjoying more popularity. These events during *Nordische Woche* could be construed as "high culture," and a program detailing just the performances in the theater was available for 12 Marks for those attendees who preferred such diversions.

This high-culture evening element across the eleven days was balanced by sport and motion picture shows, explicitly targeting the lower classes and working classes. On Sunday, September 4, for instance, football clubs staged a tournament, with Idrotts-Föreningen, Helsingborg, and Hamburg sports clubs sending teams; staging the competition on Sunday meant that laborers could come or even compete.[87] A week later, association and school teams competed against each other in track and field and fistball [*Faustball*].[88] This emphasis on physical health and activity brought German culture out of the classroom and into the outdoors, drawing on common mores of the time as well as the postwar shifts in leisure, competition, and identity. Fighting one's opponents on the pitch was at least less destructive than the battlefront, and it provided opportunities for laborers, youth groups, and even homemakers to consume festival messages in a totally different way.

That motion pictures were included spoke to the newness of film and the nascence of the German film industry. Arguably an expansion from the "magic lantern" shows of the nineteenth century, motion pictures had improved in technology and sophistication and this was expressly emphasized at *Nordische Woche*, especially in its presentation of the "Wonders of Cinematography" on September 6 in the *Stadthalle*.[89] Films from Scandinavian countries as well as Germany, especially those highlighting film as art and industry, were sponsored by the Lübeck Cinema Community [*Lübecker Lichtspielgemeinde*], with single-show tickets as well as day passes, again tiered by seats and, in this case, general versus youth admission. That this particular show happened on a Tuesday likely limited exactly who attended, but the popularity of the film in 1920s Germany only increased as the decade went on and linked cultural festivals to a variety of formats for cultural expression. Lübeck's festivals going forward tended to include film showings and festivals, especially as they became more accessible and prolific.

What is difficult to glean through these sources is what the audience looked like, who attended outside of competition winners, planners, and participants, and how widespread interest truly was in *Nordische Woche*. By all accounts, *Nordische Woche* was ultimately profitable, resulting in a surplus of funds once everyone got paid and the banners were put away. And yet, in the weeks and months after *Nordische Woche* ended, intense focus was placed on the monetary or financial results of the events and what should be done with those funds. Almost immediately, articles appeared in all the local newspapers and across Germany questioning whether or not *Nordische Woche* would be a yearly event, effusively touting its success and impacts. Communications between other festival organizers in other cities revealed discussions about the costs sunk into the different aspects of the events, particularly the *Festschrift*.[90] At the very least, the interactions between various municipalities and festival planners imply that Lübeckers were successful in advertising and promoting *Nordische Woche* amid the other festivals of the time.

Lübeck's *Nordische Woche* focused on contemporary constructions of identity and the past in the formation of current Nordic-German relations and culture. Identifying the next steps required moving beyond defining "success" in purely economic terms or a widely encompassing festival. Drawing inspiration from individual lectures and events, key municipal figures and commercial leaders in Lübeck decided to establish an organization to produce and reproduce the narratives associated with the Nordic identities that were actively constructed at *Nordische Woche*. That organization—the *Nordische Gesellschaft* [Nordic Society, or NG]—continued the work of constructing the emergent "Nordic" in-group in northern Germany in the later 1920s. Situated against the ongoing crisis of spiraling hyperinflation, the NG operated in the context of complete economic and political uncertainty. This Nordic identity was subject to negotiation and renegotiation in light of circumstances, internalizing and mobilizing entrenched racialized tropes as members framed and explained their contemporary social experiences. The events of *Nordische Woche* were recalled as part of the origin story of the NG, but over the course of the 1920s and into the 1930s, the organization increasingly expressed and reflected radicalizing attitudes.

NOTES

1. "Über den Verein," *LübeckRegatta*. https://luebeckregatta.de/index.php/ueber-den-verein/. See also "100 Jähre Lübecker Regattaverein," *LNOnline*, 31 January 2021. https://www.ln-online.de/Sportbuzzer/Sport-im-Norden/100-Jahre-Luebecker-Regattaverein.
2. "Niederschrift der Sitzung über Finanzfragen der Nordischen Woche," 6 June 1921. HAL, 1.2 NSA 2462.
3. Ibid. This is especially obvious in this memo as notations were made stating that a final budget could exceed 1,000,000 Marks in upfront costs.
4. Dr. Lange, "Bemerkungen," *Lübecker Volksbote,* 20 August 1921. HAL, 1.2 NSA 2462.
5. Dr. Lange to the *Lübecker General Anzeiger* office, "Bekanntmachung," 3 Sept. 1921. HAL, 1.2 NSA 2462.
6. Letter to Hamburg-Amerikanische Paketfahrt A.G., 8 June 1921. HAL, 1.2 NSA 2462.
7. Handarbeiten-Wettbewerb information card. HAL, 1.2 NSA 2462.
8. Handarbeiten-Wettbewerb, *Lübecker Volksbote*, 29 August 1921, 6. Digitale Bibliothek der Friedrich-Ebert-Stiftung. http://library.fes.de/luebeck/pdf/1921/1921–201.pdf
9. Ibid.

10. The borders of "Scandinavia" were shifting, at times including or excluding Iceland and Finland, which had won its independence from the Russian Empire in 1918. Visual representations of Scandinavia after the war were in flux and often relied on immediate need or circumstantial context.

11. "Programm für den Besuch der Studenten Finnlands," 2. HAL, NSA 1.2 2462.

12. "Niederschrift über die Sitzung des Arbeitsausschusses," 11 March 1921. HAL, HK 275.

13. Ibid.

14. "An das Königlich Norwegische Konsulat," 16 March 1921. HAL, HK 275.

15. Letter to Dr. Kalkbrenner, 11 May 1921. HAL, 1.2 NSA 2462: Nordische Woche 1921–1923. In this letter, the financial breakdown of "propaganda" in Scandinavian countries showed special interest in advertising to Sweden and Finland.

16. O.M., "Lübeck nach dem Krieg," *Vossiche-Zeitung*, 22 March 1921. HAL, HK 275.

17. Unsigned letter to Jan Grosse, 6 April 1921, 3. HAL, HK 275.

18. "Protokoll der 4. Sitzung des Kunstausschusses vom 31. Mai 1921." HAL, 1.2 NSA 2462. The price for exhibitions in Katharinenkirche was 500 Mark, compared to exhibitions in other Lübeck landmarks such as the Schabbelhaus, which charged 200 Marks.

19. Tom Almeroth-Williams, "Exposing a Nazi: The Exhibition Exposing a Myth," University of Cambridge, 2019. https://www.cam.ac.uk/exposinganazi.

20. Peter Selz, *Emil Nolde MoMA Exhibit Catalog,* 1963, pp. 26–27.

21. Carl Georg Heise, director of Lübeck's museums including the newly opened Behnhaus, explicitly articulated the goal to pull together Lübeck's history with its present. See Alexander Bastek, "Thomas Mann, Carl Georg Heise und die bildende Kunst in Lübeck," *Thomas Mann Jahrbuch* 26 (2013): 53–67.

22. This is especially clear in two Nolde retrospective exhibits, one at the *Behnhaus* in 2018 entitled *Emil Nolde: Farbenzauber* (see https://die-luebecker-museen.de/2018_emil-nolde) and one at the Hamburger Bahnhof—Museum für Gegenwart-Berlin in 2019 entitled *Emil Nolde: Eine deutsche Legende* (see https://www.smb.museum/en/exhibitions/detail/emil-nolde-a-german-legend-the-artist-during-the-nazi-regime/). Additional discussion in English popular press include Barry Schwabske, "The Perfect Victim: How Should We Remember the Art of Emil Nolde?" *The Nation,* 19 September 2019. https://www.thenation.com/article/archive/emil-nolde-hamburger-banhof-review/.

23. "An den Hauptausschuss der 'Nordischen Woche,'" 31 May 1921. HAL, 1.2 NSA 2462.

24. Ein deutschfühlender Freund der Kunst, "Sprechsaal," *Lübeckische Anzeiger*, 20 July 1921.

25. Alken Bruns, "Carl Georg Heise," in *Neue Lübecker Lebensläufe,* ed. Alken Bruns (Neumünster: Wachholz, 2009), 280–86.

26. Willy Pieth, *Lübish-nordische Ausstellung im oberen Chor der Katharinenkirche 1.-11. September.* Lübeck: Schmidt, 1921. HAL, NA 117.

27. See Patricia A. Baker, *The Archaeology of Medicine in the Greco-Roman World* (Cambridge: Cambridge University Press, 2013), especially Chapter 3, "Text as Material Culture." Though Baker makes the case for archaeologists analyzing texts

and text fragments about the ancient world, her larger point that textual remnants can be viewed through the lens of materiality and using material cultural methods applies to events like *Nordische Woche*, where the bulk of objects that survive are, indeed, textual while also serving as commemorative objects or souvenirs.

28. Postcard from Luther-Gesellschaft, 13 August 1921. A follow-up two days later with the printer in Lübeck indicated that the 500 copies should be sent to Pastor Knolle of Wittenberg, ostensibly the main contact of the Luther-Gesellschaft in Wittenberg. HAL, Nachrichtenamt 131.

29. Letter from Dr. Große, 7 March 1922. HAL, 1.2 NSA 2462.

30. Heinz Mahn, ed. *Festschrift zur Nordische Woche in Lübeck, 1–11 September 1921* (Lübeck: H.G. Rahtgens, 1921), 133 and 88 (of second advertisement section) respectively.

31. Ibid., 6 (of second advertisement section).

32. Ibid., n.p. (unnumbered page next to page 32 of second advertisement section).

33. Ibid., 85–86 (of second advertising section).

34. Ibid., 47 (of second advertising section).

35. St. Jakobi today hosts the chapel dedicated to the sailors lost on the *Pamir*, which sank in 1957. In 1921, it already had become the place to remember lost sailors, especially civilians.

36. Mahn, *Festschrift*, 31 (of first advertising section).

37. Ibid., 46 (of second advertising section).

38. Ibid., 23 (of first advertising section).

39. Ibid., 16 and opposite unnumbered page (of second advertising section).

40. Ibid., 41 (of first advertising section).

41. Ibid., 51 (of first advertising section).

42. Ibid., n.p. (unnumbered page opposite page 72 of first advertising section).

43. Ibid., 109–111 (of second advertising section).

44. Ibid., 5–10.

45. Ibid., 3.

46. Ibid.

47. Ibid., 4.

48. Ibid., travel insert. There are no page numbers included on this insert, as it was meant to be a mobile aid for travelers.

49. Ibid., 14–15.

50. Ibid., 16.

51. Letter to Dr. Johann Paul, 22 June 1921. HAL, Nachrichtenamt 117: Aufsätze für die Nordische Woche.

52. Letter to Dr. Stucken from Fink, 20 August 1921. HAL, Nachrichtenamt 117. By August 1921, the economic crises in Germany were deepening, clearly being felt across social and disciplinary lines.

53. Letter to Baurat Virck, 27 July 1921. HAL, NA 117.

54. HAL, NA 117. The drafts were variably handwritten, typewritten, and/or mimeorgraphed on very thin, nearly transparent paper, and finally submitted on heavier, typewritten paper. Comments were included as well as edits to the text itself.

55. Letter to director of Museum für Kunst und Kulturgeschichte from Carl Georg Heise, 26 March 1921. HAL, NA 117.

56. Adolph Goldschmidt, "Die Kunst Lübecks im 15. Jahrhundert," in Mahn, *Festschrift,* 22.
57. Walther Vogel, "Lübeck und die Ostsee im Mittelalter," in Mahn, *Festschrift,* 17–18.
58. Ibid., 19.
59. Gustav Pauli, "Die Marienkirche zu Lübekc," in Mahn, *Festschrift,* 25–29.
60. Rudolf Kelbel, "Lübecks Industrie," in Mahn, *Festschrift,* 93.
61. Rudolf Stucken, "Lübecks Verkehrslage," 103.
62. Rudolf Eucken, "Die geistige Haupaufgabe der Gegenwart," in Mahn, *Festschrift*, 44.
63. Oskar Montelius, "Altgermanischer Schiffbau," in Mahn, *Festschrift*, 60.
64. Ibid.
65. Ibid., 63.
66. Ernst Lampén, "Finnland, Suomi," in Mahn, *Festschrift*, 47. It is unclear what his profession was.
67. Ibid.
68. Ibid., also appearing on ibid., 50. The Finnish *Volk* are clearly separate from neighboring populations (including domestic minority populations, such as the Russians or Swedes).
69. Rudolf Kjellén, "Der Umgang Schwedens in alter und neuer Zeit," in Mahn, *Festschrift*, 34. He had already published *Der Staat als Lebensform* (Leipzig: S. Hirzel, 1917), which discussed geopolitics and state formation, and was a global authority on the concept.
70. Ibid., 35.
71. Ibid., 37. Kjellén also used a medieval allusion, that of searching for Excelsior, which could be achieved by emphasizing the Germanic nation in race (presumably Nordic race).
72. Fritz Rörig, "Der Markt von Lübeck: Topographisch-statistische Untersuchungen zur deutschen Sozial- und Wirtschaftsgeschichte. Mit einer Karte," 157–254 in *Lübische Forschungen: Jahrhundertgabe des Vereins für Lübeckische Geschichte und Altertumskunde* (Lübeck: H. G. Rahtgens, 1921).
73. Åbo Handelskammer, *Åbo-Turku Suomi-Finnland: Das Heft wurde von der Åbo Handelskammer für die Nordische Woche in Lübeck herausgegeben* (Åbo, Finland: Åbo Drucherei und Zeitungs Aktiengesellschaft, 1921), 1. The town of Turku was also interchangeably referred to as Åbo throughout the document, which was entirely in German.
74. Ibid., 4.
75. Ibid., 8.
76. Ibid., 12.
77. Ibid., 15.
78. Ibid., 18.
79. Ibid., 24.
80. Letter to Jan Grosse, 25 May 1921. HAL, 1.2 NSA 2462.
81. Thomas Mann, "Goethe und Tolstoi," *Deutsche Rundschau* Band 190 (March 1922), 225–246 and Thomas Mann, *Goethe und Tolstoi* (Aachen: K Spiertz, 1923).

82. Clayton Koelb, ed., *Thomas Mann's "Goethe and Tolstoy": Notes and Sources*, translations by Alcyone Scott and Clayton Koelb (Tuscaloosa, AL: University of Alabama Press, 1984), 1.

83. For examples of Thomas Mann and Ida Boy-Ed's correspondence, see Thomas Mann, *Briefe an Otto Grautoff 1894–1901 und Ida Boy-Ed 1903–1928* (Frankfurt am Main: Fischer Verlag, 1975).

84. Koelb, *Thomas Mann's "Goethe and Tolstoy,"* 7. Koelb details Mann's notes where he writes that his plan was to tour not only Lübeck but other Baltic and regional cities once the lecture was over.

85. Thomas Mann, "Freiheit und Vornehmheit," in Mahn, *Festschrift*, 39.

86. Mahn, *Festschrift*, 14.

87. Kjellén, "Der Umgang," 6.

88. Ibid., 9.

89. Flyer by the Lübecker Lichtspielgemeinde advertising the "Filmschau der deutschen und nordischen Filmindustrie," 6 September 1921. HAL, 1.2 NSA 2462.

90. Letter from Darmstadt 1922 1–18 Juni, Neudeutsche Kultur, 22 February 1922. HAL, 1.2 NSA 2462.

Chapter 3

Evolving Identity

The Nordische Gesellschaft, *1921–1938*

Breitestraße is the central market street in old inner city Lübeck; the drivable portion begins in front of the Koberg, the square in front of Heiligen-Geist-Hospital and continues as a present-day pedestrian esplanade through shops, past the Rathaus, Marktplatz, and Niederegger Marzipan to Mühlenstraße. As one of the main arteries of the old city, it was and remains the site of travel agencies, restaurants, historic sites, and government offices; in 1921, the *Nordische Gesellschaft* (NG) set up its offices first at Breitestraße 6 (next to the *Schiffersgesellschaft* restaurant) and, later, at Breitestraße 50 in the heart of the commercial district. There, it created what amounted to a chapter house with a publicly accessible Nordic Reading Room, serving as a hub for Society activities and a locally recognizable headquarters for its operations in the center of the city it claimed to represent and reflect.

Moving to its own headquarters distinguished the NG from not only the *Nordische Woche* offices in the Rathaus but also official city business. According to a report issued to the State Financial Office [*Landesfinanzamt*],

> The composition of the board of the *Nordische Gesellschaft* is similar to that of *Nordische Woche*. To strengthen their duties, the *Nordische Gesellschaft* has set up its own office and formulates comprehensive activities, whose importance to the interests of the German empire is already recognized.[1]

Building the NG from the intellectual and material foundations of *Nordische Woche* provided an already established base of support for the organization. The economic realities of the early 1920s made completely integrating the organization into state government impossible, which would also have limited the control individual men could have over the vision and day-to-day functions of the Society. The national economy continued to spiral downward, and the unregulated system of *Notgeld* drove prices and inflation upward.

The NG was established with the express purpose of continuing the work begun by *Nordische Woche*.[2] Many of the board members of the NG had been instrumental in *Nordische Woche*, especially cultural ambassadors such as local artist Alfred Mahlau and Senator Kalkbrenner. For this reason, the surplus funds that had been realized by the festival flowed directly to the new organization, with the "consent of the signatories."[3] Establishing a society to focus on solidifying cultural and economic networks meant that further sustaining finances had to be secured with a preference for community or voluntary donations. In the minutes of the September 22, 1921, meeting, Dr. Walther Schärffe (of the local firm Jost Hinr. Havemann und Sohn, later director of the Lübeck Tourist Association) included the comment that "for this purpose [that is, establishing the society], we need, above all, money and, if possible, from circles of private donors. The state should only be used in the extreme case of emergency financing."[4] A public notice, issued at the end of February 1922 by the *Nordische Woche* Finance Committee, announced the successful claims on 92 percent of the funds emanating from the event; the remaining 8 percent, if left unclaimed, was earmarked for the fledgling NG barring official objection.[5]

With the emphasis on what amounted to a public-private partnership, a pragmatic focus on private revenue sources or supporters necessitated a continuation of the dominance of individual firms and organizations. The Society itself was formed essentially as a corporation, one that would have autonomy but would bridge local businesses and city government. The institution of a salaried executive secretary, with two-thirds paid by the Society and one-third paid by Lübeck's Chamber of Commerce, meant that there would be a full-time, committed employee ensuring the work of the Society, begun at the festival, got done.[6] The Chamber of Commerce was among the first institutional members of the NG, along with emissaries or representatives of the Scandinavian nations who had participated in *Nordische Woche*, representing official buy-in of a group that highlighted shared identity, the role of Lübeck in that identity, and visions for the future.

This chapter traces the rise of the *NG* from how it was conceptualized in 1921 until mid-1938, right before a second *Nordische Woche* in October and *Kristallnacht* in November. Most importantly, this chapter analyzes how the *NG* actively constructed an in-group (as theorized by Gordon Allport) that became the hegemonic identity to the exclusion of others and was drawn into the solidifying Nazi regime. As the 1920s wore on, the activities of the Society increasingly adopted racist, propagandistic, pseudoscientific treatments of culture, race, and economy, centering German "Nordics" as a dominant and even preferred group. This reflected the polarization occurring throughout society, especially once the global depression took hold after the October 1929 stock market crash in the United States. By the time the Nazis came to power in January 1933, they had been building influence and a base of popularity before that in Schleswig-Holstein, and the exact role of the Society was in question. The inclusion of the NG into the Nazi bureaucracy expanded its influence outside of Lübeck, though individual members often felt sidelined or removed from the levers of power. The NG's activities during the Nazi period had lasting consequences for the cultural and political relationships between Lübeck and Scandinavian countries well after the war.

THE EARLY *NORDISCHE GESELLSCHAFT*, IDENTITY, AND ECONOMIC TENSION

Dr. Ernst Timm was installed as secretary of the Society effective March 1, 1922, with an annual salary of 36,000 M.[7] A note was included that, in light of the inflation, this salary should be deemed satisfactory. The acknowledgment of the difficulties associated with inflation not yet at its worst demonstrated how pervasive finances and monetary considerations were. While planning *Nordische Woche* was done in the course of civic duty, the NG was something else. The interests of the organization overlapped with those of Lübeck more broadly from time to time, but they were not completely parallel or even viewed as mutual.

The NG crafted by-laws that explicitly laid out its purpose and the way it would collect and approve membership and fees. Most importantly, according to §1 of the by-laws booklet, Lübeck was to be the permanent home for the Society and the center of its official activities.[8] This specific detail enshrined the role Lübeck was to play in the new Society and echoed one of the facets *Nordische Woche* had emphasized: that Lübeck was uniquely situated to foster and maintain German-Scandinavian cultural and economic relations. This organization, though, represented what amounted to an advocacy group outside of the city or civic political structure, constructing and stabilizing a very particular in-group based on an assertion of Nordic identity. In terms of post–World War I identity, local history was continually referenced even as the national context was defined and redefined. A trustee board was outlined as well as membership levels intended to include individual members, honorary members, and corporate members, with accompanying tiers of dues.[9]

The board of directors divided specific responsibilities among themselves, forming what amounted to departments. These men (and they were uniformly men) comprised a representation of cultural and business activity, consistent with the stated goals in the by-laws and an article from the Chamber of Commerce newsletter.[10] The first chairman of the Society was Dr. Georg

Kalkbrenner, who was also active in city politics.[11] Ernst Boie, who had led the central planning committee for *Nordische Woche* as well as Dr. Jan Grosse and Dr. Rudolf Keibel, both active in city governance, were other eminent members of a board that represented business leaders in Lübeck.[12] They also signified access to resources in the community that had been cultivated during the planning of *Nordische Woche*, such as official Society printing done by H. G. Rahtgens, printer of the *Nordische Woche Festschrift*. The aspirations of the Society required visibility, especially since economic and diplomatic realities made their ambitious goals difficult. The early steps were largely in maintaining and expanding regional networks, navigating increasingly polarized and radicalized national politics over the course of the 1920s; by the end of the decade, the NG was as much a vessel as a proving ground for racist and antisemitic ideologies, actively contributing to the intellectual landscape that fertilized and even encouraged Nazism.

The emergence of the NG demonstrates a new phase of identity formation in Lübeck in the 1920s. Individual Germans and collective localities negotiated the international system after World War I, learning and rewriting social rules against the backdrop of economic, social, and political weakness. In this context, cultural festivals moved beyond *learning* the new rules (and the strategies official institutions mobilized in enacting them) to piloting tactics individuals used to locate and consume their various identities within the system. The existence of the NG went still further and became a manifestation of those intersected identities, reacting to and attempting to shape the circumstances around it. This impacted the trajectory those ideas followed. The contours of identity proved to be malleable and situational, and the NG adjusted accordingly, often depending on political or economic factors in Germany as membership and visibility increased.

More than anything, the establishment of the NG claimed the salience of Nordic identity in German culture.[13] To transition from Nordic identity affiliation to outright Nordicism, and to construct it as a highly salient identity, three characteristics had to be associated with it. First, the identity had to be well-defined as a (or even *the*) form of "Nordic" identity. *Nordische Woche*, as a performance of that Nordic identity, represented a step on the path of identity definition from its inception to its staging, especially in terms of *cultural* parameters. The questions that persisted regarding the formulation of identity were whether or not "Nordic" would be an ethnic, racial, or social construct and how these aspects would be expressed.[14] This process was continued by the establishment of the NG. For its first five years, many Society activities developed and continuously asserted the group's role in larger German culture.

The second attribute to be associated with a highly salient Nordic identity was that it had to be generally accepted. In Germany, ethnic and/or cultural associations varied by region and demonstrated the challenge identity faced in creating national unity. As Allport argued, for an in-group to gain effectiveness or influence, "members of an in-group all use the term *we* with same essential significance."[15] For a group to have a lot of national influence, membership had to be fairly widespread, preferably outside the borders of traditional regions. In this case, affiliation with Nordic identity needed to gain acceptance beyond Lübeck's Hanseatic walls and the shores of the Baltic Sea to achieve any salience in Germany in general.

Lastly, the third characteristic to ensure a highly salient identity was that it would be easily enacted. Clearly, this step required some sort of cultural hegemony for a specific identity. Still, the presence of "others," especially Jews and "Easterners" in Lübeck, provided a ready-made contrast against which the Nordic identity could consolidate and deploy. These "significant others," as Anna Triandafyllidou theorized, provided long-standing or deep-seated contrasts, mobilized casually through idiomatic phrases and stereotyping up through virulent persecution and violent suppression.[16]

The way that an in-group manifests or codifies its identity often reacts to the society that contains it. Put another way, as Allport argued,

> in a static society it would be fairly easy to predict just what loyalties the individual will form—to what region, to what phratry, or to what social class. In such a static society kinship, status, even place of residence, may be rigidly prescribed.[17]

There was a lot about 1920s German society that wasn't static, however. For this reason, social activities that spoke to the inherent foundations of who people thought or claimed they were became incredibly important in the German context. Linkages between local, regional, national, and international identities were formed, maintained, and understood in a variety of ways by German individuals to establish where they fit in culturally. The NG was an ongoing way to do this, in a way guiding how members and member organizations reacted to the world around them.

And there was a lot to react to. The NG was established and really took root at a time when European politics and economics were volatile. Challenges to and reinforcements of imperialism impacted diplomacy and social movements, from independence in Egypt to ongoing Indian and Irish nationalist protests to the ongoing Greco-Turkish War. Political instability threatened Italy, culminating in October's "March on Rome," and the establishment of the Soviet Union fomented further worries about global communism. The Genoa Conference, convened by David Lloyd George in April 1922, revealed fractures in the British-French alliance, particularly as it related to Germany's position in Europe and its reparations bill. Lloyd George wished to involve Germany directly in crafting continental policy; Aristide Briand and then

Raymond Poincaré of France wanted to maintain Germany's secondary status and reinforce the Treaty of Versailles. All in all, the first years of the 1920s were complicated and anything but peaceful. Economics proved to be a fraught topic, one wrapped up in political power, national and nationalist politics, and broader social debates. The Genoa Conference, meant to normalize European and even global economics and politics, provided the opportunity for the Treaty of Rapallo between Germany and the Soviet Union, effectively sidelining Lloyd George's efforts and doubling down on the German view that the Entente powers sought power over them.

Back in Lübeck, NG Secretary Timm actively sought out the already cultivated commercial relationships of its early members, especially those who were located outside the city. He sent thirty envelopes and corresponding letterheads to encourage members to solicit their business contacts.[18] In an open letter to the membership of the Society, Timm reiterated the need for "continual observation of economic *life*, economic *law*, economic *policy*, transport policy between participating countries (including Germany)" and the unique diplomatic strides undertaken by Lübeck, particularly.[19] Local initiatives were the only antidote to Germany's larger problems, and despite widespread overtures, the dominant goal was a financially healthy organization in Lübeck. To do this, Timm argued, an economic news service and archive would solidify not only the efforts and reputation of the NG but also educate and interest the local public.[20]

There were practical reasons for emphasizing economic connections between "Nordic" countries and Germany and, more specifically, the NG's centrality in their maintenance. The economic climate was one of pessimism and even bitterness as inflation persisted, especially with little perceived help from the Entente. Second, festivals and the establishment of the NG cost money, and membership, especially business leaders, wanted evidence that their investment was worth it. Last, there was no guarantee that the funds available to the Society, especially to establish a news service when others already existed, would maintain their value.[21] The discussion about sponsoring an archive and economic press service arose from the stated desire to maintain Lübeck's role in northern German overtures toward Scandinavian countries. A tangible deliverable would make an easier sales pitch.

Timm explicitly pointed out that the impulse could be to argue for "all countries to be observed or attended to from one location, such as Berlin or Hamburg"; the limitation of this, however, was distance, manpower, funding, and organization, all of which Lübeck had already harnessed.[22] This contention spoke not only to economic realities that continued to plague German society but also the continued importance of regional and local identity in the previous "*Zersplitterung*" debates. Timm wanted to prevent Lübeck's relegation to second-, third-, or no-tier status behind power centers like Hamburg or Berlin. With existing financial resources dwindling, competition for foreign capital and recognition between cities meant that commercial survival depended as much on reputation and selling a location as actual profit and trade.

Tethering the purpose of the NG beyond rather ambiguous expressions of cultural correspondence proved effective and constructive. By September 1922, the NG's most concrete contribution to the cultural-commercial sphere was opening the "Nordic Reading Room," where visitors could peruse "a dozen foreign newspapers and more than 30 Nordic periodicals."[23] The Reading Room actually attracted visitors. From its inception in July 1922, interest only appeared to increase, beginning with forty-four visitors that month and increasing to 160 by September.[24] In this way, the Society provided a service to the public while simultaneously ensuring "the German public will, in time, get the impression that Lübeck is the one place where you can get the most reliable communications from the north."[25] The hope was that the NG could build on this practical foundation to collect cultural artifacts as well, including "Nordic" literature and books, for the purposes of a comprehensive *cultural* library. This also took the pressure off of the city archives in expanding and maintaining burgeoning collections.

THE INTERFERENCE OF HYPERINFLATION

The success of the Nordic Reading Room and other attempts to increase the visibility of the NG had clear challenges. One of the most difficult, especially considering the economic scope the NG quickly adopted, was in fact the economy. The NG operated in a political gray area; board member and membership were politically connected, but the organization itself wasn't *really* a municipal or policymaking entity. Activities such as economic or scientific studies and the promotion of commercial interests had the potential to realize economic gains, but cities like as Lübeck which were *not* at the center of international politics and commerce needed a push or spin to improve its prospects. In an unsigned and undirected internal memo, NG leadership recognized their deepening difficulty regarding inflation. In it, the author (most likely Dr. Timm) pointed out that cultural propaganda was necessary to shape reality in Lübeck:

> culture must also propagate something there [Lübeck]; if not, it may seem to be a bluff that cannot tolerate the light of concrete studies (a danger which there is no denying, on the one hand. This is because Lübeck's importance as a trading city, at least within Germany, is considerably overestimated on average.

> It is often difficult to utilize quantitative data without destroying such illusions.) A similar overestimation of Lübeck's current cultural significance must therefore be avoided in any case. It must be proven that the new Lübeck is culturally and economically worthy of the old (without giving the impression of the decay of a "once" major city).[26]

Put another way, the emphasis that had been placed on Lübeck's indispensable position in Germany had been exaggerated by leaders in the city in the hope that economic importance would follow claims of it.

The spiraling economy plagued attempts to move forward, however. A letter from Franz Fromme, another paid staff member of the NG board, echoed Timm's sentiments of the importance of cultural connections, especially as 1923 and hyperinflation loomed.[27] Fromme argued, "It is now more important to maintain our cultural relations with the North than ever before, because our economy suffers at the moment an undeniable, hopefully temporary, turbidity."[28] He went on to comment how Finnish trading partners complained about German business practices, making the need for cultural connection that much more necessary. Additionally, he argued, established cultural relationships would prevent England and France from gaining a foothold in Scandinavia.[29] Scandinavia and trade on the Baltic was something to be jealously guarded and Lübeck specifically had much to lose.

Constructive attempts to shore up ties to "the North" was a delicate matter. A case in point was a warning letter sent to Dr. Kalkbrenner by G. Severin, of the firm Taht & Severin and member of the Board of Directors for the NG. In it, Severin referenced an op-ed written by Dr. Timm in the *Lübeckische Blätter* entitled "Lübeck's Economic Destiny," which railed against perceived economic and trade-based injustices against Lübeck.[30] While Severin did not dispute the content of the piece, he did take issue with what he considered Timm's "lack of judgment" in the tone of the op-ed. This demonstrated the NG had cultivated a serious mission and following, at least among its members. The personal opinions of its board members, especially those perceived as in the employ of the public, had the potential to damage the reputation of the organization and even that of the city. The board of directors were split in regards to the best way to fulfill the NG's mission, especially because of its status.[31]

Walking the fine line between grievance and diplomacy impacted the Society's existence, because it relied heavily on donations and foreign membership fees for funds. By January 1923, Dr. Kalkbrenner sent a report to the Chamber of Commerce indicating that the membership fee fixed in 1921 hardly met the Society's needs, as "the Mark has dropped to 1/100 of its former value."[32] Foreign membership fees (and, better yet, foreign currency) injected capital into the flagging economy, so expanding membership, especially in Scandinavia, remained a material focus. This, however, could not compensate entirely for the Society's financial needs, and sKalkbrenner appealed to the Chamber for an increased contribution to the guaranteed fund. To put the situation in perspective, Kalkbrenner asked for 15,000 to 100,000 Marks (with emphasis on the latter rather than the former), up from the previous fixed yearly contribution of 10,000 Marks.[33]

Throughout 1923, economic pressures forced businesses, organizations, and firms to reconceptualize their finances, but little stemmed from the spiraling inflation. There were some attempts to either ignore or mitigate financial difficulties, such as sponsoring touring courses. One example, under the direction of Professor Sebastian Schwarz, targeted foreign students, teachers, and others interested in German and Lübeck history.[34] Planned for several weeks in August 1923, the course included language instruction, cultural activities such as symphony performances, the historical background of German cultural figures such as Fritz Reuter, and Lübecker art sessions led by directors of local museums (particularly Carl Georg Heise).[35] This trip in particular had several benefits. In the first place, August 1923 coincided with desperate financial issues in Germany, and charging foreigners Goldmarks had the potential to inject real reserves in the collapsing economy.[36] Secondly, and perhaps more importantly, this trip became a model for cultural tourism, highlighting art, architecture, and history, sponsored by the NG even in extraordinary times.

Ultimately, true stabilization could only occur by eliminating of *Notgeld.* On October 25, 1923, a notice appeared in the *Lübecker Anzeiger* detailing the new criteria for issuing *Notgeld*; notes had to be based on a gold loan and stamped "Approved by the Minister of Finance."[37] This applied not only to states and cities in Germany but firms as well. Notes were to be strictly regulated, and firms in Lübeck as in other cities had to apply for notes from the centralized Ministry of Finance. The transition from a poorly regulated monetary system to one that had regulatory constraints settled a major debate that captured the imaginations of *Notgeld* collectors (such as the recognized *Notgeld* authority Arnold Keller), printers, and government officials alike: the perceived difference between *Notgeld* and *Gutscheine* (vouchers). A memo by Germany's finance minister, circulated by the Lübeck Police Department, dictated that new regulations covered valid *Notgeld* issues as well as "*Gutscheine*":

> I allow myself to take this opportunity to point out that, in many places, exhibitors of unfettered emergency money may feel that they had not issued emergency money, but "vouchers"; a distinction between emergency money and vouchers does not exist. Each

> voucher, which is a monetary amount, is destined to replace money of the realm or the *Reichsbank* notes for the purposes of §1 of the said law. Viewed similarly are the banks that draw cheques on each other as emergency money, and banks that continue to issue such cheques will require my [the Minister of Finance] approval.[38]

This memo demonstrated an important step toward economic stabilization by establishing a specific hierarchy to regulate local and private currency vis-à-vis the *Reichsbank*. In Berlin, the minister of finance—Hjalmar Schacht—firmly grasped the reins of the national currency, delegating local authority to city leaders and the police department. In Lübeck, this clear chain of command made Dr. Grosse, a ranking member of the city council, a signatory to the official memo that was disseminated to the police department, which was responsible for day-to-day compliance.[39] Firms and other financial institutions that usually dealt in *Notgeld* began advertising their approved issues of emergency money in newspapers, especially the *Lübecker General-Anzeiger*.[40] Businesses such as the *Deutsche Reichsbahn* advertised specific registered notes (with descriptions and values) and the final dates they would be accepted as legal tender.[41] This regulation included the Chamber of Commerce, which had also issued *Notgeld*. Most entities able to register *Notgeld* in advance of the dissolution of the system and the introduction of the transitional *Rentenmark* accepted the notes through the end of November 1923 and even into December of that year.[42] Almost as quickly, city archives and municipal boards called on companies and businesses to retain copies of their *Notgeld*, preferably uncirculated; considering the numbers of notes that were printed at the height of hyperinflation, this request was easily fulfilled.[43]

Even as these measures were announced, hyperinflation had a massive ripple effect. Bernd Widdig pointed out that at the

> peak of the inflation, 91.6 percent of a family's budget was used to purchase food. . . . On the other hand, rent became an almost negligible outlay for many households due to strict rent-control regulations after the war. Yet for those who depended on rental income this development often meant a financial catastrophe.[44]

The focus on subsistence in 1923 was reminiscent of the deprivation at the end of the war. Spiraling economic calamity brought fresh waves of political upheaval. November 1923 was a chaotic month, between Adolf Hitler's failed Beer Hall Putsch in Munich on the 8th and 9th and rumored Communist uprisings in Hamburg and elsewhere. Shockwaves still resonated from the French incursion and occupation of the Ruhr in late 1922 through 1923 and the accompanying work stoppages.[45] All of these factors effectively shoved the Weimar Republic ever closer to collapse. Not least of these pressures was the possibility that currency stabilization would not work.

This pessimism was evident in a November 23, 1923, letter from Dr. Timm to Dr. Grosse. In it, Timm mentioned a brief detention or arrest at the hands of French picket lines after a meeting in Essen.[46] He continued his report to Grosse with an allusion to political upheaval, stating, "I do not know what the last political party events have been in Lübeck, but I do not err in the assumption that the advance of social democracy has increased aversion to profitable capital investments on the part of the State."[47] Timm's loaded statement smacked of derision against the Social Democrats, who were active in building coalition governments throughout the 1920s. It also spoke to Timm's belief that investment capital was necessary to prevent further political *and* economic catastrophe, regardless of the source. That the state represented a major investor in municipalities and cities highlighted the difficulty of a welfare state caught in hyperinflation. Persistent distrust in the system meant limited investment, skyrocketing prices, stagnant income levels, and plummeting monetary value. Previous attempts to contain *Notgeld* issues had been ineffectual, and there was little reason to believe the new measures would be any different.

THE RENTENMARK, STABILIZATION, AND A RENEWED *NORDISCHE GESELLSCHAFT*

German economic stability after *Notgeld* required draconian adherence to the *appearance* of strict currency regulation, regardless of the reality.[48] The *Rentenmark* officially entered the market on November 15, 1923 (even though, as previously mentioned, many institutions announced they would accept *Notgeld* through December). Its value was fixed and finite, based on the dollar at 1914 rates as well as existing gold reserves.[49] Just as the postwar years and inflation had affected individuals in different ways, the introduction of the *Rentenmark* similarly impacted social sectors unevenly. Individuals or firms with greater access to foreign capital, which could be exchanged at a higher rate than inflationary Marks, were able to get a larger piece of the rigidly controlled *Rentenmark* pie; those who relied on thrice-daily payments of *Notgeld* and social welfare programs were at a disadvantage.[50]

The *Rentenmark* was meant to be a transition to the *Reichsmark*, but it was important in capturing trust in the system. With this in mind, the NG produced a report on the "Economy of the Nordic Nations in 1924."[51] In it, the Society detailed, much like the Turku commemoration booklet of 1921, the expenditures and income of each Scandinavian nation as well as Germany, effectively reframing the contours of the Nordic world. The report listed top export items for each nation and compared them to the previous year's tally, in some ways completely ignoring the realities of hyperinflation that had set Germany apart from other European nations.[52] The analysis of economic structures and language provided a particular entry point for the way(s) the NG viewed its mission: reinforcing or even identifying Germany's connections north.

Identity had to add cultural meaning to structural comparisons and contrasts to become salient, however. Economic analyses of nations considered "Nordic" allowed Germany to enter metaphorical space previously occupied only by Scandinavia (especially Denmark, Sweden, and Norway—often ignoring Finland altogether). Asserting a shared heritage resonated with the German members of the NG and participants in events they were involved with. The nuance of national adaptation implied that there were multiple paths emanating from a single source; that is, different national contexts, despite similar beginnings, could manifest analogous characteristics in different ways. A variety of ventures launched, all under the umbrella of "Nordic" services and publications, formalizing in print a region increasingly referred to as Nordic.

One example was the newsletter *Nordische Pressekorrespondenz*, circulated by the *Nordische Pressebüro* and contracted with Lübeck writer Otto Weber in March 1924.[53] In the contract, Ernst Timm laid out how the editor of the *Korresonpdenz* was to be paid (two-thirds by the *Pressebüro* and the other third determined by the editors of the *Ostsee-Rundschau*); Weber acknowledged the contract, signing as "Culture Editor [*Kulturschriftleiter*]" of the NG.[54] The publications overtly sponsored by the Society began circulation January 1924, despite the tenor of Dr. Timm's earlier correspondence regarding economic and political conditions in Germany and Lübeck in particular. Creating a paid editorial position demonstrated, perhaps, some hope in currency stabilization. It also heralded a change in the identity definition of the NG. Rather than simply continue to draw borders around "the North" through economic and cultural studies, the Society began to promote cultural sameness or connection between Germany and Baltic nations.

Behind closed doors, connections were also increasingly extended to the newly established Soviet Union because of these Baltic connections. In a confidential meeting for business leaders in the NG, the Society sponsored a talk by Dr. Walter Asmis, who had been traveling in the Soviet Union over the course of two years. His older brother, Rudolf Asmis, served in the German embassy in Moscow in the early 1920s after serving the Wilhemine monarchy in Togo before World War I; he later led the Nazis' Colonial Political Office.[55] The questions to be considered were twofold. Was it likely that the new Bolshevik government would maintain control of Russia and surrounding countries, and, if so, was it advantageous for Germany?[56] The sociopolitical upheaval in Germany and its continual international disadvantage meant these questions had the potential to reshape European relations. According to the Society's report of Asmis's talk, German business leaders were encouraged to cultivate relationships in the USSR, not least because "Germany [was] the first foreign power that the new Russia [had] recognized in law."[57] The diplomatic climate regarding the Bolshevik Revolution in Russia provided the opportunity for German businesses to take advantage of new Soviet markets and relationships that Western Europe—especially former Entente members—refused to pursue due to ideological reasons and their own economic limitations.[58]

The content of Asmis's findings and the ways they were received demonstrate the complexity of international relations in 1924. Germany was on the precipice of economic stability, and that had the potential to realize political and diplomatic stability as well. This was *not* the case for the new Soviet Union. Asmis pointed out the economic difficulties that accompanied Lenin's New Economic Policy (NEP), which, he argued, represented a "collapse of pure communist economic theory."[59] Additionally, Asmis argued a political overthrow of the new Soviet structure could only occur as a result of a violent uprising, and there was no guarantee that conditions in a noncommunist Russia would remain favorable to German ventures. This built on an environment that had led to the German-Soviet Treaty of Rapallo in 1922, which provided military and economic cooperation between Germany and the Soviet Union.[60]

Despite indications that German economic interests were steadying, diplomatic interests were far from certain. Pursuing relations with the Soviet Union was thumbing the proverbial German nose at the Entente and the Treaty of Versailles. Neither Germany nor Russia was included in the Paris Peace Conference negotiations, and both were marginalized in the international community. Asmis advocated putting ideological or political fears aside, even in the wake of postwar attempts to establish Soviet communes in Germany and continued political agitation, because "the opponents of the Bolsheviks must be anti-German because they could be aligned only with the support of the Entente."[61] Persistent anger and bitterness against "the Entente" haunted German attempts to re-enter the international arena and even helped guide choices about future endeavors.

OUTREACH AND CULTURAL ACTIVITIES

In addition to framing the way business leaders pursued accelerated relationships outside of Germany, the Society took on projects with symbolic and cultural import as well. One case in point was the debated reconstruction or upgrade (*Ausbau*) of the small *Maria Kapelle am Stegel*, near the much larger landmark of *Marienkirche*.[62] The small chapel, which had been built in the

Middle Ages, was located on Mengstraße, near the commercial district and the setting for Thomas Mann's *Buddenbrooks*. Its central location, as well as its multiple uses over the centuries, led the Society to sponsor plans for its rehabilitation.[63] It also highlighted how preservation of the built environment could reflect a particular view of the past—even one that imaginary and malleable. The focus on *Maria am Stegel* expanded on the focus of Lübeck's community spaces that had been emphasized during *Nordische Woche*. It also spoke to the Society's community-oriented focus, in that it wanted to literally solidify Lübeck's history.[64] As Dr. Timm indicated in an open letter to the Society's membership, the NG sought a permanent home within which to continue the German-Scandinavian relationship. Additionally, in keeping with the Society's goals, the *Maria Kapelle am Stegel* was the perfect location, as it was built in the "old Hanseatic style" and remained a symbol of Lübeck's use of that aesthetic.[65]

Integral to the NG's mission was the continued platform of the *Ostsee-Rundschau*, which by October 1924 was

> just about to evolve into promotional material for Lübeck, of paramount importance. It is necessary to promote it by all possible means so that the uncertainty associated with the introduction such a magazine in the general public and the participating economic circles will be overcome as quickly as possible.[66]

To members of the NG and their sponsors in the Chamber of Commerce, shifting the *Ostsee-Rundschau* (later *Der Norden*) from a society newsletter to a public magazine fulfilled the goals of promoting Lübeck as well as widening the scope of potential membership. It also helped move the NG from the pet project of local elites into one more participatory. Developing the *Ostsee-Rundschau* and its accompanying advertising revenue meant that the Society could expand beyond the confines of Lübeck. In a letter to the Chamber of Industry and Commerce in Halle, Ernst Boie explicitly targeted other German communities for Society membership, if only to take "steps . . . to arouse general interest in Germany for the work of the Society."[67] Correspondence between business and society leaders in Lübeck and other municipalities in Germany increased throughout the rest of 1924.

Some of this correspondence was to increase participation in lectures and essays sponsored by the NG in Germany. Continuous publishing, especially the text of speeches sponsored by the Society, proved to be an effective way to maintain visibility in Germany and claim that the NG was providing an intellectual service. In an example of the intersection of cultural and economic attitudes, the NG published "The Problem of War Reparations" by Dr. Gustav Cassel as part of a series called *Ostsee-Schriften*.[68] Here, one can see not only the persistence of economic debates and reparations discourse but also the sense that "the Entente" and international politics had a real effect on German-Scandinavian relationships.[69] Cassel analyzed the purpose of reparation payments, especially from the Entente's strategic desire to prevent Germany's ability to wage war, though he claimed to utilize an economic, rather than political, framework.[70]

Of course, politics and economics, especially at an international level, were intertwined. The topic of reparations was inherently contentious and highlighted the interconnectedness of culture, politics, and economics. Cassel's essay revealed the Society's willingness to take on politically loaded topics and promote them as academic subject matter. Cassel's essay positioned the NG, itself, within the frame of international relations, arguing that reparations were staked on "the claim . . . that Germany alone bears the blame for the world war. But this claim is false, as anyone who knows anything about the history of the world must have realized long ago; compensation claims based on this rest on a lie."[71] Cassel's position certainly resonated with German citizens, but it was far from the impersonal, unbiased economic analysis he claimed. He went on to point out that the efforts to keep Germany dependent had in fact created an "economic burden" on the Entente, who had pursued a "primitive" policy that, like socialism, did not take into account the international picture.[72] Conflating socialism and the interests of Western Europe was a provocative way to make a cultural point using economic analysis. It also critiqued USSR-German relations, yet another reason to look north rather than east or west.

The NG set its sights much higher than becoming simply a lobby for Lübeck. In an op-ed for the *Lübecker General-Anzeiger*, the NG proudly reported that it had begun planting branch offices, such as one in Hanover and the establishment of the *Deutsch-Nordische Klub* in Berlin.[73] Simultaneously, in a move truly designed to foster cultural movement between Scandinavia and Germany, the NG expanded their sponsored tours, spearheaded by the *Deutsch-Nordische Touristenverband*. The travel board was formed to coordinate the individual trips that the Society wanted to promote, especially those that served a student population.

By 1925 the organization began to move away from merely defining or describing the parameters of its claims to Nordic identity. Part of the reason for this shift was that leaders who had been instrumental in planning *Nordische Woche* and establishing the NG, such as Jan Grosse, retired or withdrew from public life. As Grosse stated in a letter to Georg Kalkbrenner in December 1923, it was time for the Society to enter a "new bloom [*neuen Blüte*]," and he had every confidence the Society would continue to thrive.[74] Echoing Grosse's sentiments, the NG emphasized the efforts it had undertaken to promote and maintain German-Nordic relationships in a sweeping report to the Lübeck Senate. The report acknowledged the limits of nostalgia for Hanseatic times, and it argued an attempt to resurrect old glory was futile, especially considering the current circumstances.[75] Additionally, the Society had been unable to truly realize its potential until the Mark stabilization of 1924. Arguably, the goal was forward-looking, asserting new(er) ways of understanding or claiming Nordic identity rather than one simply rooted in the past. Explicitly tying that cultural identity and expansion to currency stabilization emphasized how important economic factors were in social attitudes and activity.[76]

By mid-1925, planning was underway in Lübeck for its 700-year celebration the next year. In this, the NG was invited to join a cadre of cultural and identity groups to plan and execute the celebration.[77] The Society had integrated into local circles enough to warrant an official voice in conceiving an important festival, mirroring the process that had begun in 1919 when *Nordische Woche* was first debated. As part of the city fabric, the NG occupied the unique position of extending threads across the Baltic and along internal waterways, stitching together a regional tapestry that emphasized transnational ties as an express *product* of a public festival. Even for an event as parochial as a city birthday celebration, it was about presenting a particular view of Lübeck to attendees, regardless of where they came from. This model was adapted, as well, to centering Lübeck in German context, such as exhibitions designed to highlight the economic and cultural implications of the Baltic-Rhine trading network, thereby drawing central and southwestern Germany into Lübeck's sphere of influence—and by extension that of the NG.[78]

The period between the end of *Nordische Woche* and planning the 700-year celebration represented one of ongoing identity construction and definition. This had geographic qualities, with the NG essentially mapping out who and where was included in a region whose epicenter was Lübeck. Each activity, whether it was shoring up business prospects in Denmark, Finland, or Russia, organizing student exchanges with Scandinavian universities, or inviting the general public to exhibitions of "Nordic" art (with free admission for Society members), demonstrated one more brick forming a salient identity. This construction, though, meant also mapping out who *didn't* belong more explicitly than in the early years. As Allport argued, "the very act of affirming our way of life often leads us to the brink of prejudice."[79]

The five-year period between 1924 and 1929 became the "Golden '20s" in Weimar Germany. It was an era of resurgence, cultural innovation, and international reintegration for the nation. It also represented a period, albeit a short one, of relative economic and political stability, which allowed Germans to turn their attention to other issues. For the NG, the 1920s proved crucial to establishing a foundation of operations and its role in asserting salient identity—the formation of an in-group. It was very early identity construction, and, as such, emphasized the commonalities of the group and essentially built the symbols that Allport argued group members *needed* to "make the human in-group seem real."[80]

In particular, 1926 demonstrated a turning point for Weimar Germany. Under the continued leadership and influence of Gustav Stresemann, chancellor for a time and then foreign minister, Germany conducted a series of treaties with its former World War I enemies and entered the League of Nations. This normalized international relations, at least for the time being, and it was a definite shift in Germany's fortunes. The latter 1920s saw more diplomatic advances, such as the Kellogg-Briand Pact aimed at solidifying national borders and preventing another war in Europe. At the same time, Stresemann attempted to mitigate the perception and at times traumatic effect of Germany's immediate postwar treatment by the victorious Entente, especially France. To do this, he negotiated the withdrawal of French and Belgian occupation forces from the Ruhr Valley, though Germany was still unable to rearm the Saar and the Rhineland or reassert any territorial claims.[81]

The later 1920s also represented a major shift for the NG, as the organization itself evolved. The relative economic and political stability ushered in during the second half of the decade allowed the Society time to solidify the foundations it had established earlier. In 1926, as Lübeck again prepared for a major festival, the focus on local culture reinforced the centrality of Lübeck-specific identity. A parade of local leaders and cultural organizations, a performance of the historic *Lübecker Totentanz*, and costumed depictions of scenes from medieval Lübeck (such as the "Merchant Caravan on Land with Captured Robber Barons") embodied the way Lübeckers saw their city both historically and in the modern period in the style of *Nordische Woche*.[82] The 700-year celebration was as wide-ranging as *Nordische Woche* had been, with a commemorative photo booklet documenting the parade, an exhibition catalog for events across the city, and a program and schedule. Alfred Mahlau again crafted the covers, providing a through-line from *Nordische Woche* to Lübeck's founding commemoration by way of the NG.

The NG continued to solidify its niche in Lübeck and northwestern Germany as a leading cultural voice, fostering relationships with Scandinavian entities and providing programming to demonstrate how those ties were both natural and necessary. The Society continued to sponsor lectures and film viewings that spoke to its mission. For example, beginning in late January 1926, the organization sponsored a series about the "Russian *Volk* in the past and present." Topics included analyses of classic Russian literature, the current socialist movement, and "The Realization of the Ideas of the Intelligentsia in Today's Russia."[83] The persistent interest in Russia, which was *outside* Nordic boundaries, demonstrated that the Baltic Sea remained a core geography and concept to Lübeck's economic and diplomatic activities, for the potential benefit of Germany in general and Lübeck in particular (an idea that had been introduced, it could be argued, by Thomas Mann's work on "*Goethe und Tolstoi*"). Germany's international position was still fragile and the sense that a variety of relationships must be cultivated "just in case" remained. Considering the business possibilities associated with the new Soviet state, the inclusion of lectures on contemporary Russia was a calculated move.

Film showings were another way for the NG to remain front and center in cultural activity. In conjunction with the Cinema Community of Lübeck [*Lübecker Lichtspielgemeinde*] films such as *At the Top of the World* [*Zum Gipfel der Welt: Die Mount-Everest-Expedition im Jahre 1924*] were shown for a nominal entrance fee, which was lower for members of the Society.[84] Other films or documentaries were shown as well, such as *Embers at the North Pole* [*Gluten am Nordpol*] and *The Fiji Islanders* [*Bei den Fidschi-Insulanern*].[85] This continued the process of categorizing identities through stories of adventure, colonization, travel, and including or excluding them from the Nordic umbrella. The NG capitalized on popular film trends, such as the *Berg* films, while actively situating them within Society goals. Often, a contextualizing lecture would follow, or, as in the case of a presentation on "New Swedish Art," coordinated programming with other cultural institutions was advertised.[86] This continued into 1928 and 1929, presenting lectures, exhibitions, and performances that were advertised as "traditional." One example was an "Iceland exhibition" that featured a slide presentation about Icelandic painting, followed by a performance of "Icelandic literature in the original language" by an Icelandic actress.[87] Interestingly, Iceland was not really considered "Scandinavian" and had not been included in the *Nordische Woche* proceedings. Rather, it was presented as something on the periphery, included later as part of the geographic north. Finland, too, existed in this liminal space but due to its tangible connections to Lübeck through the ferry, its participation in *Nordische Woche*, and its postwar situation it was more easily understood as a Nordic country.

The NG continued to sponsor guided tours, reinforcing a very specific narrative, with preselected locations and contexts, and it demonstrated that there was an assumption that members and the public-at-large could not only afford travel outside of Germany but also that they desired it.[88] This also established how the NG worked with other groups (such as the *Deutsch-Nordischen Arbeitsgemeinschaft Hamburg* and the *Überseeclub Hamburg*) to put large tour groups together. Building tours out of participants beyond Lübeck and in conjunction with other formal organizations showed the NG's success in impacting areas outside of Lübeck after 1924.[89] At the same time, it reflected the trend of the later 1920s toward travel and tourism, fostering physical connections between places. The *Ostsee-Rundschau* advertised these tours and also increasingly tackled the other topics Society programming did. By 1926, the NG's press bureau, guided by Walter Zimmermann, began to expressly promote Germany to Scandinavian countries, using established networks to "distribute pro-German newspaper articles by excellent personalities from the north (Dr. Sven Hedin, Professor Gustav Cassel, etc.)."[90] As mentioned earlier, these personalities had been active in connection with the NG and its programming. Most importantly, however, Zimmermann's press bureau sought to place these articles and essays in *foreign* newspapers for the benefit of German interests.[91] This was no longer about mutual understanding or benefit, as at least one branch of the NG moved from highlighting and emphasizing the concomitant heritage of Germany and Scandinavia to actively promoting Germany *to* "the north."

Due in part to steadier economic circumstances, the emergence of several business conglomerates guided German business and political interests into the 1930s. One of these conglomerates was the chemical giant I. G. Farben. In the advertising sector, a similar corporation called the *Allgemeine Anzeigen GmbH* (or *Ala*) established itself as *the* major source of advertising interests, led by business personality Alfred Hugenberg. The emergence of these vast corporations—the "cartelization of culture," as described by Peter Gay—pointed to the unresolved tensions between big-moneyed interests, liberal republicans, and revolutionaries across Weimar society.[92] For his part, Hugenberg painted a luminous figure in economic and political spheres, capturing a wide swath of the communications industry and attempting to guide public opinion using those networks.[93] Politically, Hugenberg operated on the far right, becoming a leading member of the German National People's Party (*Deutschnationale Volkspartei*, or DNVP) and hoping to reestablish authoritarianism in Germany while also framing Germanness in particular ways.

The NG, especially its press bureau, was an independent communications operation, though one that operated within the context of corporatizing interests in Germany. Publishing and travel—especially the *Ostsee-Rundschau* and the *Nordische Verkehrs GmbH*—comprised much of the NG's expenditures projected for the 1927 fiscal year.[94] By December 1926, the NG corresponded with the general director of the *Ala*, discussing not only business terms of a relationship between the groups but also the "chosen path" taken by the editors of the *Ostsee-Rundschau*.[95] The constellation of companies, organizations, and conglomerates required that the NG constantly reevaluated its tactics to stay active, to stay relevant, and even to retain a degree of independence without getting lost in the sea of voices, especially toward the end of the decade.

The conversation with the *Ala* could imply that Hugenberg and his associates either intended to influence the NG's productions, including press releases, or that high-ranking Society leaders sympathized with Hugenberg's politics and/or goals. The correspondence between the NG and the *Ala* could also be the negotiations of rivals. Support for this conclusion can be drawn from the fact that, in 1928, the *Ostsee-Presse-Korrespondenz* was sent, generally free of charge, to 300 German newspapers and magazines.[96] In this way, the subsidiary press branch of the NG acted more as a news or press release service, much like the Associate Press or Reuters. It had a stake in what was reported and how. The NG had its own agenda (and even that was a subject of internal debate) and did not want to be swallowed up by Hugenberg's empire. They did have to deal with each other, though, and were part of a growing media and communications landscape.

POLARIZING GERMAN SOCIETY AND THE TURN OF THE DECADE

The second half of the 1920s was less economically and diplomatically chaotic than the first, yet fundamental tensions persisted. Germany, while relatively independent in terms of diplomacy and politics, still relied on continued good global fortune. An international emergency could completely reverse any gains or stability. At the same time, the leftovers of economic catastrophe had created winners and losers, as Bernd Widdig adroitly explains.[97] That industry leaders like Alfred Hugenberg could aspire to consolidate a huge media empire, for example, demonstrated that the post-inflationary economy was far from an even playing field and that the inflation had not affected people equally.[98] Political advantage accompanied such an empire, and mass communication proved to move levers of power in unexpected ways, prioritizing and reinforcing the viewpoints figures like Hugenberg held. By the end of the 1920s, the explicit focus on shared heritage faded, giving way to the solidification of in-groups that defined socioeconomic and racialized stratification.

Domestic politics remained polarized, deepening cleavages in the population. Weimar democracy allowed for continued political fragmentation and a cacophony of political voices. The framers of the Weimar Constitution could not sufficiently change the social structure enough to overcome or solve the problems that had accompanied World War I and the demise of Imperial Germany.[99] Active political parties were organized variously according to region (such as Bavaria), identity or special interest (such as the Catholic Center Party), or broad-based national parties such as the Social Democrats, essentially splintering the voting base in a number of different ways. This often determined the life or death of political parties and cultural organizations alike. The motivations that guided voting behavior and political affiliation is a much-debated subject, often framing it as a binary of material considerations versus less tangible identities.[100] Rather than land on one side or the other, it is clear that material circumstances were as important as social and cultural identities. They were intertwined, rendering explanations for why people gravitated toward one side or the other complicated and even incomprehensible. It was individual, but it was also about the collective. The same was true for identity groups like the NG, which pinned its very survival on the notion that "collective identity is key to fostering commitment to the movement and thus is integral to explaining mobilization" of individuals.[101]

What makes this important is the fact that Schleswig-Holstein was a region of wider support for the Nazi Party after its reentry into politics than generally across Germany. Scholars have pointed out that border regions—and Schleswig-Holstein still was one—often breed more virulent strains of nationalism. Considering the range of experiences and the way that groups such as the NG promoted themselves by focusing on economic and cultural ties between related yet competing regions, the late 1920s presented politically divisive conditions based on identity. Even within political parties themselves, message cohesion was difficult to maintain. For example, the reformulated NSDAP after 1925 briefly attempted to build support in cities (the so-called "urban plan"), leaving behind the original target audience—rural farmers and the middle class.[102] After the national elections of May 1928 resulted in a lower return for the Nazis, the party refocused on the message of "Blood and Soil" and the pastoral ideal of the *Volk*.[103] The Nazis didn't abandon urban workers, but they reframed them within a broad rhetoric focused on imagined tradition and equally imagined racial attributes.

Schleswig-Holstein was simultaneously a manufacturing heartland and rural breadbasket. The emphasis on a Nordic identity often embraced both industry and pastoralism, and some theorists explicitly infused anthropological or pseudoscientific characteristics with nationalism and local pride. The seeds of these ideas can be seen in the rhetoric and literature produced for *Nordische Woche*. Rudolf Kjellén's concept of geopolitics discussed in Chapter III claimed that national borders and the character of the people coincided. Therefore, the Swedish *Volk* (itself a concept that fused national identity with specific characteristics) behaved differently than the German *Volk* and would act in its best interests collectively, whether it was a territorial expansion or business practices.[104] The concept of the *Volk* mobilized racial and ethnic tropes, which aided in inclusion or exclusion. For this reason, although *Nordische Woche* literature contained some of the languages of racialist nationalism, there were no indications that the festival overall was conceived to promote cohesive extremist ideology. However, the NG of the late 1920s increasingly reframed *Nordische Woche* through the lens of racialized Nordiscism.

Another important development in polarizing society was the increasing presence of racial theorists and increased attention to Social Darwinism. Richard T. Gray argued that Weimar Germany, as well as most of Europe and other parts of the "western world," were swept up in scientific notions of race, character, eugenics, and physiognomics.[105] Central to the movement to describe and categorize race scientifically were authors such as Hans F. K. Günther, who linked race, physical and mental abilities, and nationalism. For his part, Günther proposed a way to divide European populations into a type of tribal identity based on geographic, linguistic, and physical factors. Politically, Günther identified with the far-right wing of society, or what Gray considered proto-fascist.[106] For these theorists, race was imbued with spirituality rather than simply tangible attributes, connecting to mystical and nostalgic notion of *Heimat* [homeland].[107]

By the 1920s, the meaning of the term "race" was as multifaceted and complicated as *Heimat* was, at once "localized and mythicized," where the national context took on the character of the local in order to foster connection with the individual.[108] *Heimat* could simultaneously describe local, national, and international identity as a way to reconcile regional difference with national consensus, and, as James Retallack argued, "provided the means to bridge the gap between urban and rural areas, insofar as it gave the rural population access to the national discourse."[109] The nation as a concept was to be the unifier, bringing together a variety of backgrounds and disparate regions to create a large in-group, in Allport's language, in international context. This was reminiscent of so much of the discourse surrounding *Nordische Woche* in 1921: its motivations, the reasons for pursuing wide-ranging and even intangible outcomes, and the connections to material gain. Race, operating as a category, could be used in the same way. It simultaneously *included* members of a nation and *excluded* others, though there were gray areas. Those who were historically excluded, such as Jews, Roma, and Africans, remained excluded even as the language evolved.

Hypernationalist parties on the right and social-political theorists focused on race as a criterion of belonging, though it was difficult to positively define. Going back to Günther and his associated ideologues, the desire to conclusively categorize "races" and discern their physical and intangible characteristics led to an explosion of anthropological ethnographies of Europe and the wider world.[110] Günther identified a number of "races" in Germany, and prime among them was the "Nordic race" concentrated in northwestern Germany and Scandinavia.[111] The presence of identity groups in Lübeck and surrounding areas self-described as "Nordic" lent some credence to the idea that Schleswig-Holstein had different inherent characteristics than, say, Bavaria, Austria, or France. Coupled with the fact that Schleswig-Holstein was a border region and Lübeck was a border *city*, contemporary racial studies opened the door to shift the focus of cultural groups away from regional notions of identity toward racialized ideology. It built on the foundations constructed by *Nordische Woche* but mobilized an evolving vocabulary.

Racist or *völkisch* parties were generally still relegated to the fringe of political and social life throughout the 1920s, though reactionary protests and frustrations with the Weimar Republic roiled beneath the surface. Until 1929, though, international and economic forces were enough to prevent extremist views from replacing mainstream ideas. This did not mean that *völkisch* ideology was repudiated, though. Racialist and pseudoscientific theorists published and lectured throughout Europe, and proponents of eugenics policies were common in the United States, Western Europe, Australia, and Japan, adjusting their language and stated goals to fit within a centrist or liberal worldview. Antisemitism was never truly under the surface, and it was concentrated in discussions about the "Jewish question" focused on whether or not Jews could ever be part of the national community. Anthropological studies were combined with phenomenology or spiritualism to formulate a more transcendent notion of racial characteristics. L. F. Clauß, a student of Hans F. K. Günther, wrote along these lines, arguing that race was more about internal attributes and less about physical appearance.[112] This fueled debate over how to best discern one's race and created tension within the *völkisch* community (including within the Nazi Party).

October 1929 was a bad month, one that catalyzed destabilization going into the 1930s. First, Gustav Stresemann died on October 3, eliminating a major figure of stability from the Weimar government and freezing Germany's complete reentry into European and global affairs. Adding to this, beginning on Friday, October 24, the stock market in New York experienced a catastrophic downturn, losing a percentage of overall market value. The situation deteriorated as investors panicked, withdrew funds, sold investments, and—worst of all—lost faith in the system. By October 29, global markets continued to hemorrhage, due in part to the fundamental suspicion people held against the international economy. The ramifications for Germany were dire. The United States, through its expansive monetary plans in Europe designed to keep reparation and war-loan payments flowing, had effectively made itself the creditor and financial foundation of Europe. With the American economy crippled, the ripple effect meant that tenuous diplomatic and economic relationships in Germany had few options to offset the loss of American capital. The supportive buttress to the German economy and even its currency collapsed, pitching Germany headlong into a new abyss of economic crisis with the hyperinflation of 1923 barely in the rearview mirror.

Despite the economic difficulties brought on by global depression, the NG continued to promote travel to Scandinavia as cultural literacy and enrichment. Even in April 1930, well after the initial shockwaves of the stock market crash six months earlier, the *Ostsee-Rundschau* produced a pamphlet on economic output and other work undertaken by the NG with an eye on the future. Tracing the emergence of the society through its activity in Lübeck, the editors (unnamed, though most likely the board of directors) highlighted *Nordische Woche* and the 700-year celebration as milestones both for the city and the organization. They also discussed the NG's desired international impact rather than being confined to one regional or even national context.[113] They claimed that the celebrations had turned into "German-Nordic rallies [*deutsch-nordische Kundgebung*]."[114] The pamphlet ended with a view toward 1931 and the hope that the Society and its subsidiary or related offices would continue the business that had begun nearly a decade earlier.

This demonstrated a subtle yet important shift. Attending rallies (rather than festivals) was a political activity. To celebrate one's "Nordic" heritage, according to the NG, was elevated to a political statement above all else and proclaimed one's membership publicly in that identity. The focus in planning the celebrations of the 1920s had explicitly been on local identity and how that locality fit into the national, "Nordic"/Baltic, and international context. Reframing local celebrations as "German-Nordic rallies" implied that more was at stake than simply commemorating history. After 1930, a generalized "Nordic" identity began to take precedence in Society literature and correspondence, as the centrality of Lübeck's receded even further than it already had been. The differing functions of the organization were delegated to departments, the largest of which controlled publishing (advertising, essays, and the like) and "cultural" activities, such as membership activities.[115]

By April 1930, Ernst Timm had fully taken on control of the NG as executive director, though the NG's direction was still debated by its founders. In a short note, Jan Grosse critiqued the 1930 edition of the *Deutsch-Nordischen Jahrbuch*, which highlighted Society activities as well as cultural endeavors throughout Scandinavia and northwestern Germany. Finland was completely missing, despite the great care to include Finnish culture and traditional connection to Lübeck. Though much ado was made of the society's *Nordische Woche* origins, an entire portion of the festival—the *Deutsch-Nordische Verkehrskonferenz*—was completely dismissed in favor of a new conference, held in Copenhagen in 1930.[116] While this may seem nitpicky and even querulous, it shows that the leadership of the NG was deviating from the initial scope of the organization as put forth by the founders in favor of centering more ideological conceptions of Nordic lands, culture, and identity. Timm asserted more overarching authority, rather than simply being an administrator hired partially by the Chamber of Commerce. The NG had gained a life and agenda of its own, reflecting the positions of evolving membership and sociopolitical circumstances.

By utilizing and adapting traditional notions of local, national, and international identity, the NG had crafted a discourse about Germanness and Germany. An opinion essay that appeared in the *Hamburger Fremdenblatt* reflected on the challenge presented by the postwar years and subsequent economic turmoil—the "isolation into which Germany fell due to war"—arguing this had been rectified to a small degree, building larger and more interconnected networks.[117] To a lesser degree, NG programming allowed members to reconsider their more individualized place in the recast contexts. On December 31, 1931, nearly the last hour of the year, the NG conducted a meeting in which the board of directors hoped to pilot efforts to avoid a replay of the immediate post–World War I years.[118] 1932 promised little but a deepening economic crisis; this time, however, there was no global plan along the lines of the Dawes Plan or even a currency transition supported by a strong economy as there had been in 1924. 1932 was an election year in Germany, with presidential voting occurring in March and April and federal elections in July and November. Political forces were as fluid and volatile as the economy. It was during the July elections that the Nazi Party—as well as other extremist parties—saw an uptick in support as the patience for the Weimar coalition governments ran out. By 1932 and 1933, Germany was again poised on a precipice of change sweeping through the nation, affecting localities and individuals in different ways, and requiring a new set of strategies which German citizens and organizations had to navigate.

THE NAZIS, *GLEICHSCHALTUNG*, AND EARLY NAZI POLICY

The Nazis entered electoral politics in the late 1920s after a four-year ban following the Beer Hall Putsch. By 1928, the party focused on actually being a political party, rather than overthrowing the Weimar Republic in a Mussolini-style takeover. That election saw them net 2.5 percent of the electorate; in 1930, that percentage rose to around 18 percent.[119] Their most effective victory, however, occurred during the July 1932 federal elections, when they became the largest party in the Reichstag. Though Adolf Hitler lost the presidential election, he was able to make a play for the office of the chancellor because of the Nazis' electoral gains, to the tune of approximately 37 percent. The months following the July elections were hardly peaceful, with mainstream institutional parties unable to harness a popular following while solidifying their own positions and, as Detlev Peukert argued, flirting with authoritarianism and *coup d'état*.[120]

Hitler's ascension to the office of chancellor on January 30, 1933, accelerated the collapse into a one-party state. The Nazis exploited the trauma of the previous year's series of elections and falling governments as well as the Reichstag Fire of February 1933. The Enabling Act of March 1933—by then just one more period of rule-by-decree—made further Nazi measures possible, without the pesky resistance of the Reichstag or other parties. In short order, an organized boycott was launched against Jewish businesses on April 1, and the regime turned to enshrining ideology in law with the "Law for Restoration of the Professional Civil Service" in April and the "Law Against the Formation of New Parties" and the "Law for the Prevention of Genetically Diseased Offspring" in July. The foundations of the Nazi state were fundamentally anti-democratic and racial. From the time the Nazi Party claimed control over the government, a program of coordination known as *Gleichschaltung* was conducted to determine which local and regional organizations could be integrated into the state; those outside the Nazis' ideological worldview or representing a challenge to Nazi control were abolished, marginalized, or even criminalized. It was a racial state, but one subject to the nuances of regional identity, individual agendas, and ongoing national and social discourse.[121]

The *NG* was wrested from the control of regional leaders and placed under Alfred Rosenberg, who aimed to stake out his own niche in the regime and the Party more broadly. Rosenberg fancied himself an ideologue, one who had unique abilities to appeal to the intellectual foundations of a Nazi-controlled Europe and was positioned to influence foreign policy. The NG presented Rosenberg with an opportunity to exploit the established groundwork for propagandistic purposes in Scandinavia, especially in spreading his own interpretation of Nazi ideas and centralizing his own power in relation to other Nazi leaders.[122] By the end of 1933, many prominent leaders of the NG professed Nazism or were at least sympathetic, in part because the original directing committee was forced to resign.[123] This hints at the fact that *Gleichschaltung* was not a smooth or even desired process, one that even like-minded leaders may have been opposed to.

Those who showed a willingness to go along were allowed to remain. Ernst Timm, for example, was viewed as having at least some enthusiasm for the new regime. Whether this was a function of the shift in social norms in Germany or long-held beliefs is difficult to ascertain.[124] What followed was a year of shuffling, reshuffling, and transition, not only for the NG but also for Lübeck. Otto-Heinrich Drechsler, who was appointed Mayor (*Oberbürgermeister*) of Lübeck in June of 1933, was a Nazi loyalist who had joined the party in 1925. Hinrich Lohse, Nazi *Gauleiter* for Schleswig-Holstein, had also been a party member since 1925, and he took control of the NG directly under Rosenberg by September 1934 as "President and Leader of the *Nordische Gesellschaft*," while Timm retained the title of executive director (*Reichsgeschäftsführer*).[125] Timm was still able to publish with and speak for the NG, but he was no longer *the* voice of the organization. Rather, he was asked to stay out of Lohse's way.[126]

Because of its traditional emphasis on foreign relations and contact between Lübeck and Scandinavian countries, the NG was poised to serve as a gateway northward for the new regime, especially in nations that seemed relatively impervious to Nazi overtures.[127] Timm argued that it could serve as an organ by which to "find or recruit new men who are fit to work for the Nordic idea on a small scale. One could summarize this whole activity under the concept of systematic training."[128] The connection between the NG and Party and state structures took time to define, but the evolution of the Society after 1926 had laid the groundwork by cultivating membership increasingly sympathetic to the Nordic idea and Nordicism more broadly. Timm encouraged party leadership in April 1934 to attend the NG rally in order to highlight the importance of the group to the *Reich*, even if no formal connection beyond Rosenberg had yet been made.[129]

While large-scale events such as major rallies for NG members from across Germany and even abroad were an indelible feature of Nazi Germany, it is worth mentioning that more subtle, so-called "small-scale" efforts were considered equally if not more important for the survival and growth of the Reich. The June 1, 1934, meeting of the complete board of the NG including Drechsler presented an action plan for the following six months, highlighting not only the work that had been completed but also the trajectory for the Society going forward. The plan was prefaced with the statement:

> Preliminary remark: It is assumed that the *Nordsiche Gesellschaft* is not an organization for its own sake, but only a means to promote the ideas it represents. As a matter of principle, therefore, any activity that is not strictly necessary and has the sole purpose of propagating the society as such must be avoided. Both in Germany and especially in Scandinavia, the emphatic anonymous work on a small scale is more important than pompous events. Of course, a public propaganda appearance cannot be avoided as long as certain membership advertising is required. But the management is aware that this is not the real task of society.[130]

The NG itself was explicitly viewed by the party, at least, as less important than the ideology it promoted. This also hints at the fact that the process of *Gleichschaltung*—coordination or alignment within the Nazi state apparatuses and its ideologies—was bumpy, challenging, and even involuntary. The NG, with its own history, agenda, and personalities, could be competition for the Nazi Party unless it could be subordinated to *its* control and *its* agenda. Further complicating this situation was the fact that the Party was a tapestry of individual interests, pitting high-ranking members against each other as they jockeyed for position and proximity to Hitler and the mechanisms of power.

Whatever Society work was being done in Germany at this time—especially lectures from other ministries and initiatives, such as Strength through Joy, the SS, the SA, and the National Socialist Teacher's League, to name a few—was not meant to attract attention from Scandinavia or even from the general public.[131] Rather, these party connections were meant to shore up influence and assure coordination within Germany, aided by pre-packaged materials and utilizing the networks already cultivated by organizations such as the *Institute für Weltwirtschaft* and the German Academic Exchange Service (DAAD). In this way, the NG appeared to retain the research-oriented agenda it had begun with as much as possible, but it was adapted to suit the needs of the consolidating state. The NG succeeded in hosting its first national rally of the Nazi era on June 1 and 2, 1934.

Among the dignitaries invited were the leaders of the major state offices, including the SS, SA, and the ministries. Many of these leaders were invited to become individual members of the NG, distinct from the group memberships (and higher membership fees) that could be collected from entities such as Chambers of Commerce and city senates.[132] Whether it was pursuing ranking Nazis or institutional memberships, more than anything the NG was seeking wide-ranging patronage and legitimacy. In the case of the Lübeck Senate, Timm essentially shamed it into subscribing to a membership that the Senates of Hamburg and Bremen had already obtained.[133] For 1934, the Lübeck Senate paid a RM100 fee. That December, Timm argued that the membership fee should increase to RM1000, since the society had exploded in scope and action, and the headquarters of the group was Lübeck; Hamburg, he said, had paid RM200.[134] It is clear from this letter that, especially after the Nazi Party began incorporating the NG into its bureaucracy, the organization would have much more of an integrated and less autonomous orientation than before. The old competitions, though, remained.

The post-1933 NG evolved along with the regime, and its leaders had to consider the role of factions in the government. The person who served most (or claimed status) as patron determined who the group aligned with and/or how the group was used in the bureaucracy. It also, potentially, determined which organizations could serve as foils or obstacles to even the most banal activities. For example, Ernst Röhm of the SA was invited as a matter of course to the NG's First *Reichstagung*, but by the end of that month, the purge of the SA during the "Night of the Long Knives" eviscerated his influence and that of the SA as a whole.[135] Fortunately for the NG, alignment was clearly with the SS leadership by September, demonstrated by Lohse's solidifying role, making it less vulnerable to early power struggles within the regime.

The rally staged by the NG in June 1934 served as the major event of the year for the organization, much in the same way as the NSDAP party rallies in Nuremberg did in September. For the following five years, up until the declaration of war in September 1939, the NG staged rallies in Lübeck in June, bringing upper-level Nazis and state ministries together with society members and leaders from across Germany and Scandinavia at the beginning of the summer season. Rather than staging a week-long public festival like the 1921 *Nordische Woche*, the NG opted to produce shorter rallies more frequently at less cost (one letter from 1936 soliciting funds for the Third *Reichstagung* asked for a RM20,000 contribution from the Lübeck Senate).[136] The yearly congresses held by the NG dealt with specific themes in German-Nordic culture. The Second Congress, for example, focused on Lübeck and its history. A wooden three-dimensional model of the *Altstadt* was carved specifically for the event, as well as a renovation of the iconic *Holstentor*; that carving is now housed in the *Holstentor*, taking up nearly a whole room. The Fourth Congress in 1937, in contrast, was a traveling tour of archaeological digs in Northern Germany and Denmark.[137] They were meant to be a short introduction for NG members to applications of Nordic thought and an analysis of the influence Nordic architecture of prehistory on Germany. The party had a similar model, though the national party rally in Nuremberg was a longer, more high-profile affair, and the 1934 Nuremberg rally was filmed and released the following year as *Triumph of the Will.*

ACCELERATION: THE NUREMBERG LAWS TO *KRISTALLNACHT*

By the end of 1934, especially after Hindenburg's death in August, the Nazi regime moved from a period of consolidation and organization to developing a faster pace on policy and legalizing Nazi ideological goals. The introduction of the Nuremberg Laws in advance of the 1935 annual party rally in Nuremberg initiated a new phase of Nazi rule, especially as it related to citizenship, the legal construction of "Aryan" and "other," and increased persecutions of Jews. In this context, Fred J. Domes edited *Die Schicksalsgemeinschaft der Ostsee* (The Baltic Sea Community of Destiny) and argued in the preface that a "community of destiny" could only be found through the analysis of individual questions apart from social constructions of commonality (such as the nationalist rhetoric that was so important in the 1920s).[138] The contributing authors, among them Alfred Rosenberg, went on to discuss the ideal role of Germany in Europe especially as it related to connecting and leading Aryan communities.[139] In many ways, this was akin to the broad brush strokes Rosenberg favored in his own writing, especially in 1930s *The Myth of the Twentieth Century*. Rosenberg himself was viewed as overly romantic, even ridiculous, and many in Hitler's inner circle including Hitler himself were reported to merely tolerate him. Domes and Timm focused primarily on Lübeck and the Baltic Sea, situating the region and the NG itself in broader Nazi-defined context.[140]

Local leaders were still preoccupied with proximity to power, and especially how individual communities fit into German racial identity. Higher-level bureaucratic leaders like Rosenberg were more concerned with Germany in general and how it related to other nations. Still, this was inconsistent with the previous year's action plan, which de-emphasized the NG as anything other than a vessel of Nordicist nationalism. This tension remained a constant challenge throughout the Third Reich, despite the Nazis' attempt to portray a single-minded, racially ordered state through propaganda like *Triumph of the Will*, released in March 1935. The existence of the Nordic movement, centered in northwestern Germany, was a subtle indication that even the Aryan identity was more complex and bureaucratic than ideologues and officials let on.

September 1935 was an important month, not only because it heralded another annual party rally but also because it was when the Nazis stepped up their persecutions of Jews beyond boycotts and individual or local action. The introduction of the Nuremberg Laws, coinciding with the annual rally,

> defined in detail who was a "Jew," limited the rights of Jewish and non-Jewish Germans to have sexual relations with or to marry the partners of their choice (the "Law for the Protection of German Blood and Honor"), and revoked Jewish legal rights to full citizenship ("Reich Citizenship Law").[141]

Marion Kaplan pointed out that these laws by and large reinforced broad German practice anyway, considering that Jews were increasingly segregated from non-Jewish Germans beyond the settlement of neighborhoods.[142] This was clear in Lübeck, where signs posted as early as August 30, 1935 (predating the official release of the Nuremberg Laws) declared Jews unwelcome and unwanted in in city limits.[143] It built on the city's already existing reputation for anti-Jewishness and outright antisemitism, especially in the old *Innenstadt.*

It could be argued this environment had developed over a previous couple of years of Nazi governance or even late 1920s political polarization, but turn-of-the-century scholarship argued that Lübeckers exhibited antisemitic attitudes early on. Gotthard Deutsch, in his article on Lübeck for the 1906 volume of the *Jewish Encyclopedia*, stated,

> In 1900, it had a population of 82,813, including 663 Jews. Like most of the free cities of Germany, Lübeck did not tolerate the Jews. In 1350, the city council wrote to Duke Otto of Brunswick-Lüneburg requesting him to exterminate the Jews living in his territory, as they were responsible for the plague. . . . In 1499 the local chronographer, Reimer Kock, states expressly that "there are no Jews in Lübeck, as they are not needed here.[144]

Deutsch detailed the back-and-forth status of the Jews in and around Lübeck, at first concentrated in the Moisling neighborhood, outside the city walls, then variably allowed a degree of toleration depending on the status of the city in wartime and who had control of the territory.[145] It wasn't until 1850 that Jews were permitted to consecrate a synagogue in the inner district rather than in Moisling, and the community remained small. The Nuremberg Laws did not result in an outright expulsion from Lübeck proper as it had in the past, but they were both a warning and a way to signal to Lübeck Jews that their community currently was and had always been outsiders. It also alerted non-Jews to changing norms and what was permissible, whether it was those who actively embraced the Nazi Party or who viewed the situation as something that didn't affect them.

Writers and thinkers who highlighted Nordic superiority, *völkisch* thought, and enthusiastic Nazism found more and more outlets to do their work. Hans Friedrich Blunck, friend of Fred Domes and legal scholar from Altona, was one example. He had been an active writer throughout the Weimar period, marshaling interest in regional Hanseatic history with emergent Nordicist ideologies.[146] Blunck enjoyed continued exposure throughout the Nazi period, in part because he enjoyed the patronage of Hinrich Lohse and connections to the NG and other Nazi writers' circles. He had two plays included in the 1936 version of the *Volksspiel und Feier* guide, which focused on the foundational work of the NG in Lübeck and provided official sanction to specific work.[147] Gunnar Gunnarsson, Icelandic author and novelist, also enjoyed extensive exposure in NG publications and on the lecture circuit. Many of these figures were established writers and thinkers; after the war, many of them had to grapple with a difficult pro-Nazi legacy.

Nazified policies were put into place throughout Germany, attempting to permeate all aspects of life and every layer of society, especially once they were codified into law. It was through public performance that political and cultural entities expressed their perspectives and demonstrated alignment with Nazi directives. Public spectacle was necessary to make Nordic identity indelibly connected to Nazi ideology, because as Brigitte Almgren and others argued, "As recently as the 1920s, it was by no means a foregone conclusion that the Nordic idea would be integrated into the Nazi ideology."[148] NG-affiliated groups, such as the *Plattdeutsch Volksgill* (Low German Society) and its theater-performance arm *Niederdeutschen Bühne* (Low German Stage),

> appointed to perform work for the purposes of National Socialism's cultural renewal of the empire. National Socialism leads us back to the source of our strength, to our foundations and folklore, and to the values of the *Heimat* and the healthy bases of all cultural life.[149]

Connecting folk and dialect groups to the broader mission of the NG served again to reflect the centrality of the Nazis in a rewritten "tradition," one that was as illusory as it was contradictory. Ongoing debates over identifying racial makeup kept Günther and Clauß in the discourse. As early proponents of the "Nordic Idea" (*Nordische Gedanke*), they were able to expand theoretical debates over race into regime-supported professorships, academic departments, and research agendas.

Clauß argued that race, especially the Nordic race, was expressed through personality and characteristics rather than appearance, which made it possible for even siblings to "often feel each other as absolutely foreign, as a foreign race."[150] He felt that race was more ephemeral, a soul rather than slate of set characteristics. On the other hand, Hans F. K. Günther advocated the concept that race was a physically expressed characteristic, that one could outwardly identify another person's "race."[151] The role of the NG in this context was to signal how membership and even the general public could understand these intellectual arguments, which formed the foundation for law and procedure in the regime. The Günther/Clauß split mirrored the ongoing competition between Rosenberg, Josef Goebbels, Heinrich Himmler, and others in guiding the direction of the party and its initiatives.

As early as 1936, Günther claimed that the NG was the "racial idea [*Rassegedanke*] in Gobineau's sense."[152] In many of the speeches at NG congresses or functions, the Nazi Party was explicitly hailed as the savior of the Nordic Idea (and, indeed, the Nordic race), rather than highlighting the efforts of the NG specifically. At the NG's Third *Reichstagung* in June 1936, speaker Erich Hilgenfeldt stated that although "the German *Volk* had been alienated to the Nordic Idea before 1933," the National Socialists viewed it as "self-help" and integral to "public welfare."[153] The society thereafter associated itself with the *Nordische Bewegung* and the *Nordische Ring*, which utilized and expanded the work of Clauß and Günther. So much of the NG's effectiveness depended on networking across the country, especially in light of the fact that Nordicism broadly navigated inconsistencies and even contradictions, especially from a nationalistic standpoint.[154] The NG embarked on presenting its view of Nordic identity as a stark foil to the enemies of the Nazi regime; this can be seen in a memo from December 1936 where "suggestions" for a speech opening an art exhibit in Lübeck focused on the "importance of Nordic beauty ideals and Nordic thought" in contrast to the "degenerate" Expressionist art of the postwar period.[155] The memo went on to detail that a strong nation holds onto its ideals, implying that the chaos of the early 1920s could be traced to "the people's" detachment from their traditional archetypes of art and beauty.

After a brief respite from accelerating antisemitism and political violence due to international attention the 1936 Olympics got, the second half of the

1930s entrenched antisemitism as the law of the land as well as attempts to (re)define racial in-groups, social and cultural norms, and political culture. By 1937, the NG was added as a sponsoring group with editing powers of the journal *Rasse*, its members were afforded a special subscription price.[156] In addition to articles focusing on eugenics and pseudoscientific analyses of "race" in Europe, *Rasse* reported on the NG's congresses every year. It included lists and advertisements of other journals by affiliated and/or approved organizations, consistently including *Der Norden* (the renamed monthly missive of the NG) and the *Nordische Rundschau* as outlets to further research and read about advances in racial and eugenic theory, especially the Nordic movement. The NG increasingly published and sponsored books dealing with a variety of facets of "Nordic culture" that were viewed as distinguishing features of a superior group, including *Der Norden Lacht: Humor des Nordens* (The Northern Laugh: Northern Humor). The forward of the book, published in October 1938 and coinciding with the *Nordische Woche* event in Hamburg that same month, linked even unique humor to the formation of a *völkisch* identity, saying: "The *Volk* cannot manage without humor."[157]

By 1938, the NG was firmly established in the regime and active in a variety of ways, ranging from cultural work and lectures to mobilizing Scandinavian networks in pursuit of diplomatic relations. Its utility to the Party was still debated, but this only motivated Society leaders and their patrons more to demonstrate effectiveness and potential. The NG's Fifth Congress in late June 1938 was much like a Nazi rally, comprised of two days of official speeches and political theater. NG regional directors including Dr. Timm spoke with keynote speeches by Alfred Rosenberg on Monday, June 20, and Heinrich Himmler on June 21.[158] At the same time, there was the sense that foreign participants in the event would go back and tell their friends and neighbors what they had seen of Germany for themselves.[159] The later part of the year was a turning point in many ways for Nazi Germany. The Munich Conference in September and the violence of Kristallnacht in November accelerated the pace with which the Nazis made life miserable and dangerous for Jews. The march toward war through rearmament, annexation, and invasion continued alongside ongoing legal and social measures to solidify the nation as a racial in-group.

NOTES

1. Dr. Schärffe, "Bericht über die Besprechung zur Gründung einer Nordischen Gesellschaft in Lübeck," 1.

2. Letter from 25 October 1922, HAL, 1.2 NSA 2462. See also the *Nordische Gesellschaft's* file at the *Deutsch Kongress-Zentrale* (DKZ) list the date of

establishment as September 1921: DKZ collection, Hoover Institute, Stanford, CA: Box 227, Folder *Nordische Woche* 1938.

3. Letter from 8 August 1922. HAL, 1.2. NSA 2462. There was, however, some debate about the taxable status of these funds, derived from the general or guaranteed fund. It appears that there was a question about taxing the funds as a donation, though the status of the *Nordische Gesellschaft* as an organization deriving from and originating during *Nordische Woche* precluded the funds from being considered distinct.

4. Dr. Schärffe, "Bericht über die Besprechung zur Gründung einer Nordischen Gesellschaft in Lübeck," 22 September 1921, p. 1. HAL, HK 144.

5. Public Notice from Finanzauschuss, End of February, 1922. HAL, 1.2 NSA 2462.

6. Letter from the NG to membership, 11 March 1922. HAL, NSA 639: Staatsrat Dr. Grosse.

7. Ibid.

8. "Nordische Gesellschaft Lübeck Satzung," no date. HAL, HK 144.

9. Ibid. Individual memberships were priced at 20 M, corporate or institutional memberships at 200 M, and honorary memberships obligation-free.

10. "Aufgaben der Nordischen Gesellschaft auf wirtschaftlichem Gebiete," *Mitteilungen der Handelskammer zu Lübeck*, 15 March 1922. HAL, HK 144.

11. Gerhard Schneider, "George Rudolf Reinhold Kalkbrenner," in *Lübecker Lebensläufe aus neun Jahrhunderten*, ed. Alken Bruns (Neumünster: Wachholz, 1993), 196–198. Kalkbrenner, as we will later see, occupies contentious space in Lübeck history especially as it related to the Nazi period. Though he was extended "honorary citizenship" to Lübeck in the 1950s, this was revoked in 2015 due to his activities during the Nazi era.

12. "Nordischen Gesellschaft in Lübeck," 9 Februrary 1922. HAL, HK 144. The appointment of Dr. Ernst Timm as a salaried secretary seemed to give much of the day-to-day responsibilities of running the Society to him rather than Dr. Kalkbrenner, who, as chairperson, assumed a role much like a commercial patron or sponsor. However, Kalkbrenner clearly represented a powerful force in the continued organization of the *Nordische Gesellschaft*.

13. Identity salience is broadly defined in the work of Richard Serpe and Sheldon Stryker as the probability that an identity is invoked in any given situation or set of circumstances. Additionally, identity salience implies a hierarchy of identities, where a highly salient identity is more likely to be invoked across situations. See, for example, Richard Serpe and Sheldon Stryker, "Commitment, Identity Salience, and Role Behavior," in *Personality, Roles, and Social Behavior*, ed. William Ickes and Eric S. Knowles (New York: Springer-Verlag, 1982). My working application of salience derives from Allport's implication that identities that are strongest, most important, and significant are salient in a sociological sense. What defines a salient identity is, on one hand, an individual issue. Allport, as a social psychologist, sought to reconcile what drove individuals to identify each other with patterns that occur in society. For example, to illustrate this point, Allport argued that "tolerant" people tend to "have no interest in group distinctions. To them a person is a person. But this benign lack of awareness is difficult to achieve in our society, where human relations

are so largely framed in terms of caste and class. As much as one might wish to treat a Negro [*sic*] simply as a human being, circumstances force an awareness of race. The prevalence of social discrimination tends to make ethnic attitudes salient" in *The Nature of Prejudice*, 428.

14. For example, the manifestation of a racial identity would be a biological expression of identity, based on scientific notions of race. At the same time, an ethnic construction of "Nordic" could be construed as a set of common cultural norms that could transcend biological attributes. Lastly, social attributes of an identity, one that appeared very early, was expressed in terms of economic activity of a specific country, especially those considered Scandinavian. This also demonstrated how specific historical context factored into identity formation.

15. Allport, *The Nature of Prejudice*, 31.

16. The historic difficulties Jews had in Lübeck was described in a 1904 encyclopedia of Jewish history, identifying the inconsistent tenor of German-Jewish relationships in the city, reaching back to the early modern period. This will be expanded upon in Chapter 5. See Gotthard Deutsch, "Lübeck," *The Jewish Encyclopedia*, Vol. 8 (New York: Funk and Wagnalls, 1904), 198. Available at archive.org, accessed 11 June 2018. https://archive.org/details/b29000488_0008. See also Anna Triandafyllidou, *Immigrants and National Identity in Europe* (London: Routledge, 2001), especially Ch. 1.

17. Allport, *The Nature of Prejudice*, 31.

18. Dr. Ernst Timm, "An die Herren Mitglieder des Kuratoriums!" 11 March 1922. HAL, NSA 639.

19. Dr. Ernst Timm, "An die Herren Vorstandsmitglieder der Nordische Gesellschaft!," 24 April 1922, p. 1. HAL, NSA 639. Emphasis original.

20. Ibid., 2–3.

21. Ibid., 6. Timm laid out a rough estimate of how much it would cost to post correspondants, trying to allow for the "possibility of further devaluation [*etwaige weitere Geldentwertung*]."

22. Ibid., 1.

23. "Die Taetigkeit der Nordischen Gesellschaft vom Maerz bis September 1922," 26 September 1922, 1. HAL, NSA 639.

24. Ibid.

25. Ibid., 3.

26. "Lübecker Kulturpropaganda 1923," no date, p. 2. HAL, NSA 639.

27. Fromme was appointed as head of cultural affairs, according to a letter from Dr. Grosse to Professor H. Schumacher, 30 January 1922. HAL, 1.2 NSA 2462.

28. Memo from Franz Fromme, no date, 1. HAL, NSA 639.

29. Ibid.

30. Letter from G. Severin to Dr. Kalkbrenner, 7 December 1922. HAL, NSA 639.

31. Ibid.

32. Dr. Kalkbrenner, "An die Handelskammer," 4 January 1923. HAL, HK 145: Bewilligung von Beiträge für die Nordische Gesellschaft, 1922–1925.

33. Ibid.

34. Nordische Gesellschaft, "Ferienkurse für Ausländer." August 1923. HAL, NA 283: Nordische Gesellschaft 1921–1925 (mit 1 Plakat).

35. Ibid., 3.

36. Ibid., 4.

37. "Bedingungen für wertbeständiges Geld der Länder," *General Anzeiger*, No. 249 (25 October 1923). HAL, PA 3769.

38. Memo from Der Reichsminister der Finanzen, 26 September 1923, p. 2. HAL, PA 3769.

39. Throughout the Polizeiamt file dealing with Notgeld (3769), there are multiple examples of attempts to monitor or regulate *Notgeld* between 1918 and 1923. Vouchers, checks, emergency notes, and other scrip were identified as unfortunately necessary for day-to-day municipal (and later private) operation. The *Polizeiamt* was the place where an accounting was made of the municipal notes issued to rectify any shortfall, though that required a degree of self-reporting and regulation, hence the penchant to overprint and overspend.

40. HA, PA 3769.

41. Memo to Dr. Grosse from Gröner, 17 August 1923. HAL, PA 3769.

42. HAL, PA 3769.

43. Dr. Gundlach, Tgb. Nr. 2080, 11 March 1924. Stadtarchiv Kiel [SAK] 36065: Kieler Notgeld, 1917–1954.

44. Bernd Widdig, *Culture and Inflation in Weimar Germany*, 46–47.

45. Detlev K. Peukert, *The Weimar Republic: The Crisis of Classical Modernity* (New York: Hill and Wang, 1987), 59–75. Peukert outlines concisely the challenges confronting the Republic in November 1923.

46. Timm's identification of his location came in a previous letter, dated 2 November 1923, to Dr. Keibel. HAL, NSA 639. Essen, as part of the Ruhr Valley, was close to the Belgian border was subject to the combined French/Belgian incursion into the Ruhr industrial region that precipitated the German strikes and work stoppages.

47. Letter to Dr. Grosse from Dr. Timm, 23 November 1923. HAL, NSA 639.

48. Contemporary scholars and commentators, including the Dawes Report issued by the United States, viewed the *Rentenmark* as "a precarious and artificial solution to the German monetary problem," as described by Constantino Bresciani-Turroni in *Economics of Inflation*, 338. Bresciani-Turroni argued that the perception of stabilization—the view that the German government was getting a practical handle on inflationary notes—led to increased consumption and the appearance of increased purchasing power, even as, temporarily, the number of notes in the system in Germany actually increased.

49. Widdig, *Culture and Inflation*, 48. Widdig argued that hyperinflation virtually disappeared overnight, "as quickly as it had arrived." While this does not imply a smooth transition without economic pain, it does speak to the extreme volatility of German currency.

50. See Gerald D. Feldman, *The Great Disorder*, 754–835. In Chapters 16 and 17, Feldman convincingly lays out the social and political factors that contributed to economic choices and consequences.

51. Bengt Paul, “Die Wirtschaft der nordischen Länder im Jahre 1924,” in *Das Jahr 1924. Ostsee-Schriften Heft* 2 (Lübeck: Nordischer Verlag/Nordische Gesellschaft, 1925).

52. Ibid., 24.

53. “Anstellungsvertrag zwischen der Nordischen Gesellschaft und dem Schriftsteller Otto Weber beide in Lübeck,” 28 March 1924. HAL, NSA 639.

54. Ibid.

55. See Daniel T. Bullard, “‘*Vergiss nicht unsere Kolonien!*’: German Colonial Memory from 1919 to 1943” (PhD diss., York University, 2012), accessed 14 June 2022, https:// https://www.collectionscanada.gc.ca/obj/thesescanada/vol2/002/NR90358.PDF?is_thesis=1&oclc_number=910984548.

56. “Vertraulich!,” 16 February 1924. HAL, NSA 639.

57. Ibid., 1.

58. Ibid., 2.

59. Ibid., 5.

60. For a discussion of the controversy surrounding the Rapallo Treaty, see Peter Krüger, “A Rainy Day, April 16, 1922: The Rapallo Treaty and the Cloudy Perspective for German Foreign Policy,” in *Genoa, Rapallo, and European Reconstruction in 1922*, ed. Carole Fink and Axel Frohn (Cambridge: Cambridge University Press, 2002), 49–62.

61. Ibid., 1. Asmis continued to discuss monetary policy and how the Entente powers conducted immigration policy with an eye on reparation and war-debt payments, both regarding Germany and the Soviet Union.

62. “Zeichnung für den Ausbau der Kapelle am Stegel bei St. Marien Mengstraße Lübeck für Zwecke der Nordischen Gesellschaft.” HAL, HK 146: Ausbau der Kapelle Maria am Stegel für Zwecke der Nordische Gesellschaft 1924.

63. Johann Baltzer, F. Bruns and H. Rahtgens, eds. *Die Bau- und Kunstdenkmäler der freien und Hansestadt Lübeck, Bd 4* (Lübeck: H. G. Rahtgens, 1928), 361–369. This volume of architectural history, published by the same publisher as the *Nordische Woche Festschrift*, discussed the historical details of the building at length and its uses.

64. Though there is no evidence that the planned-for rehabilitation occurred and the chapel was destroyed in the Palm Sunday 1942 RAF air raid in Lübeck, the site and its foundation outline have been included in the UNESCO World Heritage Site information presented throughout the city.

65. Dr. Timm, “An unsere Mitglieder!” 2 February 1925. HAL, HK 144.

66. Dr. Keibel, “Betrifft: Zahlung an die Nordische Gesellschaft aus dem Werbefonde,” 4 October 1924. HAL, HK 144.

67. Ernst Boie, “An die Industrie und Handelskammer, Halle,” 6 October 1924. HAL, HK 144.

68. Gustav Cassel, “Das Problem der Kriegsentschädigung,” *Ostsee-Schriften* Heft 1, 1924. HAL, HK 144.

69. Ibid., 3.

70. Ibid.

71. Ibid.

72. Ibid., 4.
73. "Mitgliederversammlung der Nordischen Gesellschaft," *Lübecker General-Anzeiger*, 14 December 1924. HAL, HK 144.
74. Jan Grosse, "An das Kuratorium der Nordischen Gesellschaft," 19 December 1923. HAL, NA 283. The construction of "new bloom" is also close to that of "new blood [*neues Blut*]," both implying and promoting not only a new infusion of personalities in the NG but also the flowering of the NG's efforts.
75. "An Einen Hohen Senat!" February 1925, 4. HAL, NSA 639.
76. Ibid., 2.
77. Letter from Dr. Timm, 31 July 1925. HAL, NSA 639.
78. H. Mahn, "Plan einer Ausstellung auf dem Holstentorgeländ in Lübeck," March 1925, 1. HAL, NA 283.
79. Allport, *Nature of Prejudice*, 25.
80. Ibid., 44.
81. Peukert, *The Weimar Republic*, 193–204. Peukert deftly explains the factors at work during the later 1920s, and, more specifically, Stresemann's role in them.
82. Lübeck 700-Feier Festumzug Folio, 1926.
83. Notice to Membership from Dr. Timm, 16 January 1926. HAL, HK 144.
84. Ibid.
85. Notices to membership from Dr. Timm, 6 February 1926 and 7 April 1926 respectively. HAL, HK 144. Reports on the production of films such as *Gluten am Nordpol*, now considered a lost film, appeared in trade magazines such as *Kinematograph*; see *Kinematograph*, 5 September 1925, 32.
86. Notice to membership from Dr. Timm, 5 March 1926. HAL, HK 144. In particular, this specific program was presented in conjunction with the Behnhaus, while also drawing attention to the home institution of the lecturer Dr. Pauli in Hamburg, the *Hamburger Kunsthalle*.
87. Notice to institutional members from Dr. Timm, 2 January 1928. HAL, HK 144.
88. Depending on the length and distance of the trip, tours could cost up to 450 Mark, depending on mode of transportation, who was leading the trip, and when it occurred. "17tätige Sonderreise," July 1927. HAL, HK 144.
89. Letter to "Den Deutschen Industrie- und Handelstag, Berlin" 19 November 1927. HAL, HK 144.
90. Letter to *Reichszentrale für deutsche Verkehrswerbung* from Eschenburg, 6 April 1926. HAL, HK 144. This phrasing also appeared in an unsigned, unaddressed draft that included notes from Dr. Timm dated 29 March 1926.
91. Ibid. In the letter, Eschenburg emphasized that "*German* interests [*deutsche Interessen*] was of utmost importance, especially in the foreign [*Auslande*] press. Eschenburg's use of *Auslande* rather than *fremde* is interesting as well, avoiding the connotation of a completely alien culture or land as compared with Germany.
92. Gay, *Weimar Culture*, 133.
93. Ibid., 133–134; see also Peukert, *The Weimar Republic*, 170–171 and 220; Widdig, *Culture and Inflation*, 51.
94. Voranschlag 1927, n.d. HAL, NSA 639.

95. Letter to Thorndyke (*Ala*) from Board of *Nordische Gesellschaft* 2 December 1926. HAL, NSA 639.

96. Letter to Dr. Cords from Otto Weber, 3 October 1928. HAL, HK 144.

97. Widdig, *Culture and Inflation*, 49–52.

98. Hans Mommsen discussed how elite members of right-wing and ultranationalist parties worked in tandem with other fringe groups, like the Nazis, hoping to establish a base of support while manipulating the political system (such as Hugenberg's idea that Hitler could be used, essentially, as a tool in government after 1932). See Hans Mommsen and Elborg Forster *The Rise and Fall of Weimar Democracy* (Chapel Hill, NC: University of North Carolina Press, 1998), 334.

99. For a concise discussion of the domestic political situation in the Weimar Republic, especially from an organizational point of view, see Gay, *Weimar Culture,* 16–22.

100. See Manfred Kuechler, "The NSDAP Vote in the Weimar Republic: An Assessment of the State-of-the-Art in View of Modern Electoral Research," *Historical Social Research/Historische Sozialforschung*, Vol. 17, No. 1 (1992): 22–52; Christian Stögbauer, "The Radicalisation of the German Electorate: Swinging to the Right and the Left in the Twilight of the Weimar Republic," *European Review of Economic History*, Vol. 5, No. 2 (German Cliometrics: August 2001): 251–280; Brian Ault, "Joining the Nazi Party before 1930: Material Interests or Identity Politics?" *Social Science History*, Vol. 26, No. 2 (Summer 2002): 273–310; and Gary King, Ori Rosen, Martin Tanner, and Alexander F. Wagner, "Ordinary Economic Voting Behavior in the Extraordinary Election of Adolf Hitler," *The Journal of Economic History*, Vol. 68, No. 4 (Dec. 2008): 951–996.

101. Ibid. Ault critiques various sociological approaches to explaining political behavior, particularly from the standpoint of social movements, arriving at the conclusion that identity politics, in conjunction with other modes of analysis such the Rational Choice (RC) approach and others, more compellingly explains how the Nazis built a viable support base in Germany at the end of the 1920s.

102. Mommsen, *Weimar Democracy*, 334–335.

103. Ibid.

104. Rudolf Kjellén, "Der Umgang Schwedens in alter und neuer Zeit," in Mahn, *Festschrift*, 34–37 and Rudolf Kjellén, *Der Staat als Lebensform* (Leipzig: S. Hirzel, 1917).

105. Richard T. Gray, *About Face: German Physiognomic Thought from Lavater to Auschwitz* (Detroit: Wayne State University Press, 2004), 177.

106. Gray, *About Face*, 178.

107. For a clear discussion on the elements of *Heimat*, see Celia Applegate, *A Nation of Provincials: The German Idea of Heimat* (Berkeley: University of California Press, 1990); Peter Blickle, *Heimat: A Critical Theory of the German Idea of Homeland* (Rochester, NY: Camden House, 2004); Elizabeth Boa and Rachel Palfreyman, *Heimat: A German Dream. Regional Loyalties and National Identity in German Culture, 1890–1990* (Oxford: Oxford University Press, 2000); Alon Confino, *The Nation as a Local Metaphor: Württemberg, Imperial Germany, and National Memory, 1871–1918* (Chapel Hill: University of North Carolina Press,

1997); Willi Oberkrome, *"Deutsche Heimat:" Nationale Konzeption und regionale Praxis von Naturschutz, Landschaftsgestaltung und Kulturpolitik in Westfalen-Lippe und Thüringen(1900–1960)* (Paderborn: Verlag Ferdinand Schöningh GmbH, 2004); James Retallack, *Saxony in German History: Culture, Society, and Politics, 1830–1933* (Ann Arbor: University of Michigan Press, 2000); and others.

108. Blickle, *Heimat*, 47.

109. Retallack, *Saxony*, 168. Though Retallack analyzed the region of Saxony in particular (just as Applegate focused on the Palatinate), the ideas about how *Heimat* functioned on national and local levels are applicable.

110. Though he began writing between 1919 and 1920, Günther's breakthrough work was *Rassenkunde des deutschen Volkes* (München: J. F. Lehmann-Verlag, 1922), which made him a leader in German ethnography and racial science. He solidified this reputation with the publication and translation of *The Racial Elements of European History* (London: Methuen & Co., 1927). For discussion of his ideas in the context of developing Nazi culture, see George L. Mosse, *Nazi Culture* and Geoffrey Field's "Nordic Racism."

111. Gray, *About Face*, 178.

112. Ibid. Evidence of this is Clauß's work *Rasse und Seele* from 1937.

113. "Wirtschaftliche Ausgabe," *Ostsee-Rundschau*, April 1930, 1. HAL, HK 144. The pamphlet had no explicit authors, but the board of directors (comprising of Ernst Timm, *Ostsee-Rundschau* editor Walter Zimmerman, Fred J. Domes, Alfred Mahlau, and Prof. Mahn) was listed, including a copy of by-laws.

114. Ibid., 2.

115. Flowchart of 1931 *Nordische Gesellschaft*. HAL, HK 144.

116. Letter to Ernst Timm from Dr. Grosse, 2 September 1930. HAL, HK 144.

117. "Zehn Jahre 'Nordische Gesellschaft in Lübeck,'" *Hamburger Fremdenblatt*, 12 December 1931. HAL, HK 144.

118. "Rundfrage Neujahr 1932: Die Forderung der Stunde," 31 December 1931. HAL, HK 144.

119. Peukert, *The Weimar Republic*, 236. For a thorough discussion of electoral politics in the later Weimar period see in particular chapters 11, 12, and 14 of Peukert's book.

120. Ibid., 264–265. Much has been written about the last elections of the Weimar Republic, including analyses of voter demographics and ongoing electoral volatility. See especially Thomas Childers, *The Nazi Voter: The Social Foundations of Fascism in Germany, 1919–1933* (Chapel Hill: University of North Carolina Press, 1983) and Eric D. Weitz, *The Weimar Republic: Promise and Tragedy* (Princeton: Princeton University Press, 2007).

121. See both Michael Burleigh and Wolfgang Wipperman, ed., *The Racial State: Germany 1933–1945* (Cambridge: Cambridge University Press, 1991) and Devin O. Pendas, Mark Roseman, and Richard F. Wetzell, *Beyond the Racial State: Rethinking Nazi Germany* (Cambridge: Cambridge University Press, 2017).

122. For a thorough explanation of Rosenberg's interest in the *Nordische Gesellschaft*, see Birgitta Almgren et al., "Alfred Rosenberg und die Nordische Gesellschaft," 7–51. See also, for explanation of Rosenberg's *Außenpolitisches Amt* and

the organization of the ministry, including the *Nordische Gesellschaft*, see Jacobsen, *Nationalsozialistiche Außenpolitik, 1933–1938.*

123. Jacobsen, *Außenpolitik*, 488–489.

124. Brandt and Due, "A Humourist in the Shadow of the Swastika," *Perspective.* Brandt and Due cite a letter from the Royal Danish Consulate in Hamburg to the Danish Ministry of Foreign Affairs from October 1924 labeling Timm as a "fervent Nationalist." The article goes so far as to describe Timm as a "vociferous agitator of National Socialist ideas," evident in his dealings with Danish cartoonists during his Nordische Gesellschaft tenure and after at Interpress.

125. "Fragebogen für Genehmigungsantrag," 30 May 1938, DKZ collection, Hoover Institute, Stanford, CA, Box 227.

126. Jacobsen, *Außenpolitik*, 489.

127. Several studies have analyzed Scandinavian nations' responses to Nazism and specifically the *Nordische Gesellschaft*'s role in each country, considering the range of political parties including extremist positions. By and large, scholars argued the Society had little impact in each country, though international members participated in German festivals. While most combatant countries in Western Europe had Nazi parties, authors such as Henrik Lundbak argued that other far-right and nationalist parties in Scandinavia pursued visibility and a voice in international politics in *Danish Unity: A Political Party between Fascism and Resistance, 1936–1947* (Copenhagen: Museum Tusculanum Press/University of Copenhagen, 2003).

128. Letter from Dr. Ernst Timm to Reichstatthalter Hildebrandt, 7 April 1934. HAL, NSA 1.2 2468: 1st Reichstagung Nordische Gesellschaft..

129. Ibid. Timm went so far as to include preliminary plans for the rally itself to entice leadership to make an appearance in Lübeck.

130. "Arbeitsplan der Nordischen Gesellschaft für die nächsten sechs Monate," 1, enclosed in 7 May 1934 letter to Oberbürgermeister Drechsler from Dr. Timm. HAL, NSA 1.2 2468.

131. Ibid., 2–3.

132. Letter to Senat der freien und Hansestadt Lübeck from Dr. Timm, 9 January 1934. HAL: NSA 1.2 6618—Mitgliedschaft der Stadt bei den NG.

133. Ibid.

134. Letter to Senat der freien und Hansestadt Lübeck from Dr. Timm, 31 December 1934. HAL, NSA 1.2 6618.

135. The so-called Night of the Long Knives, June 30, 1934, saw a purge of high-level SA members and Ernst Röhm himself. It was argued the SA was gathering too much power and represented a threat to Hitler himself; scholars have demonstrated that the consolidation of power around Heinrich Himmler and the primacy of the SS began after June 1934, leading to a sprawling sub-bureaucracy that included the Gestapo, the concentration and death camp system, the police, the elite Waffen-SS, and various ministries related to racial policy. Many leaders of these ministries were members, themselves, of the SS, and so this helped maintain the SS as the premier organization in the Nazi state.

136. Letter to Senat der Freie und Hansestadt Lübeck from Pfundtner, 3 February 1936. HAL, NSA 1.2 Kammereiamt [KA] 414—Reichstagungen der Nordischen Gesellschaft.

137. Alexander Funkenberg, *Haus und Hof im Nordischen Raum* (Lübeck: C. Kabitzsch,1937). This congress was carried out in conjunction with the Sixth Nordic Archaeological Meeting in 1937, discussed in Steffen Stummann Hansen, "The Wandering Congress: The Sixth Nordic Archaeological Meeting in Denmark 1937," *Acta Archaeologica,* Vol. 74, No. 1 (Oct. 2003), 293–305.

138. Fred J. Domes, ed., *Die Schicksalsgemeinschaft der Ostsee* (Berlin: Gerhard Stalling, Verlagsbuchhandlung/Nordischen Gesellschaft, 1935), 3.

139. For further discussion German-Scandinavian connections see Robert Bohn, ed., *Deutschland, Europa und der Norden: Ausgewählte Probleme der nordeuropäischen Geschichte im 19. und 20. Jahrhundert* (Stuttgart: Franz Steiner Verlag, 1993), especially Fritz Petrick, "Der 9. April 1940 und die 'Neuordnung' Nordeuropas," 97–106 for particular analysis of Rosenberg's ongoing work regarding Scandinavia and Domes' volume.

140. Domes, *Schicksalsgemeinschaft*, 35. In fact, Ernst Timm wrote an essay about the role and tasks of the *Nordische Gesellschaft* in particular, rather than the bigger picture of the *Außenpolitisches Amt.*

141. Marion Kaplan, *Between Dignity and Despair: Jewish Life in Nazi Germany* (New York: Oxford University Press, 1998), 42.

142. Ibid., 43.

143. "Der deutsch-nordishche Verein und die Judenverfolgungen," Korrespondenz "Nordschleswig" Flensburg, Hansestadt Archiv Lübeck, NSA 05.02 Nordische Gesellschaft Band 2, 1938–1944. The unnamed writer explained that Jews were expressly warned away from theaters, restaurants, and public spaces.

144. Gotthard Deutsch, "Lübeck," *The Jewish Encyclopedia*, Vol. 8 (New York: Funk and Wagnalls, 1904), 198. Available at archive.org, accessed 11 June 2018. https://archive.org/details/b29000488_0008

145. Ibid., 198–199. Deutsch points to the Thirty Years' War as well as French occupation of the city during the reign of Napoleon, when variably the French, the Danish, or the Prussians controlled the land around the free city.

146. For a detailed discussion of Blunck's impact before and during Nazism, see W. Scott Hoerle, *Hans Friedrich Blunck: Poet and Nazi Collaborator, 1888–1961.* Studies in Modern German Literature Vol. 97 (Bern: Peter Lang, 2004).

147. Hans Friedrich Blunck, "Das Deutsch-Nordische Schriftstellerhaus: Worte des Grußes," in Domes, *Schicksalsgemeinschaft*, 43.

148. Almgren et al., "Rosenberg und *Nordische Gesellschaft*," 6.

149. "Werbevorstellung der Niederdeutschen Bühne auf der Freilichtbühne," E. Hinrichs, n.d. [August 1933]. HAL, NSA 1660: Plattdeutsch Volksgill zu Lübeck.

150. Ludwig Ferdinand Clauß, *Die Nordische Seele* (Berlin: J. F. Lehmann, 1932), 8.

151. Hans F. K. Günther, *Der Nordische Gedanke unter den Deutschen* (Berlin: J. F. Lehmann, 1927).

152. Hans F. K. Günther, "Zur dritten Reichstagung der Nordischen Gesellschaft," *Rasse* III, Heft 6.

153. Erich Hilgenfeldt, "Der Nordische Gedanke in der deutschen Wohlfahrtspflege: Auszug ans der Rede auf der dritten Reichstagung der Nordischen Gesellschaft in Lübeck, Juni 1936," *Rasse* Heft 7/8 (1936), 286–287.

154. For a detailed study of the evolution of "Nordic Idea" and Nordic movements more generally, see Stefan Breuer, *Die Nordische Bewegung in der Weimarer Republik* (Wiesbaden: Harrassowitz, 2018).

155. Letter to Dr. Boehmcker from Wolff, 6 December 1936. HAL, Schul- und Kulturverwaltung [SKV] 699: Die Reichstagungen der Nordischen Gesellschaft in Lübeck 1936–1940.

156. Lutzhöft argued that Clauß, in fact, was much less ideologically sympathetic to the Nazi Party and that he did not want his work to "serve any political party": Lutzhöft, *Nordische Gedanke*, 47. Whether or not this is true is debatable, but Günther's work was much more in line with Nazi policy and mindset than Clauß's was in general.

157. A. Eskil Avenstrup, *Der Norden Lacht: Humor des Nordens* (Berlin: Wilhelm Limpert-Verlag, 1938), 7.

158. Nordische Gesellschaft, *Tag des Nordens* (Lübeck: H.G. Rahtgens, 1938), back cover. DKZ collection, Hoover Institute, Stanford, CA, Box 227.

159. Letter from Hermann Funk, 23 June 1938. HAL, 1.2 NSA 2473: 5th Reichstagung der Nordsiche Gesellschaft.

Chapter 4

Nazi Nordicism in War and Occupation

Two houses of worship and community embody the Lübeck experience of World War II and the Nazi regime. On the eastern side of the old city, situated between St. Aegidien and St. Annen Museum, is the synagogue of the *Jüdische Gemeinde Lübeck*. Completely restored only in 2020, it stands as a memorial to the Jewish Lübeckers who weathered pogroms, persecution, deportation, and resurgence. Across the island in the center, Marienkirche and its towers occupy a block next to city hall and the *Marktplatz*. Built as a basilica, it anchors the central district as one of its main churches. It also sustained incredible damage during the 1942 Royal Air Force air raid and became a major site of memory for Lübeck's local wartime experience. Two melted bells, which crashed through the ceiling of the south tower, remain where they fell as a remembrance to the flames that hollowed out a portion of the city and took decades to rebuild.

The historic inner city reveals just how complex the war was for Lübeckers in terms of memory. Marienkirche tells only part of the story, but it is one that persists into the present day and is a tangible reminder of the devastation of World War II and how it came home. Other sites throughout the central district, such as the consecrated parish dedicated to the Lübeck Martyrs (*Propsteikirche Herz Jesu*), the medieval Armory across the street which served as Gestapo headquarters during the Nazi era, and the *Stolpersteine* ("stumbling stones") throughout the city begin to piece together Lübeck's experiences before, during, and after the war. The remains of the wartime experience are in many ways still visible, and the influence of groups like the *Nordische Gesellschaft* (NG) subtly persists in design and in museums new and old; a copy of the NG's monthly journal *Der Norden* was displayed in the European Hanseatic Museum's History Lab when it opened in 2015.

This chapter traces parallel movements—the incorporation and maturation of the NG, Nordicism in Nazi ideology and in the regime more generally, Lübeck's wartime experiences, and early occupation by the British. Part of the story is how the Hamburg chapter of the NG mounted its own *Nordische Woche* in October 1938, challenging the authority of the central office in Lübeck and reorienting the NG's mission to include cities other than Lübeck. It was attended by high-ranking Nazis and occurred just as actions against Jews escalated. It also engaged the cultural and political theater strategies the Nazis used to define the contours of German society, such as the so-called Degenerate Art traveling exhibit of 1937. The "new" *Nordische Woche* was an example of how the Party continued to incorporate regional groups into the bureaucracy as different officials grew their patronages and fiefdoms. The competition between these men—sometimes to curry Hitler's favor, sometimes to maintain or increase their own power—impacted policy and the place(s) the NG existed in it.

The NG's relocation to Travemünde in 1942 after the RAF bombing in Lübeck ended the peak of its influence; its headquarters as well as its archive went up in flames just as the Nazi war effort experienced setback after setback. At the end of the war, the NG was just one more faded component of a criminal enterprise, and Germany lost all sovereignty as the Allies occupied the country. The Allied military authority set about establishing order and undoing the Nazis' influence on the population and institutions as it navigated refugee and displaced person camps in the wake of continent-wide genocide. In northwestern Germany, British occupation officials enacted laws related to the control of property, identifying and arresting Nazis, and conducting denazification proceedings. At the same time, Lübeck's position on the border with the Soviet zone—contentious to say the least—led to debates over the region's trade, its position, and the livelihoods of its populations. The assertions to Nordic identity, seen as crucial to recovery after the World War I, now was tainted with deadly, racialized Nazism, in part because of the activities of groups like the NG during the Nazi regime.

HAMBURG'S *NORDISCHE WOCHE,* 1938

Nordische Woche 1938, held in Hamburg, was different from NG congresses because it was aimed at the general population rather than members much like the *Nordische Woche* of 1921. The event was planned by the NG bureaucracy, requiring paperwork to ask for and receive permission to host the event from the *Deutsche Kongress-Zentrale* in Berlin. In a letter from October 1, 1938, the Commissioned Manager of the Hamburg NG office argued for a multiday and multisite event, rather than the more limited day-long congress.[1]

Press releases announced some of the planned activities for Hamburg's *Nordische Woche* (in conjunction with "folkloric" societies) as well as an NG rally.[2] From the outset, the NG took visible control in the organization of *Nordische Woche*. Official correspondence regarding *Nordische Woche* originated with or was received by the Hamburg NG office, including maps and registration forms for both *Nordische Woche* and the Society.[3] In addition to Hamburg's *Nordische Woche*, the NG still hosted its annual congress in Lübeck in June, though the estimated attendance was only 300 German citizens and 200 "foreigners."[4] This number seems small, especially when one takes into consideration the ambitions for both the organization itself and the *Nordische Woche* it planned for later in the year. Invitations and press releases were sent to other states in Germany, demonstrating a desire to host a formal yet well-advertised event, although some state leaders expressed a wish for more warning.[5]

The program for *Nordische Woche* 1938 was not a *Festschrift* in the style of Heinz Mahn's booklet from 1921. The booklet included on its back cover the wish of the organizers that participants and recipients act as advertisers, providing word-of-mouth to assure "participation of the friends living in our town and those from the lands of the North."[6] Advertisements from Hamburg's businesses were largely absent, making the booklet purely functional to guide participants through the week rather than serving an economic or collectible purpose. It also made clear who the sponsor of the event was: the NG, as a component of the Nazi regime. The advertisements that *were* included a list of Hamburg's museums, travel to Denmark sponsored by the Society, and books by Hans Freidrich Blunck.[7] The booklet directed potential participants to visit the Hamburg NG office to purchase entrance tickets for lectures, concerts, theater performances, or films; the prices for each event were included in the itinerary.[8]

The booklet itself opened with a note from Karl Kaufmann, the head of the Hamburg NG office. In it, he expressed the desire to make *Nordische Woche* a yearly event "dedicated to Nordic thought and the significant achievements of the people of the north."[9] He discussed how the festival provided a connection between Hamburg and Scandinavia, including the aid such a connection would provide in the "future destiny of the [German] people and the people of Europe."[10] The festival was departure from previous NG functions that centered on Lübeck, and though the headquarters remained there the Hamburg office had its own agenda. It also demonstrated that locality was still important, even in tension with national identity and Party ideology. Following this note, an article about the "Nordic Idea and the *Nordische Gesellschaft*" exalted the role of the European person in the past and the future, claiming that "They [those of Nordic blood] plow up the ground of the past and new life arises in new form. . . . A thousand years later, the

European person discovers and conquers the world."[11] The article ended by tying together the resurgence of the [Northern] European with the work of the NG, which sought to "educate the German person of the consciousness of Nordic thought on the one hand . . . [and] on the other hand care for the relations with the north," embodied in the form of *Nordische Woche*.[12] In this way, the goals of Hamburg's *Nordische Woche* were clear and fit within the scheme of Nazi diplomatic ambitions even as it deviated from the origins of the NG itself in Lübeck.

What was considered "Nordic" was again expanded in Hamburg. For example, the *Nordischer Abend* on October 16 was comprised of "songs and music from Norway, Sweden, England, and Finland."[13] By October 1938, Hitler had annexed portions of Czechoslovakia, Austria, and moved back into the Rhine in order to consolidate all people of "Germanic" blood and language. Including England in a heritage of cultural achievement and racial similarity can be easily construed as a political move, especially in a festival that was supposed to attract international attention. If England was linked to Germany culturally, politically, and diplomatically, it was possible there would be less resistance to German expansion or the *Anschluß* in Austria. In the event of war, England could possibly be neutral or even an ally.

Whether or not English representatives were invited to Hamburg's *Nordische Woche*, though, is unclear.

Hamburg's *Nordische Woche* events included plays or performances that harkened back to classical Greece or medieval Europe, creating the illusion of a generic European but clearly non-Jewish heritage that echoed the opening ceremonies of the 1936 Olympics. Rather than emphasizing the achievements or character of specific nations, the plays and selected topics highlighted common foundations of European culture. For example, Sophocles's *Antigone* was performed on October 18.[14] The previous day, a 1935 play by Wilhelm Schöttler called "Nibelungen-Not" was performed, bringing to mind the *Niebelungenlied* and Wagner's Ring cycle.[15] Lectures on aspects of Nordic culture, such as Finland's industry, were present as they were in 1921, but with greater emphasis on its relation to Germany broadly. All of these were implicitly labeled as at least precursors to Nordic culture.

Hamburg's *Nordische Woche* seemed to look more into the future than Lübeck's had though it totally reflected the Nazi present. It constructed an amalgam of past and future in ways that underscored the worldview of the Party. Lectures and events that paired "Nordic" culture with a German writer or painter served to conflate the two. One of the free lectures discussed Danish pictures of Goethe and portrayals of Goethe in the Danish context, reframing imagined communities from the outside.[16] While the text of the lecture was not included, it was presented on a day that featured an Ibsen play and an analysis of Ibsen, Björnson, and German drama.[17] In the same vein, a lecture dealt with "Nordic Language and its Germanic Characteristics," clearly trying to convince attendees and observers of Germany's centrality to Nordicism.[18] On the last day, the City Orchestra and Philharmonic performed a Sunday concert featuring the "Nordic Masters" of music, especially Brahms and Grieg.[19]

By 1938, the NG featured regional offices spread throughout Germany. The central office, though, was still located in Lübeck despite the relocation of *Nordische Woche* to Hamburg. The reason for this is not clear, as Lübeck had been written into the foundational by-laws. One could presume, for instance, that it would be easiest to locate the offices of the NG in Berlin or even Munich amid the other central offices staffed by the top levels of Nazi bureaucracy. It could, however, denote that regionalism still persisted to an extent, and the proximity of Lübeck to Scandinavia fit in more with the goals of the NG than a move to Berlin would. It also could indicate that the NG and its patron Alfred Rosenberg were not only poorly understood, they were marginalized in the context of Nazi bureaucracy and influence and most Nazis didn't know or care about the NG. This was no longer the case once Germany invaded Poland and France and Britain declared war.

Mere weeks after Hamburg's *Nordische Woche*, the Nazis unleashed a coordinated pogrom against Jews on November 9, 1938. Ostensibly due to the assassination in Paris of Ernst vom Rath, Third Secretary in the German embassy in Paris. What followed was a widespread escalation of persecution, violence, and terror against the Jews in Germany and the incorporated territories. Euphemistically called the "Jew Action" but more widely known as *Kristallnacht*, the pogrom led many Jews, in Lübeck and elsewhere, to finally emigrate to wherever they could. Thousands of businesses were destroyed, and nearly 30,000 Jews across the country were rounded up and sent to concentration camps. The response of non-Jews, as described by Marion Kaplan, ranged from "rampant viciousness, studied ignorance, and occasional kindness."[20] In Lübeck, the synagogue was ransacked and destroyed on the inside, due to its location between St. Aegidien (a Lutheran church) and St. Annen, a medieval church-turned-city-museum. In the wake of the violence, Nazi officials in Lübeck continued to be inconsistent, as described by Christiane Pritzlaff, regarding day-to-day life in the city, especially for school children. On the one hand, Jewish children could not be without their lessons; on the other, however, Jewish children could not attend classes with or be taught by non-Jews, and no private Jewish schools would be supported by state funds.[21] It became steadily harder for Jews to leave, especially once World War II in Europe began in September 1939, and daily life was increasingly restricted, punctuated by escalating persecution, terror, and dispossession.

WAGING TOTAL WAR

Once World War II became a reality, the NG represented a potential avenue into Scandinavia to ensure peace—or at least quiet—to the north. There is little evidence that the NG of the Nazi era was at all effective in swinging "brethren Nordics" to support the Nazi Party; most Scandinavians regarded Nazism, characterized by German hypernationalism, as at odds with their own interests. Those who did embrace Nazism were in the minority and had their own challenges in their home countries over the course of the war.[22] At the same time, there was little evidence that Nazi leadership was interested in cultivating extensive relationships with some of these Scandinavian Nazis in general, preferring instead to control the local populations with imported Germans. Where there was space to advocate in Scandinavia, Rosenberg in particular claimed it was really "only the Nordic Society" positioned well and interested.[23] There was little room for other nationalisms in a Germany-centered Nordicism. As Nazi Germany sought to re-form Europe along its own ideological lines, it was clear all other nationalisms and identities were subordinated to a particular iteration of racialized Germanness.

The war commenced after years of build-up and annexation on September 4, 1939. What this actually meant to Germans was unclear, as the collapse of the Polish government at the end of September led to another period of consolidation, organization, and coordination in the east. War had been waged against German Jews since at least 1933 with increasing aggression, but the onset of armed conflict in Poland signaled uncertainty.[24] Per the Ribbentrop-Molotov Agreement (often called the Nazi-Soviet Non-Aggression Pact), the regime set to officially annexing and aligning Polish territory into the existing German state. The next eight months, often called the *Sitzkrieg* or "Phony War," saw extensive plans drawn up to conquer Western Europe and protect the borders of Germany itself while expanding ideological policy in the occupied "Greater Germany."[25] The NG planted new offices, in Vienna as well as Prague, arguing for the historic legitimacy that Nordicism had in these areas. In the opening ceremony in Prague on March 28, 1941, Hinrich Lohse referenced the collaborative work between Tycho de Brahe and Johannes Kepler in Prague, claiming that "since March 15, 1939, it was time for the Nordic Society to gather all those forces involved in the cultivation of Nordic ideas in this age-old center of German spiritual life."[26] The NG was actively asserting a role in integrating eastern territories into *thinking* the nation and setting the stage to apply its in-group criteria to the populations there.

Nazi officials, led by Josef Goebbels, mounted propaganda campaigns, waging war on an intellectual and informational level as they had throughout the 1930s.[27] In some ways, the ideological but incohesive core was a reflection of the disorganized and chaotic political structures that were being implemented, east and west, resulting in "overlapping jurisdictions and competing authorities."[28] This was particularly obvious in the east, where territory seized in the invasion of Poland was now incorporated into the Reich, installing regional governors, Party leaders, and SS and military bureaucracy. Intimately connected to control in Poland was the destruction of the intelligentsia and the first whispers of the Final Solution. Resettlement of so-called ethnic Germans into "cleared" territory began a pattern that persisted during the war: eliminating Polish partisans and Jews (and later Latvians, Lithuanians, and many others) to make way for German Jews who were deported and German settlers. This multistep process meant establishing ghettos, conducting mass executions, and employing stopgap measures to handle the "problem."[29] Goebbels went so far as to note, after a tour of the Lodz ghetto on November 2, 1939, that the conditions in Lodz were terrible and "indescribable. These are no longer human beings, they are animals. For this reason, our task is no longer humanitarian but surgical. Steps must be taken here, and they must be radical ones, make no mistake."[30]

The implementation of the T-4 or Euthanasia Program, aimed at "cleansing" Germany of "life unworthy of life" in a radical application of eugenics and racial hygiene as well as ghettoization in the east moved Nazi racial policy forward.[31] Backdated to coincide with the invasion of Poland, the T-4 program targeted physically and mentally disabled people in an effort to purify the national (Aryan) gene pool. Beginning with disabled children and progressing to include adults, institutionalized Jews, and camp inmates, the program medicalized ideology in an attempt to strengthen "Aryan" Germans.[32] The program spread across "Greater Germany" and sparked protest among clergy members, especially the bishop of Münster and Pope Pius XII, in 1940 and 1941.[33] In part, it was the transports that called attention to what was happening, as well as the fact that the targets of the program still had family and social ties. Hitler ordered a suspension of the program in August 1941, but other actions, such as Operation 14f13, replaced it and essentially moved it underground throughout the war.[34] The lessons from the T-4 program, such as not operating completely in the open, as well as the machinery to kill more than 200,000 people shaped the way the Nazis undertook the destruction of the Jews.[35]

The war was fairly quiet in Lübeck until April 1940. While the Winter War of November 1939 pitted Finland against an invading Soviet Union, it was still a conflict that didn't actively include Germany and aroused little sympathy for either side among Nazi officials. By April 1940, though, the invasion of Denmark and subsequent conquest of Norway really drove home the war aims of the Nazi regime. Presented as a way to prevent a French or British invasion of Scandinavia in support of Finland (and to protect Germany's own borders on the continent), the German military and navy moved into Copenhagen and Oslo. Denmark capitulated quickly, in part to prevent harm to Danish citizens, and this ushered in a period where resistance, acquiescence, and control existed simultaneously. Norway in particular had an interesting experience, which demonstrated the fluid nature of Hitler's war aims and plans for after the war was over. On April 9, 1940, Vidkun Quisling, nominal leader of the Norwegian *Nasjonal Samling* (National Union), declared himself prime minister upon German invasion, though he tried for the title of "*Fører*," the Norwegian word for *Führer*.[36]

Quisling, however, never achieved the prominence in Norwegian politics he craved. His Party never got more than 3 percent of the vote and never elected a representative to the *Storting*, Norway's legislature. The royal family refused to appoint him prime minister and instead exhorted Norwegians to continue resisting.[37] Quisling was never the complete authority in Norway, though he was finally awarded the title and did have some power regarding civilian matters. The power of the Party in Norway during the war was the *Reichskommissar* for Norway, Josef Terboven, beginning April 24, 1940, though Norway itself wasn't overtaken until June 1940. Though he did not have authority over the military forces for the duration of the war, he did command his own force and had paramilitary authority. More than anything this highlighted the view that Norway was to be a province of a Germanic Europe, rather than an independent country of brethren Nordics.[38] This was the outgrowth of how the NG and the Nazi Party mythologized and then subordinated "Nordic" lands; a passing comment from the June 1940 issue of *Der Norden* remarked that the Economic Research Council, established in Kiel in 1935, would have to "examine in particular new possibilities for expansion between the economic areas of Greater Germany and Northern Europe aris[ing] from the situation created by England and France declaring war on the German Reich."[39] Permanent policy was to be decided after the war, but the process by which Norway and Denmark were to be integrated into the Nazi state required Party-level control, especially over matters of population.

In 1941, press releases celebrated the twenty years of the NG, "developed by the initiative and energy of imperial leader Alfred Rosenberg to a full-scale organization" which "instructed the care of interstate relations with the north and the support and deepening of Nordic thought."[40] This effectively rewrote the history of the Society to begin with the Nazi era and Rosenberg specifically, rather than connecting its emergence to 1921. Additionally, the NG expanded to include a German-Flemish Working Group, widening the intellectual footprint of the Society to include the Netherlands, with which "Lübeck, historically always active economically and culturally" connected to "Low German spaces."[41] Two weeks earlier, on September 1, policy ensured that Jews would be identifiable in public through the compulsory use of the yellow star in the Reich, including in western Poland (then called Warthegau), Alsace, and Austria. Measures building on the policy that already existed—removing Jews from everyday life and explicitly identifying them in public space—contributed to the constant permeation of antisemitism in a way that marked Jews as "other" and detached them from potential support. This was further reinforced by an article from the December 1941 issue of *Der Norden*, which linked the Jews' supposed pursuit of gold and power with that of the United States, set in stark contrast with "Europe."[42] That same issue featured pictures and descriptions of winter in Scandinavia, orienting Germans to the north and simultaneously segregating Jews and non-Germans elsewhere.

The timing of this wasn't coincidental. On December 6, 1941, deportation orders came for Lübeck Jews. Already by late November, trains carrying Jews had traveled through Lübeck's main train station on at least two occasions destined for Poland.[43] The regions of Lübeck, Hamburg, and even western Mecklenburg were "evacuated" in 1941, variably destined for Riga, Minsk, and even Lodz. The deportees were to pay for their trip, some accounts stating up to 25 percent of their liquid assets.[44] Christopher Browning accounted for this action by tracing it to the policy enacted in October 1941, where Jews were to be expelled from the Reich and moved further and further east following the front lines of Operation Barbarossa.[45] For the Jews of Lübeck, this had dire consequences. Otto-Dietrich Drechsler, Lord Mayor of Lübeck, was *Reichskommissar* of Latvia, operating under the authority of the NG's Hinrich Lohse, who was now *Reichskommissar* for all the Baltic States in addition to being *Gauleiter* of Schleswig-Holstein. Drechsler, specifically, oversaw the ghetto in Riga as well as the construction of the concentration camp outside the city, Jungfernhof. In late October 1941, Lohse and Drechsler met with Rudolf Lange, detachment commander associated with *Einsatzgruppe* A in Latvia, in part to reconcile policy and practice regarding Jewish deportation from Germany and what to do with them once they got to Latvia.[46]

The various puzzle pieces—Lohse and Drechsler, deportation orders, and the quickening pace of Nazi extermination policy—determined that Lübeck's Jews would be deported to Riga on December 6. In the following two days, Pearl Harbor was bombed by the Japanese and the first extermination camp at Chelmno began operation, beginning a new phase of the Nazis' war on the Jews. The number of Jews in Lübeck had decreased between 1933 and 1941 especially after Kristallnacht, with many families (or parts of families) emigrating before deportation orders were issued. Siegbert and Florenze Camnitzer and their son Ludwig, for example, reportedly escaped to Uruguay in 1939, after the harrowing experience of Kristallnacht and the dispossession of the family's department store.[47] They along with their extended family lived at Breitestraße 41, several doors down and across the street from the NG headquarters. The Jewish community in Lübeck remained small but tight-knit, driven by its rabbi and other leading figures. At the same time, though, Lübeck's local Evangelical Lutheran Church was a strong supporter of National Socialism and its policies, with few exceptions dismissing clergy critical of the state church and employing those willing to radicalize.[48] By December 1941, the deportation order swept up perhaps ninety people, according to the sole Lübeck survivor of the transport Josef Katz; they amassed at St. Annenstraße, boarded a train at the central train station, and hooked up with a train coming from Hamburg with deportees from Kiel and Hamburg at the Hanover Station.[49] The community was decimated, and the Jews who were deported faced harrowing circumstances.

They arrived in Riga on December 9, reportedly met by Rudolf Lange himself, and were herded from the platform to the concentration camp Jungfernhof, some three kilometers away; there they were guarded by Latvians and SS alike.[50] Jews from Hamburg, Nuremberg, Danzig, and Kiel mingled with the Lübecker Jews, including the family of Rabbi Joseph Carlebach, who had ties to both Hamburg and Lübeck.[51] Betty Wilner of Nuremberg recalled how the prisoners set to occupying the children, as Rabbi Carlebach "immediately summoned together those camp inmates with educational training. There were neither books nor writing material. . . some of the melodies he [Carlebach] sang together with the children still ring in her ear to this day."[52] The camp at Jungfernhof was an old estate and truly a temporary measure, though the number of prisoners swelled to between 4,000 and 5,000 people.[53]

Some of the transport was moved to the Riga ghetto while others were selected for work, such as working to build the Salaspils concentration camp. Josef Katz was one such worker and recalled that to survive one had to *look* like he or she was working while "shirking the work" as much as possible.[54] Through all of this, summary executions, mock trials, and death from illness and overwork plagued life in Jungfernhof, Salaspils, and Riga. Transports continued to bring German Jews to Latvia throughout the winter of 1941 and 1942, rounding up whole communities at a time. Herta Rosenthal of Leipzig, who was deported in mid-January 1942, recalled that "everybody saw it, and they were screaming bloody murder. All the Jews were leaving Leipzig, and they [the Germans] were happy a lot of them. . . . They brought us during the day, not at night. There were both SA and ordinary citizens there."[55] Rosenthal's recollections demonstrate that she thought most of the Jews brought to Riga were from southern Germany and indicate that Jews tried to stay with their immediate communities and support systems as much as possible. Riga and the camps surrounding it saw at least two waves of transports between November 1941 and February 1942, originating from the major cities of Germany and some from Austria and Czechoslovakia.[56]

Even as deportations progressed, Nazi officials were constructing a more organized policy behind the scenes out of the public confusion and chaos that accompanied deportations from Germany. On January 20, 1942, Reinhard Heydrich staged the Wannsee Conference to inform the various ministries of the Reich about the "Final Solution" and the official policy of extermination. Among the attendees was Rudolf Lange of *Einsatzgruppe A* in Latvia. Christopher Browning argued that policy was still incoherent regarding *how* to kill the Jews in the east and also extract their labor, and this reflected again the unevenness and competition in ministry jurisdiction.[57] Mass shootings had occurred throughout the east behind the advancing lines of the Wehrmacht from the onset of the invasion of the Soviet Union. It continued until extermination centers (other than Chelmno) could be built as a more industrial and experimental (euphemized as "humane") method of achieving the ultimate goal of Nazi policy: a "Jew-free" Europe organized according to Nazi interests.

Actions against the German Jews in Riga occurred in late February and late March 1942. Masked as the "Dünamünder canning factory action," Jews who were deemed unfit for work were told they were moving to a canning facility for lighter assignments. On March 26, 1942, approximate 1,800 Jews from Jungfernhof, Salaspils, and the Riga ghetto were taken to the Bikernieki Forest and shot.[58] Josef Katz was the only survivor from Lübeck from his transport; the rest, including Rabbi Carlebach, perished in the forest. It is estimated that up to 5,000 victims were executed there.[59] Lohse and Drechsler, Party and municipal functionaries as well as NG leaders, were the immediate reason Lübeck's Jewish community was deported so quickly and to Latvia specifically. Nazi policy had always sought a way to remove Jews from German life, and it did it in the open in a variety of ways, building on years of indoctrination and training. Some of that ideology had been incremental, moving by inches, making it possible to enact overt and genocidal policy while assuring everyday Germans' acquiescence and silence. Many Germans materially benefited as they increasingly had since 1933, dispossessing Jews of their property, their business, and now their lives; sometimes the promise of this benefit was enough.[60] The connections between strands of ideology, such as that mobilized by the *Nordische Gesellschaft* and increasingly radicalized over time by high-ranking Party members, made it possible to take historic modes of identity and adapt them to genocidal outcomes. It was not Lübeck alone that succumbed to this, but the structural power that accompanied local and regional figures shows how Nazi policies operated across the Reich with deadly effectiveness.

Two days after the massacre of Lübeck's Jews in Latvia—Palm Sunday that year—Lübeck was bombed by the British Royal Air Force, touching off a firestorm that destroyed much of the historic inner city and the residential neighborhood of St. Lorenz. The NG's headquarters on Breitestraße was reduced to rubble, as was much of the commercial district. Three of the churches—Marienkirche, St. Petri, and the Lübecker Dom—were virtually destroyed, and the destruction in Lübeck deeply wounded and shocked local morale. Lübeck itself was not so much a strategic target, though it did have a Luftwaffe base in Travemünde (on the Priwall peninsula) and some heavy industry. Rather, it was a cultural and historic target, meant to strike at the heart of the populace's will to make war. Other cities fitting the same profile, notably Rostock, were similarly targeted. The subsequent months witnessed tit-for-tat bombing in England as well as Germany, the so-called Baedecker raids that focused on cities of cultural and historical import such as Canterbury and Wismar.

The impact of the bombing was felt in the upper levels of the Nazi bureaucracy. The strategy of bombing widely regardless of military import frustrated Nazi officials, not because of any attachment to Lübeck itself but because of the necessity of maintaining some semblance of unity and single-minded support for the war. On March 30, 1942, two days after the bombing, Josef Goebbels noted in his diary that

> This Sunday [the 28th] is thoroughly spoiled by an exceptionally heavy air raid by the RAF on Lübeck. In the morning I had already received a very alarming report from our propaganda office there, which I at first assumed to be exaggerated. . . . Kaufmann believes that no German city has ever before been attacked so severely from the air. Conditions in Lübeck are in part chaotic . . . but he isn't being given the proper support from Berlin.[61]

The following day, he noted that "Eighty per cent of the old part of the city must be considered lost."[62] While that estimation proved to be too high—extreme damage was later estimated at around 17 percent, and minor damage a further 40 percent or so—the fact that Goebbels remarked on it and mourned for the art that was inevitably lost demonstrated the effectiveness of the NG's efforts. Lübeck itself wasn't a powerhouse and wasn't terribly important in terms of military aims (nearby Bremen was viewed as much more strategic in that way) despite its location on the Baltic. Goebbels was preoccupied with the feared loss of art and architecture, detailing the churches that were destroyed or damaged, the churches that escaped destruction, and the fate of other landmarks like the Holstentor.

On April 4, 1942, Goebbels wrote that

> the English claim they dropped one thousand-pound bombs on Lübeck. The damage done there is indeed enormous. I am shown a newsreel of the destruction. It is horrible. One can well imagine how such an awful bombardment affects the population.[63]

The bombing of Lübeck meant a new phase of the war, one that brought increasing payloads of destruction to cities that usually remained outside the scope of military action. Similar attention to destruction in Rostock nearly a month later warranted Goebbels's plan to drop

> handbills printed with pictures of the damage done by the English in Lübeck and Rostock, and under them the Führer's announcement of his Reichstag speech that reprisal raids are coming. . . . I expect quite a psychological effect from this stunt.[64]

The successful attack on Lübeck and other cities like it, some deep in Germany, became a feature of the war until its conclusion, and the persistence of bombing raids had to be addressed in propaganda to prevent collapse of morale. This later extended to popular films produced in Germany, some of which were active in framing perceptions of the home front during the war. Mary-Elizabeth O'Brien noted, "Fewer than twenty feature films produced in Nazi Germany treated the contemporary Second World War experience."[65] Of these, films like *Die Degenhardts*, directed by Werner Klingler in 1944 and set in Lübeck, situated family life and struggle in the context of the war, strangely ending with the Palm Sunday bombing.[66] Films like this attempted to twist the bombing from a morale-killer into a reason to continue the war at all costs, particularly for the *Volk* and, as Goebbels put it, the "North German population, which on the whole is much tougher than the South German or the Southeast German population."[67] Goebbels's comments recall the late 1930s debates over ethnic hierarchy in Nazi hierarchy; his passing comment demonstrated again the success the Nordicist groups had in national identity construction. It also revealed ongoing tensions between factions. Rosenberg backed Quisling in Norway and grew frustrated over Terboven's focus on "his impending protectorate" and lack of concern for "*völkisch* necessities."[68] What was considered the "real" priority for the Nazi regime was still incoherent and in some ways divorced from the realities of war.

The rubble and loss in Lübeck was an all-too-real physical challenge, and it became the backbone of wartime memory. In Lübeck itself, services were conducted on Palm Sunday in the churches that had not been destroyed, including Katharinenkirche which had served more as community space than church in the late nineteenth and early twentieth centuries. Clergy sought to give comfort and support to those impacted by the bombs; the attack on Lübeck destabilized Germany as well as the city itself, however. On April 7, 1942, over a week after the bombing, one of the Lutheran clergymen of the Luther Church (affiliated with the Evangelical Lutheran Church, the state church), Karl Friedrich Stellbrink, was arrested for preaching against Germany. Though he had originally been appointed to the Luther Church in 1934 as a supporter of the state church and was a member of the Nazi

Party, by 1937 he had been dismissed from the Party and was critical of Nazi policy toward the churches.[69] In his interrogation, he stated that he had said in the aftermath of the bombing, "'In the distress of our hometown we hear God's voice.' I'm sorry if the people understood that phrase to mean that we heard God's judgment. I did not mean it that way."[70] He claimed he did not feel the bombing was just recompense for Germany, stating rather he meant to castigate the English for the "cultural crime" they had committed against Lübeck. Following his arrest, the synod expelled him, leaving him with little structural support.

After Stellbrink's arrest, three more clergymen, priests from the *Herz-Jesu-Gemeinde* in central Lübeck, were detained and questioned. Johannes Prassek, Hermann Lange, and Eduard Müller all served in various roles for the parish and all arrived in 1939 or 1940; they each had met Stellbrink by 1941. Prassek served as vicar and administered to Polish forced laborers in Lübeck.[71] Eduard Müller worked closely with local youth and actively tried to serve as a foil to the Hitler Youth, allowing discussion of the regime and its policies.[72] Perhaps the most open of the three was Hermann Lange, who preached that participation in the war was completely irreconcilable with Christian faith.[73] The Catholic Church, especially the Bishops of Osnabrück and Münster, had already protested the T-4 program. Now Bishop Berning of Osnabrück sent letters of support to the three Catholic priests and visited them in prison. Given the shock of an attack on a non-military target—and one that was incredibly effective—the regime jumped to action to make the point that to be German was to actively and fully support the war. To be anything less than an advocate for the war was to be un-German and an outsider. Thus, membership in the racial community was predicated on behavior as well as race, and there were many ways to betray the *Volksgemeinschaft*. The Lübeck Christians' Trial of June 23, 1943, saw all four men convicted, and, despite Bishop Berning's plea for clemency, all four were guillotined in Hamburg on November 10, 1943.

THE FINAL DAYS OF WAR AND CAPITULATION

In the midst of all this, the NG was forced to relocate to Kaiserallee 6 in Travemünde, right on the beach of the Baltic Sea after its headquarters was completely destroyed. Rosenberg began to complain in his diary of the "Lübeck clique" in Riga (referring to Drechsler and Lohse) by November 1942, as they argued over the status of Hugo Wittrock, Lord Mayor of Riga; Rosenberg increasingly considered the Lübeckers "philistines" and saw them, much as he did Terboven, as attempting to ensure personal power at the expense of Party and even NG goals.[74] While it continued to publish *Der*

Norden through 1944, by and large, the Society's influence and visibility faded, especially as the fronts in Europe, Northern Africa, and the Soviet Union began to collapse. In the east, the pace of extermination continually ramped up, often dispensing with selection in favor of murdering entire transports of Jews and Roma. The movement of prisoners between camps and uprisings in ghettos and death camps challenged Nazi efficiency. The German war effort in the Soviet Union was a disaster, and by late 1943 and early 1944, the Red Army began advancing toward Germany. Ahead of the advance, the Nazis liquidated camps and conducted evacuations and death marches. Josef Katz, who had survived along with twenty-nine others from his transport, was moved to Danzig via ship in Fall 1944, thus beginning the steady removal of refugees, prisoners, and retreating soldiers toward the Reich from across the occupied territories.[75] Coupled with the success of the D-Day invasions in June 1944 in Normandy, the war effort against the Jews continued even as the military campaigns crumbled.

On May 2, 1945, British forces entered Lübeck city limits and immediately began imposing martial law in order to secure the region. Northwestern Germany had thousands of refugees, workcamp inmates brought from Eastern Europe, and people fleeing advancing armies. The effort to reach the German heartland had been difficult, the Allies fanning across the western half of the continent in an effort to secure France, Belgium, the Netherlands, and Germany itself. Along the way, Allied infantry liberated countless camps. In the east, the Red Army liberated Auschwitz in January 1945 and had swept through former ghettos and mass graves. By March 1945, Hitler issued an order to begin destroying installations and infrastructure, as well as documents and evidence. As Jeremy Noakes and Geoffrey Pridham pointed out, Hitler felt that "if the Third Reich was to be destroyed", then neither did the German people deserve to survive.[76] In his political testament, dictated before committing suicide on April 30, 1945, Hitler exhorted Germans, civilians and soldiers alike, to be obedient to the Reich unto death.[77] This order was borne out in hastily-assembled paramilitary units [*Volkssturm*] comprised of children and the elderly defending Berlin and other cities even as surrender became inevitable.[78]

The end of the war came amid confusion and chaos, with some German units surrendering, and others fighting on. The Canadian Occupation Force reported that German commanders had no idea who their soldiers were or where they were from, and the civil government had collapsed providing no help.[79] For Lübeck, occupation policies were in full force by May 4. Overall surrender on all fronts was secured by May 7, and the following day was heralded as "Victory in Europe" Day. What followed was more uncertainty, the pursuit of both high-ranking and middling Nazis, and the physical devastation of land and people. The cultural forays of the prewar NG that had been forged in the wake of World War I and Nazified over the course of a decade or more were now annihilated in global conflagration. Most importantly, Germans had to grapple with the devastation wrought on fellow people—Jews, Roma, political opponents, communists—who could never be rescued or replaced. Circles of identity would again be tested economically, politically, and culturally in another postwar period, this one in a world that witnessed, however silently, the Holocaust.

BRITISH OCCUPATION AND PREPARING FOR THE NUREMBERG TRIALS

If the end of World War I was considered traumatic, the end of World War II in Europe was simultaneously indescribable and inescapable. The British sought to consolidate control of the entire north, though there were still German forces ensconced in Norway. The same forces that occupied northern Germany liberated Denmark, in advance of the full surrender of the German military. Even as the British encountered surrendering Wehrmacht, they also had to deal with scores of refugees of varying backgrounds, some of whom had been fleeing the advancing Red Army since February 1945. The influx of refugees, as well as the discovery of ever-increasing numbers of slave laborers from Eastern Europe, concentration and death camp victims, and the last gasp of Nazi militarism that gripped portions of the civilian population complicated an already chaotic situation.[80] The logistics, policies, and procedures governing British military occupation have been extensively analyzed, demonstrating the complexity of establishing an occupation force as well as operating as one of the "Big Four."[81] One of the overarching factors regarding local British occupation was the fact that British military officials were simultaneously operating in local, national, and international ways; Lübeck was once again a city on many borders. The primacy of tracking down, arresting, and questioning Nazi officials—especially those deemed "high level" and Hitler's inner circle—was an important priority, and the Allies agreed that a tribunal bringing the architects of Nazi aggression to justice was paramount.

Some of the highest-ranking Nazis, notably Hermann Göring, Alfred Rosenberg, and Albert Speer had been captured or surrendered. Others, like Heinrich Himmler, attempted to negotiate a separate surrender and their own escape. What was even more daunting was the middle level of the machinery, the various ministries in Germany, those who had administered and run camps across Europe, the myriad industries that benefited from slave labor, and the organizations like the NG that operated both inside and outside the government. Most difficult of all and perhaps the most underestimated task was unraveling Nazism from everyday life and from Germans' worldviews while figuring out the degree to which individuals and communities could be "rehabilitated." This obviously meant a web of policy and procedures, aimed at attacking Nazi ideology on every level and in many ways. Nazism proved to be structural and systemic, precisely the goal of the Nazi hierarchy in remaking German society. This meant that the process of denazification would be long, difficult, and uneven at best. Regional history and identity in a post-Nazi Germany, in the context of Allied occupation, were as important as they had been in the creation of the Nazi state and its concomitant ideologies. For Lübeck, this meant detaching its "Nordic" identity from its Nazi connotations, difficult indeed after the previous two decades spent embedding and emphasizing the exclusionary racialism in it.

The first step was the International Military Tribunal beginning in late 1945 in Nuremberg and the subsequent trials that followed. Interviews with the main defendants representing all corners of the Nazi bureaucracy were conducted by American psychologist Leon Goldensohn, whose notes were aimed at unpacking the defendants' motivations, justification, and reflections as well as individual defendants' character traits and psychological profiles.[82] Goldensohn interviewed not only the highest-ranking officials but also middling functionaries who ensured the Final Solution was carried out. Included in these interviews were Alfred Rosenberg and Hjalmar Schacht, whose work and policies had impacted the intellectual foundations as well as the financial policies of the Reich; in Schacht's case, he had been instrumental in ending hyperinflation. Robert Gellately acknowledged that the interviewees were seen as subjects to be studied, rather than patients in the traditional sense; the trials sparked interest, a flurry of books, and newsreels, making the defendants characters on a world stage in the context of war crimes trials designed to mete out justice.[83]

When interviewing Alfred Rosenberg on February 3, 1946, Goldensohn noted that Rosenberg

> was dressed in an American field jacket, tweed trousers, shoes without laces, colored shirt without tie. He greeted us with superficial amiability, moved his papers from the cot, and so forth, and invited us to sit down. . . . His face is a costume of sobriety and philosophic calm, smiling understanding, broad vision, and reflective of the true philosopher, who looks on all that is transpiring with critical, but not bitter, detachment.[84]

At the same time, though, Goldensohn noted that Rosenberg steadfastly held to his ideological perspectives; his opinion on the *Protocols of the Elders of Zion*, for example, had not changed, "nor did he seem particularly interested in whether it was factual or not."[85] That Rosenberg lacked remorse was clear, and he maintained that his philosophy—which Goldensohn repeatedly referred to—was academic and reflective in nature, not fanatical or "pornograph[ic]" like Julius Streicher's work in *Der Stürmer*.[86]

Rosenberg's tenor in the interviews with Goldensohn mirror the ways groups like the NG had fit into national culture and a sense of what was "true"; perhaps some of this was precisely because of his patronage of the NG and ideological Nazism more broadly. According to them, difference was obvious and real, racial, bloodborne, mystical, and palpable. To acknowledge this was simply to identify and promote one's heritage, allowing for the perpetuation and apology of the ideology and the ends it brought. Rosenberg was certainly not alone in this. Many of the interviewees unsurprisingly downplayed their own agency in bringing about war and genocide, even as they detailed their actions as part of a larger political machine. This also occurred in lower levels of the Nazi bureaucratic state, not least local and national leaders of the NG.

Another Goldensohn interviewee was Oswald Pohl, who had been chief of the SS Economic and Administrative Main Office (WVHA), which oversaw everything from concentration camps to factories connected to the war effort. Pohl argued he didn't actually hate Jews or participate in events such as *Kristallnacht* because he remained unconvinced of its necessity. Rather, he argued, "All I did was follow orders. My conscience is clear. I never ordered the death of a Jew or personally killed one. I have explained how the extermination program was not part of my command, but skipped me."[87] Schacht echoed this perspective, referring to Jewish friends as a way to prove ambivalence toward or even a challenge to Nazism. Schacht reacted with defensiveness when Goldensohn mentioned that other defendants pointed to antisemitic economic policy as a foundation for Jewish dispossession and persecution; he claimed that his reason for staying in Hitler's government—or even Germany in the first place—after 1935 was because he "felt that at least one honest man in that government might serve as a check on Hitler."[88]

Regardless of how individual defendants and witnesses in the Nuremberg Trials framed their innocence or guilt, the transcriptions provided a foundation regarding the criminality of Nazism in general and the mindsets of individual Nazis and government officials specifically. This included organizations incorporated into the bureaucracy like the NG. In this postwar period, unlike the one that followed World War I, Nazi guilt was clear and necessitated a program designed to eliminate it from German society. That guilt was also necessary to justify ongoing occupation and the lack of national sovereignty. The twelve "subsequent" trials conducted in Nuremberg after the International Military Tribunal were important to emphasize how multifaceted and deep-seated the Nazi bureaucracy was, and it framed the policies and procedures the Allies adopted in their individual zones and collectively. Ultimately, the number of death sentences, meted out in October 1946, as well as the range of prison sentences and the three exonerations prevented the narrative that Germany had not really been defeated nor held guilt for the execution of the war.

DIPLOMACY, LAW, AND LOCAL CONCERNS

Even before the war ended, cracks and outright fractures appeared in the alliance against the Nazis. Much of the tension had to do with spheres of influence and the way Europe would be divided up after the war. Few decisions regarding administration and even timelines regarding postwar justice and logistics were amiable. The borders of the occupation zones and the procedures that would cover them all were announced beginning June 5, 1945. Borders were particularly politicized, most notably the borders between the British and Soviet zones in the north and the American and Soviet zones in the south. The British military authority itself had to conduct internal and interzonal diplomacy between cities and states, especially due to the American administration that governed Bremen and Bremerhaven; there was also extensive American presence in Hamburg, indicating its prominence regionally. The open question of the relationship between the British and Soviet zones led to a patchwork of initiatives, policies, and uncertainties, especially for Lübeck, located as it was directly on the border with the Soviet zone.

That uncertainty extended across the German-Danish border as well. Though Denmark was sovereign following liberation on May 4–5, 1945, British occupation authorities in the northern states of Germany had authority over German POWs and operated camps in the wake of capitulation. This connected to the questions surrounding ethnic German refugees in Denmark and northern Germany, Eastern European refugees, and victims of Nazi persecution and genocide. The war years presented a complex memory, one that simultaneously involved collaboration and resistance. After the war, all of Scandinavia, not just Denmark, was viewed as a contested arena of economic and ideological competition—very much reinforcing prewar motives of groups like the NG. The British wished to establish a firmer foothold in Scandinavia and viewed the war as an interruption to these overtures; they additionally did not want to cede ground to the Americans either in terms of trade or diplomacy.[89]

British occupation proceeded in phases, guided both by geography (such as the boundaries laid out by Allies before the capitulation at Yalta) as well as logistics. All the while, though, preparations were made to support a long-lasting occupation of indeterminate length, one that could occur even after a peace treaty was signed. Foundational to British occupation were short- and long-term goals, which involved complete demilitarization and pacification, repatriation of prisoners of war and displaced persons, and the complete reeducation of youth, former Nazis, and the German populace at large.[90] From the outset of martial law and the installation of Allied military personnel, proclamations began rolling back Nazi law and its structure of civil society. The first two laws issued by the Allied Control Authority simultaneously repealed Nazi laws and dissolved all Nazi organizations.[91] From there, laws related to marriage, scientific research, the protection of property and taxation, the import of materials, and even the flag flown by German ships under Allied control all warranted individual proclamations.

Military authorities were completely supreme in terms of decision-making and had a complex landscape to navigate at the end of the war. Authorities had to address the issue of Holocaust survivors and victims of Nazi aggression. They also had to establish a process to assign guilt or innocence as it related to the Nazi state. Often, occupation administrations dealt with institutions and resources first, because the issues related to the human cost of war were going to be long-lasting. Some of these resources were, surprisingly, cultural heritage and archival materials. As early as May 24, 1945, the British military asserted protective authority over art and other treasures, seeking to rehome them as quickly as possible for the purposes of preservation.[92] While this may seem like an odd inclusion, it was vital to the British to inventory and assess everything about the localities they controlled. This also related to the Military Government of Germany's Law Number 52, which detailed the control of property, particularly that held by state or local government, any organizations that had been dissolved by the military government (such as the NG), or individuals who were identified as people of interest.[93] A variety of subsidiary proclamations were produced regarding banking, property transfer, and other assets; German officials responded with detailed lists of SS members, suspect business owners, and others whose activities were particularly governed by Law No. 52, sealing the communication with an official stamp, the swastika scratched off.[94]

Occupation authorities in all zones operated on at least three levels at once. The first was international, dealing with issues of diplomacy and borders, restoring trade ties where appropriate, and ensuring that the emergent global community saw unequivocally that Nazism was a criminal organization from end to end. The Nuremberg Trials were assuredly part of this. The second level was national, establishing protocols and structures across Germany to assert occupation authority and get control of resources and people. The third level was local. Individual military authorities took up residence in their zone, becoming emissaries in some ways between Germans and the military hierarchy. They also began figuring out the ways in which *local* people would answer for their activities during the war, if they had anything to answer for.

DENAZIFICATION

Though it ended up being a stilted, uneven process, denazification became a hallmark of occupation in the years immediately after the war. It was intimately connected to Allied goals for any German state(s) going forward, and the various Allied powers approached the process and the end goal in different ways.[95] At times, the varied mindsets Allied personnel had regarding Nazism and the probability of rooting it out diverged, resulting in a cacophony of policies and procedures that often contradicted or did not jibe with other Allied goals. At the same time, however, unraveling Nazism from German society proved to be a gargantuan task. Nazism had sought to completely remake Germany—and indeed much of the rest of Europe—according to Nazi ideologies. This underscored the need to expunge the Nazis' influence over organizations and individuals if there was any hope of a functional Germany after the war. This was discussed in ambiguous terms and related more generally to postwar policy regarding Germany outlined in the Moscow Declaration, then at the Tehran Conference in 1943 and in subsequent conferences between the Big Three.[96] The processes by which Germany would be rid of Nazi influence and ideology, however, were incohesive. Perceptions about the proceedings as well as uneven judgments and outcomes from zone to zone.

Overall, the practice was to categorize and sort Germans into tiers of ideological enthusiasm, ranging from Group I (considered "major offenders") to Group V (exonerated). Many Germans fell into Group IV: followers. The Americans conducted the most widespread denazification efforts, requiring most if not all of the Germans in their zone to fill out a lengthy questionnaire (*Fragebogen*) regarding their wartime activities and attitudes.[97] Other zones did not have this blanket requirement. In the British zone, only those Germans who endeavored to work in politics, business, and administration had to submit to denazification proceedings. Military authorities engaged already cleared German leaders to process denazification hearings beginning in 1946, though this development was also slow-going. Those cases determined to be egregious and high-profile—those labeled Group I or II—were handled by the military occupation authority. Individuals proposing to serve on the boards, according to the Deputy Regional Commissioner for Schleswig-Holstein R. U. J. Martin, had to "have a sense of objectivity with regard to the necessity to remove the Nazi and Militarist influence from German life."[98]

German denazification boards operated at the pleasure of occupation authority, and at times occupation personnel felt the need to remind German board members who was truly in power. The British did not want to have to tie up resources in conducting denazification hearings. It was just one more thing resident authorities had to do, and it seemed to get in the way of other pressing matters, such as addressing food shortages and assessing damage across the country. At the same time, however, they did not like the perception that the military was out of the loop regarding the hearings, or that it was completely a German-led effort, though to an extent it had to be to have any real lasting effect. In March 1947, the Kreis Resident Officer in Lübeck, H. G. Sullivan, noted that board members were not *elected* to serve on denazification committees, but rather "nominated," those "nominations . . . subject to the approval of Public Safety and Intelligence *before the nominees can begin to serve*."[99] He went on to say that "Much to my surprise I was informed yesterday that the 'Panel' had functioned on 7th March. The proceedings of that meeting are of course null and void, as they were carried out by an unconstitutional body."[100]

In many ways, the British approach to denazification was an attempt to reestablish some functioning German economy due to its own postwar pressures such as ongoing rationing and the breakdown of imperial control in India and Pakistan. This is evident in the communication from British Occupation Headquarters in Kiel to the Schleswig-Holstein Denazification Committee on August 7, 1947. Authorities set parameters for denazification in the agriculture and farming sector, stating that "due to the strained food situation, the denazification of farmers has to be carried out with the utmost care. There should be no errors that could affect agricultural production."[101] The missive went on to say that only those "influential" farmers—of twenty hectares or more, employing more than ten workers—should even be vetted through denazification proceedings, as to have questionnaires for everyone would unnecessarily slow down the process and exacerbate the shortages. At the same time, though, firms in other industries were given the all-clear to resume activity, especially utilities, printing firms (such as the large Lübeck publishing house Schmidt-Römhild), and transportation.[102]

The denazification process produced conflict and public debate in the British zone. In Lübeck, the committee was required to travel throughout Schleswig-Holstein, which highlighted the shortage of gasoline, the need for food vouchers beyond typical rations, and space to conduct the proceedings.[103] Beyond these material concerns were the ways in which Germans interacted with the boards and the way the boards themselves interacted with each other. Though the British military authority largely handed the proceedings over to German boards by mid-1947, the military was still ultimately in charge. Cases could be handed between local boards and the British, depending on the progression of the case, the controversy associated with it, or the category of the defendant. This was also true of interactions between city level, *Land* level (state or province level), and appeals boards.[104] It did not help that some individuals served on a variety of committees, causing confusion and questions about which entity they spoke for in official communication. Individual cases got caught up in the back-and-forth tug of war between the different levels of the hierarchy, either by simple lack of communication or because one board was asserting authority over or in place of another. An example of this was Werner Rautenberg's case from 1946 to

1947, which dragged on for more than a year because of contested jurisdiction and authority.[105]

Further divisions in denazification proceedings had to do with local political memberships. The Social Democratic Party (SPD) was a dominant force on the denazification boards, led by Senator Dr. Luise Klinsmann, who became a leading political and cultural figure following the war. She quickly emerged as a capable leader in local politics, free from problematic associations from the Nazi period, and she committed herself to rebuilding Lübeck's cultural life.[106] Klinsmann's presence on the denazification board, as well as in the Lübeck Senate and as a cultural ambassador for the city, lent a bit of stability and continuity (if overlap) to the various committees. She broadly connected the two phenomena—denazification and a rejuvenated cultural life—and drew on her doctoral work on Lübeck's industrialization to address postwar challenges.

Yet all was not smooth on the denazification committees, nor could it be. To start, though the SPD enjoyed the greater proportion of representatives on the committee (after January 1947 ostensibly to reflect the makeup of the citizenry of Schleswig-Holstein and/or the populations who would come before the boards), the Christian Democratic Union (CDU) made strides in electoral politics, especially in 1949.[107] Additionally, the uncertain status of the German Communist Party (KPD), which eventually was outlawed in the western zones, made a communist representation in denazification tenuous and, in some cases, targets of political pressure. Lastly, the remnants of the far-right, hardly negligible though certainly a smaller proportion of voters after the fall of the Nazis, maintained a presence both on the boards and in political life, complicating the desire to "put Nazism behind them" and move forward as a rehabilitated Germany.[108]

The process of denazification in Lübeck was fraught not only because of the unclear jurisdictions and fluidity regarding procedures. The sectors marked for quick denazification led to challenges from the public, as individuals moved from the shock of defeat (or the relief of liberation) to ongoing and persistent conditions that made everyday life difficult at best. At the same time, the old personal and political divisions drove perceptions of the proceedings, and denunciations continued to flow in, now reporting former (or not-so-former) Nazis instead of Jewish neighbors and dissidents. One correspondent requested the ability to establish a new hotel, arguing that most established guest houses were run by Nazis and or even a "fanatical synagogue stormer," and therefore should not be able to continue operation.[109] Denazification processes were complicated and led many Germans to believe that proving anti-Nazi sentiment should bring them special privileges in the new military regime; it also could be a mechanism by which to mete out revenge.[110] Denazification has conventionally been deemed a failure and, at best, stilted, but the context of local confrontation with the recent past (and the uneven or retaliatory results that came out of the proceedings) provides an important backdrop to all of the economic and political debates going forward, especially in the 1950s.[111]

NOTES

1. Nordische Gesellschaft Hamburg-Kontor, 1 October 1938. DKZ collection, Hoover Institute, Stanford, CA, Box 227.
2. "Nordische Woche in Hamburg," 15–23 October 1938, press release, DKZ collection, Hoover Institute, Stanford, CA, Box 227.
3. DKZ collection, Hoover Institute, Stanford, CA, Box 227, *Nordische Woche* 1938 folder.
4. "Fragebogen für Genehmigungsantrag," 30 May 1938, DKZ collection, Hoover Institute, Stanford, CA, Box 227
5. "An den Reichsgeschäftsführer der Nordischen Gesellschaft Herrn Dr. Ernst Timm," 31 May 1938, DKZ collection, Hoover Institute, Stanford, CA, Box 227.
6. Nordische Gesellschaft, *Führer durch die Nordische Woche in der Hansestadt Hamburg vom 15 bis 23 Oktober 1938* (Hamburg: Nordischen Gesellschaft, 1938), back inside cover.
7. Ibid., 19–20. The booklet was more of an advertisement for the *Nordische Gesellschaft*, selling its ideas and ideology.
8. Ibid., back cover and 6–14.
9. Ibid., 1.
10. Ibid.
11. C. A. Claussen, "Nordischer Gedanke und Nordische Gesellschaft," in *Nordische Woche 1938*, 2.
12. Ibid., 3. It should be noted that Claussen cited Hitler's *Mein Kampf* when describing the cycle of humanity, and that, in many ways, the Nordic man would be capable of changing history.
13. Nordische Gesellschaft, *Nordische Woche 1938*, 7.
14. Ibid., 9.
15. Ibid., 8.
16. Ibid., 11.
17. Ibid.
18. Ibid., 12.
19. Ibid., 14.
20. Marion A. Kaplan, *Between Dignity and Despair: Jewish Life in Nazi Germany* (Oxford: Oxford University Press, 1998), 123. Kaplan's description of *Kristallnacht* punctuates her contention that the pogrom was the end of even illusory security for the Jews in Germany.
21. Christiane Pritzlaff, "'Zu guten Juden und zu guten Deutschen': Die jüdische Volksschule in Lübeck (1934–1940)," in *Menora und Hakenkreuz: Zur Geschichte der Juden in und aus Schleswig-Holstein, Lübeck und Altona (1918–1998)*, eds.

Gerhard Paul and Miriam Gillis-Carlebach (Neumünster: Wachholtz Verlag, 1998), 405–406. For further discussion of the Jewish community specifically in Lübeck in the same volume, see also Albrecht Schreiber, "'Ich seh schon, ich muß mir noch allein begroben': Das Ende der jüdischen Gemeinde Lübeck," 265–282.

22. Joachim Joesten wrote extensively, and contemporaneously, of the Nazi threat toward Scandinavia (including Sweden, Denmark, and Norway), and argued that Scandinavians were largely committed to keeping the Nazis out of their territory, even discounting the "Nordic" commonality between them racially. See Joachim Joesten, "The Nazis in Scandinavia," *Foreign Affairs*, Vol. 15, No 4 (July 1937), 720–728.

23. Jürgen Matthäus and Frank Bajohr, eds., *The Political Diary of Alfred Rosenberg and the Onset of the Holocaust,* Documenting Life and Destruction: Holocaust Sources in Context (Lanham, MD: Rowman & Littlefield/USHMM, 2015), 195.

24. The scholarship on Jewish life before World War II is vast. For further reading, see Karl Christian Führer, "Contradiction Nazi Propaganda: Classified Advertisements as Documents of Jewish Life in Nazi Germany, 1933–1938," *Media History* Vol. 18, No. 1 (2012): 65–76; Marion A. Kaplan, *Between Dignity and Despair: Jewish Life in Nazi Germany* (Oxford: Oxford University Press, 1998); Jürgen Matthäus and Mark Roseman, eds., *Jewish Responses to Persecution, Vol. 1: 1933–1938* (Lanham, MD: Altamira Press, 2010); Francis R. Nicosia and David Scrase, eds, *Jewish Life in Nazi Germany: Dilemmas and Responses*, Vermont Studies on Nazi Germany and the Holocaust (New York: Berghahn Books, 2010); Gerhard Paul and Miriam Gillis-Carlebach, *Manora und Hakenkreuz: zur Geschichte der Juden in und aus Schleswig-Holstein, Lübeck, und Altona, 1918–1998* (Neumünster: Wachholz Verlag, 1998);

25. At the time, this included Austria, which had been formally annexed as a province of "Greater Germany" and renamed *Ostmark*, Czechoslovakia, and western Poland (the *Warthegau*).

26. "Gründung eines Kontors Prag der Nordischen Gesellschaft," *Leipziger Neuester Nachrichten,* 30 March 1941.

27. Josef Goebbels, *The Goebbels Diaries, 1939–1941*, trans. and ed. Fred Taylor (New York: G. P. Putnam's Sons, 1983), 38. Goebbels discussed his efforts extensively throughout the 1939 portion of his diary, referencing the circulation of the *Protocols of the Elders of Zion* and a "Jerry-Letter" campaign, falsified anti-French letters claimed as captured from English soldiers in France.

28. Doris Bergen, *The Holocaust: A Concise History* (Lanham, MD: Rowman & Littlefield, 2009), 104.

29. Bergen, *The Holocaust*, 106–114. The ghetto at Lodz, for example, was established in the winter of 1939, sealed by April 1940, and utilized slave labor.

30. Goebbels, *Goebbels Diaries 1939–1941*, 36.

31. Many studies have analyzed the process and impact of the Tiergartenstrasse 4 (T-4), or Euthanasia, Program. For further reading see Susan Benedict, Linda Shields, and Alison J. O'Donnell, "Children's 'Euthanasia' in Nazi Germany," *Journal of Pediatric Nursing* Vol. 24, No. 6 (Dec 2009), 506–516; Christopher Browning, *The Origins of the Final Solution: The Evolution of Nazi Jewish Policy,*

1939–1941 (Lincoln: University of Nebraska Press and Yad Vashem, 2004); Michael Burleigh and Wolfgang Wippermann, *The Racial State: Germany, 1933–1945* (Cambridge: Cambridge University Press, 1991); Henry Friedlander, *The Origins of Nazi Genocide: From Euthanasia to the Final Solution* (Chapel Hill: University of North Caroline Press, 1995); Robert Jay Lifton, *The Nazi Doctors: Medical Killing and the Psychology of Genocide* (New York: Basic Books, 1986);

32. Browning, *The Origins of the Final Solution*, 190–192.

33. Bergen, *The Holocaust*, 132.

34. Browning, *Origins of the Final Solution*, 192.

35. The number of victims associated with the T-4 program are constantly revised, usually higher than before, as documents and mass graves are continually unearthed in Austria, the former East Germany, and Eastern Europe. Yad Vashem, in 2018, released a statement drawing on testimony from the Nuremberg Trials that indicated a number around 275,000. Jefferson Chase, in an article for *Deutsche Welle* discussing the Bundestag's remembrance ceremony in 2017, also discusses how uncertain an accurate total is and how it relates to collective memory of the program. See Jefferson Chase, "Remembering the 'forgotten victims' of Nazi 'euthanasia' murders," *Deutsche Welle*, 26 January 2017, accessed 12 June 2018, URL: http://www.dw.com/en/remembering-the-forgotten-victims-of-nazi-euthanasia-murders/a-37286088

36. Hans Fredrik Dahl, *Quisling: A Study in Treachery*, trans. by Anne-Marie Stanton-Ife (Cambridge: Cambridge University Press, 1999).

37. William L. Shirer, *The Challenge of Scandinavia: Norway, Sweden, Denmark, and Finland in our Time* (New York: Little, Brown, 1955).

38. This attitude was reflected in the treatment of Austria as well, which, while annexed, served as a distinct *province* of a Greater Germany. Hitler pronounced such sentiments on occasion, echoing some tenets of Pan-Germanism but adapting it to European territories and populations under German control.

39. "Wirtschaftswissenschaftliche Forschungsgruppe der Nordischen Gesellschaft beim Institut für Weltwirtschaft an der Universität Kiel," *Der Norden,* Vol. 17, No. 6 (June 1940), 186. HAL, 05.02 Nordische Gesellschaft—Allgemeines (Zeitungsschnitte), Band 2 (Akte Weltwirtschafts Instituts Kiel), 1938–1944.

40. "20 Jahre Nordische Gesellschaft," *Diplomatisches Bulletin*, 15 September 1941, DKZ collection, Hoover Institute, Stanford, CA, Box 227.

41. "Flamenbesuch in Lübeck: Deutsch-flämischer Arbeitkreis gegründet," *Deutsche Zeitung in den Niederlanden*, 2 Sept. 1941. DKZ collection, Hoover Institute, Stanford, CA, Box 227.

42. "Der Norden und Europa," *Der Norden*, Vol. 18, No. 12 (Dec. 1941), 365.

43. Struan Robertson, "A History of Jews in Hamburg—Hamburg Transports," quoting Wilhelm Mosel of *Deutsch-judische Gesellschaft*, 2008. https://web.archive.org/web/20080528230706; http://www1.uni-hamburg.de/rz3a035//depor-trans.html; this site is accessible via archive.org's "Wayback Machine," where sources related to the destruction and commemoration of Hamburg's Jews (and areas surrounding it) were digitzed, largely inspired by Wilhelm Mosel of Hamburg (1937–1999).

44. Struan Robertson, "A History of Jews in Hamburg—Riga," attributed to Fritz Benscher's recollection. https://web.archive.org/web/20080922202328; http://www1.uni-hamburg.de/rz3a035//Riga.html.

45. Browning, *Origins of the Final Solution*, 300–303.

46. For extensive discussion regarding ghettos and deportation sites in Riga, as well as Lodz and Minsk, see Browning, *Origins of the Final Solution*, 330–334. Lange, who later attended the Wannsee Conference on 20 January 1942, was a member of the SS and SD, and was instrumental in applying the "Final Solution" in Latvia.

47. Heidemarie Kugler-Weiemann, "The Camnitzer Family Lived at Breite Straße 41," *Intiative Stolpersteine für Lübeck*, 2008, accessed 12 June 2018. https://www.stolpersteine-luebeck.de/index.php?id=21&F=2&L=1.

48. Stephan Linck, "Christen und Juden 1933–1945," *Gesellschaft für Schleswig-Holsteinische Geschichte,* 2018. Linck details how the Lübeck Evangelical Lutheran Church issued a constitutional amendment in 1933 to allow the state full access to its affairs.

49. Robertson, "A History of Jews of Hamburg—Deportation from Hamburg to Riga."

50. Ibid.

51. Peter Freimark, "Joseph Hirsch Carlebach," in *Lübecker Lebensläufe aus neun Jahrhunderten*, ed. Alken Bruns (Neumünster: Wachholz, 1993), 67–70.

52. Ibid.

53. Ibid.

54. Robertson, "A History of Jews in Hamburg—Riga."

55. Herta Rosenthal, "All the Jews Were Leaving Leipzig," in *What We Knew: Terror, Mass Murder, and Everyday Life in Nazi Germany—An Oral History*, eds. Eric A. Johnson and Karl-Heinz Reuband (Cambridge, MA: Basic Books, 2005), 68.

56. Browning, *Origins of the Final Solution*, 376–377.

57. Ibid., 397.

58. Robertson, "A History of Jews in Hamburg—Riga."

59. Ibid. For further reading on the Holocaust in Lativa—and how it engulfed German Jews—see Andrej Angrick and Peter Klein, *Die "Endlösung" in Riga: Ausbeutung und Vernichtung, 1941–1944* (Darmstadt: Wissenschaftliche Buchgesellschaft, 2006); Andrew Erzegailis, *The Holocaust in Latvia, 1941–1944: The Missing Center* (Riga: Historical Institute of Latvia, 1996); and J. A. S. Grenville, *The Jews and Germans of Hamburg: The Destruction of a Civilization, 1790–1945* (New York: Routledge, 2012).

60. For an in-depth analysis of the material gains of the Holocaust, see Götz Aly, *Hitler's Beneficiaries: Plunder, Racial War, and the Nazi Welfare State.*

61. Josef Goebbels, *The Goebbels Diaries, 1942–1943*, edited and translated by Louis P. Lochner (Garden City, NJ: Doubleday & Co., Inc, 1948), 154. "Kaufmann" is Karl Kaufmann *Gauleiter* of Hamburg 1933–1945, and the previously mentioned *Vorsteher* of the Hamburg-Kontor *Nordische Gesellschaft,* who wrote the forward for the 1938 *Nordische Woche* booklet.

62. Ibid.,155.

63. Ibid.,160. See also "Royal Air Force Bombing Command, 1942–1945, *Imperial War Museum*, 2018, accessed 13 June 2018, https://www.iwm.org.uk/collections/item/object/205023090. The RAF reportedly dropped 400 tons of bombs, of which 2/3 were incendiary.

64. Goebbels, *Diaries, 1942–1943*, 193.

65. Mary-Elizabeth O'Brien, "The Spectacle of War in *Die große Liebe*," in *Cultural History through a National Socialist Lens: Essays on the Cinema of the Third Reich*, Robert C. Reimer, ed. (Rochester, NY: Camden House, 2000), 211n4.

66. Ibid., 197. See *Die Degenhardts*, directed by Werner Klingler (Tobis Filmkunst, 1944).

67. Goebbels, *Diaries, 1942–1943*, 160.

68. Matthäus and Bajohr, eds., *The Political Diary of Alfred Rosenberg*, 199.

69. Ökumenischer Arbeitskreis "Lübecker Martyrer," Archdiocese of Hamburg, "Karl Friedrich Stellbrink," *Lübecker Martyrer,* 2018, accessed 13 June 2018, http://www.luebeckermaertyrer.de/de/geschichte/portraet/portraet-stellbrink.html, Stellbrink's history matched others', especially Martin Niemöller and Dietrich Bonhöffer. Stellbrink, unlike Niemöller and Bonhöffer, was not involved in the Confessing Church, but like them his criticism focused on the Nazis' policy and actions toward the church, rather than the treatment of the Jews or other "undesirable" populations.

70. Karl Friedrich Stellbrink, "Vernehmungsprotokoll Pastor Stellbrinks," *Lübecker Martyrer*, 2018, accessed 13 June 2018, http://www.luebeckermaertyrer.de/de/geschichte/dokumente/vernehmung-stellbrink.html. See also Martin Thoemmes, "Karl Friedrich Stellbrink," in *Neue Lübecker Lebensläufe*, ed. Alken Bruns (Neumünster: Wachholz, 2009), 569–572.

71. Ökumenischer Arbeitskreis "Lübecker Martyrer," Archdiocese of Hamburg, "Johannes Prassek," *Lübecker Martyrer*, 2018, accessed 13 June 2018, http://www.luebeckermaertyrer.de/de/geschichte/portraet/portraet-prassek.html. See also Martin Thoemmes, "Johannes Heinrich Wilhelm Prassek," in *Neue Lübecker Lebensläufe*, ed. Alken Bruns (Neumünster: Wachholz, 2009), 500–503.

72. Ökumenischer Arbeitskreis "Lübecker Martyrer," Archdiocese of Hamburg, "Eduard Müller," *Lübecker Martyrer*, 2018, accessed 13 June 2018, http://www.luebeckermaertyrer.de/de/geschichte/portraet/portraet-mueller.html. See also Martin Thoemmes, "Eduard Müller," in *Neue Lübecker Lebensläufe*, ed. Alken Bruns (Neumünster: Wachholz, 2009), 455–457.

73. Ökumenischer Arbeitskreis "Lübecker Martyrer," Archdiocese of Hamburg, "Hermann Lange," *Lübeck Martyrer*, 2018, accessed 13 June 2018, http://www.luebeckermaertyrer.de/de/geschichte/portraet/portraet-mueller.html. See also Martin Thoemmes, "Hermann Lange" in *Neue Lübecker Lebensläufe*, ed. Alken Bruns (Neumünster: Wachholz, 2009), 364–367.

74. Matthäus and Bajohr, eds., *The Political Diary of Alfred Rosenberg*, 298, 320–321.

75. Robertson, "A History of Jews in Hamburg—Riga." Many collections of testimonies from survivors, especially available through the USC Shoah foundation and oral histories collected by Yad Vashem and the United State Holocaust Memorial

Museum detail individuals' experiences in the broader context of the contracting area of German control after Fall 1943.

76. Jeremy Noakes and Geoffrey Pridham, eds., *Documents on Nazism, 1919–1945,* 676.

77. Adolf Hitler, "My Political Treatise," in *Documents on Nazism, 1919–1945*, eds. Jeremy Noakes and Geoffrey Pridham, 678.

78. For further reading on the end days of the Reich and the role of the *Volkssturm*, see Stephen Fritz, *Endkampf: Civilians, Soldiers, and the Death of the Third Reich* (Lexington: University of Kentucky Press, 2004) and Ian Kershaw, *The End: Hitler's Germany, 1944–1945* (New York: Penguin Books, 2011), among others.

79. Historical Section, Canadian Military Headquarters, "Report No. 174: The Canadian Occupation Force in Germany, May 1945 to June 1946," 12.

80. For further description of the end of the war and the challenges confronting Allies and Germans alike, see Ian Buruma, *Year Zero*, especially Part I, "Liberation Complex," as well as Richard Bessell, *Germany 1945: From War to Peace* (New York: HarperPerennial, 2010) and Frederick Taylor, *Exorcising Hitler: The Occupation and Denazification of Germany* (London: Bloomsbury, 2011).

81. The history of Allied occupation, especially that of the British, has had much scholarly attention, especially Konrad Jarausch, *After Hitler: Recivilizing Germans, 1945–1955* (Oxford: Oxford University Press, 2006) and Giles McDonough, *After the Reich: The Brutal History of the Allied Occupation* (Cambridge: Basic Books, 2009), among other listed in the introductory chapter.

82. Robert Gellately, "Introduction: Nuremberg—Voices from the Past," in Leon Goldensohn, *The Nuremberg Interviews: An American Psychiatrist's Conversations with the Defendants and Witnesses*, ed. Robert Gellately (New York: Alfred A. Knopf, 2004), xix.

83. Ibid., xxii–xxiii. On pages xxiv and xxv, Gellately mentioned that his editing took the form of making dates and spelling consistent, and correcting "obvious mistakes." This type of editing retains the integrity of the interviews as they existed, including the ways interviewees remembered or even lied about events, contributing to the record of the way collective memory, framed in the immediate postwar period, has evolved and been challenged over time.

84. Leon Goldensohn, *The Nuremberg Interviews: An American Psychiatrist's Conversations with the Defendants and Witnesses*, ed. Robert Gellately (New York: Alfred A. Knopf, 2004),197.

85. Ibid., 198.

86. Ibid., 199.

87. Ibid., 405.

88. Ibid., 228.

89. Rasmus Mariager, "'British Leadership Is Experienced, Cool-Headed and Predictable': Anglo-Danish Relations and the United States from the End of the Second World War to the Cold War," *Scandinavian Journal of History*, Vol. 37, No. 2 (May 2012), 246–260.

90. Historical Section, Canadian Military Headquarters, "Report No. 174: The Canadian Army Occupation Force in Germany, May 1945 to June 1946," 9. This

report indicated that the Canadian government authorized Canadian soliders to participate in British Occupation in Germany at the end of the war.

91. Office of Military Government for Germany, *Enactments and Approved Papers of the Control Council and Coordinating Committee for Germany for Year 1945*, Vol. I. Library of Congress Digital Collection, https://www.loc.gov/rr/frd/Military_Law/Enactments/Volume-I.pdf.

92. Abschrift: Museen der Hansestadt Lübeck signed by Director Schröder, 24 May 1945. HAL, 04.01 Hauptamt [HA] 1127: Städtische Museen-Verschiedenes

93. Military Government—Germany: Supreme Commander's Area of Control, "Law No. 52: Blocking and Control of Property," June 1945. HAL, HA 0101–2.1 Militärregierung; Kontrolkommission (CCG).

94. Letter to Lord Mayor of Lübeck from Schmidt, Landesversicherungsanstalt Schleswig-Holstein, 18 June 1945. HAL, HA0101.

95. Jarausch, *After Hitler.*

96. Robert Gellately, *Stalin's Curse: Battling for Communism in War and Cold War* (Oxford: Oxford University Press, 2013).

97. Interestingly, Herbert Marcuse, of Frankfurt School fame, was one of the authors of the *Fragebogen* in the American Zone.

98. Memo on De-Nazification, Selection of Members of Panel from R. U. J. Martin, 22 October 1946. HAL, HA 04.01 0597: Denazification.

99. Memo to Oberstadtinspektor from RKO H. G. Sullivan, 13 March 1947. HAL, 04.01 HA 0597. Italicized portion original to the document. Incidentally, many of the documents included in this file have both German and English versions, indicating the varied audiences of each documents. Clearly, many of the English officers did not speak German, and many German civilians did not speak English.

100. Ibid.

101. To Denazifizierungausschusses Schleswig-Holstein from British CCG HQ Kiel, 7 August 1947. HAL, 04. 01 HA 0592—Entnazifizierung. Interestingly, the word for "denazification" in German vacillated between the more-Anglicized "denazifizierung" and the more grammatically-German "Entnazifizierung," at times with both appearing in the same document (such as a letter from the Lübeck Denazification Committee to the Schleswig-Holstein state administration from 2 December 1947). As the British Military Government was the presiding entity of all denazification programmes in the British zone, it appears when communicating with military or state authorities, boards would revert to the Anglicized title when referring to themselves, while using the German construction when identifying the process more generally.

102. HAL, 04.01 HA 1673: Politische Überprüfung der freien Wirtschaft. This file contains several lists of firms and individuals from Lübeck either requiring questionnaires, dismissal from their positions due to wartime activities or membership in the Nazi Party, or an all-clear to resume their work. These lists are from a variety of dates, ranging as early as May 12, 1945 to 1947.

103. Many letters pleaded with military authorities to requisition rooms for denazification proceedings as well as transportation, gas, and meals for the denazification boards. See HAL, 04.01 HA 0596: Denazification and HA 0597.

104. Ibid.

105. In Rautenberg's case, the local denazification board came to a different conclusion than an appeals board at the *Land* level, causing a struggle for each to assert its own agency. See Entnazifizierungsverfahren gegen Werner Rautenberg: Ihr Schreiben vom 21.11.1947. HAL, 04.01 HA 0592.

106. Sabine Jebens-Ibs, "Luise Klinsmann," in *Lübecker Lebensläufe aus neun Jahrhunderten*, ed. Alken Bruns (Neumünster: Wachholz, 1993), 205–208. See also Lübecker Lexikon, Lipp, Christine. *Frauen in der Lübecker Geschichte: Lübecker Frauenportraits im Laufe der Jahrhunderte; Katalog zur Wanderausstellung*. 2005.

107. Memo on Denazification Panel and Review Board from KRO H. Sullivan to Oberstadtdirektor Lübeck. HAL, 04.01 HA 0597.

108. Ibid.

109. Memo to Wirtschaftsgruppe Gaststätten- und Beherbergungsgewerbe from Städt. Verwaltungsrat, 27 November 1945. HAL, 04.01 HA 1673.

110. Exemplifying this situation was communication to the British Occupation authority in August 1945 by Robert Schmidt, who detailed his continual anti-Nazi sentiment, as well as his sons, both doctors who had been harassed and rendered penniless by the SS and the advancing Red Army. HAL, 04.01 HA 1673.

111. Many scholars have discussed the specific policies regarding denazification in the four occupation zones and the differences associated with each occupier. By 1946, the British occupation authority engaged traveling denazification boards comprised of Germans, reserving their involvement for only Categories I and II (the highest levels of participation and zeal for Nazism); see Jill Jones, "Eradicating Nazism from the British Zone of Germany: Early Policy and Practice," *German History* Vol. 8, No. 2 (1990): 145–162; Konrad H. Jarausch, *After Hitler: Recivilizing Germans, 1945–1995* (Oxford: Oxford University Press, 2006); Frederick Taylor, *Exorcising Hitler: The Occupation and Denazification of Germany* (New York: Bloomsbury Press, 2011); and Francis Graham-Dixon, *The Allied Occupation of Germany: The Refugee Crisis, Denazification, and the Path to Reconstruction* (London: I. B. Tauris, 2013), among others.

Chapter 5

New Nordic Days

Lübeck's coastal district, Travemünde, is a short train ride away from the central station and features holiday apartments, several beaches on the Baltic, and access to the ferry port. At the turn of the century, the business elite went to Travemünde to summer and played at the casino. During World War II, the Luftwaffe maintained a base on the Priwall peninsula and forced laborers from eastern territories were housed there as well. In the mid-twentieth century, Travemünde was the northern terminus of the inner-German border, effectively becoming an island only accessible by ferry from the mainland once the border was sealed. Travemünde and other outlying districts like Schlutup were important to midcentury Lübeck, representing proximity to the Soviet bloc as well as a potential entry point for trade with the east. Travemünde's location on the Baltic coast as the connection point to Scandinavia as well as visibly adjacent to the German Democratic Republic (GDR) embodies the complicated and fluid nature of borders, their impact on social, cultural, and political matters, and shifting contours of identity. Today, Priwall serves as one of the two Cold War sites of memory in greater Lübeck, though the concrete remnants have long since disappeared.

Julia E. Johnsen noted in 1948 that

> Postwar Germany has been a major problem to the Allied nations undertaking its occupation since V-E Day. A healthy Germany is essential for the welfare of Europe; but reconstruction policies for Germany and surrounding countries must avoid the disastrous errors made by the Allies after World War I which led to a revived Germany strong enough to challenge the world.[1]

The collapse of the Third Reich and the military occupation of Germany and Austria had thrust Germans into a position that was at once familiar and completely foreign. Those who had lived through the end of World War I and the subsequent economic and diplomatic challenges anticipated something similar to the wake of World War I. Yet, this was a world that knew about the Holocaust, that had witnessed far greater destruction than the previous world war, and was at war in the Pacific months after V-E Day. For Lübeck, the main evidence of the war being over was persistent British occupation and oversight, as well as the presence of refugees and former slave laborers. Germans had to grapple with the national and personal guilt of the Holocaust and aggressive war, even if they wanted to deny it. Their nation had ceased to exist, reduced to occupation zones with little sense of what would come next. The connections that had been forged during the Weimar and Nazi periods necessarily had to be reconfigured, and that would take time. Would it be possible to rehabilitate Germanness, to say nothing of German nationalism?

After the initial years of denazification proceedings and the onset of the Cold War, Germans relearned the tactics of everyday life, gradually asserting more agency in the very construction of the postwar state. This meant, even, a reevaluation or reconstitution of everyday language, resuscitated from Nazified forms and frames of reference. As De Certeau argued in *The Practice of Everyday Life*, Just as in literature one differentiates "styles" or ways of writing, one can distinguish "ways of operating"—ways of walking, reading, producing, speaking, etc. . . . These "ways of operating" are similar to "instructions for us," and they create a certain play in the machine through a stratification of different and interfering kinds of functioning.[2] The conflicts that arose in the postwar period, in Germany as well as on the continent and globally, related to diplomacy, identity, leadership, and the reflection of Germany's "possible selves" in the wake of the war and the intensification of the Cold War.

This chapter details not only the processes by which 1950s Lübeckers reconstituted their event-planning playbook but also the ways in which they produced new "Nordic Weeks" (*Nordische Tage*) as products of the Cold War, a way to solidify West German Lübeck identity and combat economic and social difficulties Lübeckers perceived. By the end of the 1950s, *Nordische Tage* events had outlived their usefulness, identified as more expensive than their worth, and were shuttered with one exception—the *Nordische Filmtage Lübeck*, or Nordic Film Days Lübeck, which continues to the present day. Festival culture did not disappear from Lübeck, but it changed and stabilized after 1956, even as the inner German border calcified as a political assumption. The resurrection of the Nordic in-group in Lübeck tried to distance itself from Nazification connotations, even if echoes of racism and antisemitism persisted. This all contributed to the way Lübeck managed its relationship with the West German state, its border with East Germany, and a bipolar global environment.

ZONAL CONFLICT, THE BORDER, AND POSTWAR DIPLOMACY

Almost from the moment of capitulation, the issue of the border zone was an ever-present issue for Lübeckers. As the biggest city directly on the border as well as directly on the Baltic, border security dominated early British military policy. Some of this had to do with British-Soviet relations, but it was increasingly flavored by an east-west orientation.[3] The logistics of occupation and occupiers' ideologies impacted policy, in specific zones as well as over all of Germany and Austria. The presence of political economy and the indelible link economics had to political outcomes led to debates over what type of local governance to pursue and how best to rebuild according to ideological needs. As stated before, in the British zone the goal was to resurrect a functioning German economy (and, proceeding from that a state) as quickly as possible in part to lessen the financial burden on the British, but this at times clashed with French, Soviet, and more importantly American goals after the war.

By 1946, the gulf between the Western Allies clearly dominated by the United States and the Soviets widened, articulated in speeches and print. Winston Churchill's March 5 speech "The Sinews of Peace" argued that

> a shadow has fallen upon the scenes so lately lighted by the Allied victory. Nobody knows what Soviet Russia and its Communist international organization intends to do in the immediate future, or what are the limits, if any to their expansive and proselytizing tendencies. . . . If now the Soviet Government tries, by separate action, to build up a pro-Communist Germany in their areas, this will cause new serious difficulties in the British and American zones, and will give the defeated Germans the power of putting themselves up to auction between the Soviets and the Western Democracies.[4]

Lübeckers felt this threat acutely. Travel between zones, regulated by Zonal Travel Permit documents after June 30, 1946, was easier to navigate between British and American zones, where border checks were sporadic. For all intents and purposes, though, the border between the British zone and the Soviet zone was closed and travel documents were difficult to procure. That September, James F. Byrnes, the American secretary of state, traveled to Stuttgart to present his "Restatement of Policy on Germany," more subtly echoing the concerns Churchill had already bluntly articulated:

> It is not in the interest of the German people or in the interest of world peace that Germany should become a pawn or a partner in a military struggle for power between the East and the West. German militarism and Nazism have devastated twice in our generation the lands of German neighbors. It is fair and just that

> Germany should do her part to repair that devastation. Most of the victims of Nazi aggression were before the war less well off than Germany. . . . The United States is firmly of the belief that Germany should be administered as an economic unit and that zonal barriers should be completely obliterated so far as the economic life and activity in Germany are concerned. . . . The time has come when the zonal boundaries should be regarded as defining only the areas to be occupied for security purposes by the armed forces of the occupying powers, and not as self-contained economic or political units.[5]

It was clear that the Western zones were more in lockstep with each other, despite zonal variations. This extended to local elections, which varied widely from zone to zone in terms of participation. In an article for *The Spectator*, Alan Bullock deconstructed German politics by zone, including the parties that participated in the elections (especially those in Berlin in October 1946) and the circumstances that contextualized them. Acknowledging the differences between urban and rural populations, Bullock emphasized that the British zone "with its many big towns and its unsolved industrial problems" faced political upheaval that the Americans were able to ameliorate in the South.[6] The impact of these elections, as well as the outcomes in Berlin that resulted in a loss of communist-held seats on the city council, showcased how important economics and political systems were to institutional processes.

The Soviet zone grew more isolated from more unified American-British policy. Byrnes's speech prepared the ground for zonal economic unification, but it also raised the political stakes for it, signaling that the assertion or reduction of political power followed on the heels of economic strategy. The American and British zones became the "Bizone" on January 1, 1947, fulfilling an agreement brokered by Byrnes and British Foreign Secretary Ernest Bevin in December 1946. The calcifying "inner-German" border persisted, though, on Lübeck's doorstep. The areas adjacent to the border between the Western and Soviet zones became a special Zone Border Area [*Zonengrenzgebiet*], with policies and economic aid considered separate issues from the rest of Germany.

Rebuilding decimated Germany, while important to achieve Britain's goal to resuscitate the German economy and self-reliance as quickly as possible, was not something the British government could afford despite its concerns. The centrality of the economy in creating and maintaining political stability led to American-dominated policy, especially in the proposal of the Marshall Plan for Economic Recovery, and this would have important ramifications for the zonal border area. In a June 5, 1947, speech at Harvard University, George Marshall proposed a program to encourage political stabilization through economic recovery, stating,

> The truth of the matter is that Europe's requirements for the next three or four years of foreign food and other essential products—principally from America—are so much greater than her present ability to pay that she must have substantial additional help or face economic, social, and political deterioration of a very grave character. The remedy lies in breaking the vicious circle and restoring the confidence of the European people in the economic future of their own countries and Europe as a whole. The manufacturer and the farmer throughout wide areas must be able and willing to exchange their products for currencies the continuing value of which is not open to question.[7]

More than anything, as it had been after World War I and hyperinflation, Marshall and others hoped to restore *confidence* in the system, whether or not it was as strong as it was believed. The key to social, cultural, and political stability was economic, according to Marshall, falling in line with the Western Allies' goals for their zones as well as their priorities related to denazification. Considering Churchill's and Byrnes's speeches from the year before, the Marshall Plan proceeded as an outgrowth of unprecedented American control in Europe and idealistic strategies for integration. Applying Marshall Plan funds to Germany had a dual benefit for Britain; it could help rebuild or redeploy *British* resources while simultaneously accomplishing the goals set out by occupation authorities in northwestern Germany.

This imperiled Soviet expansion in Europe, despite Marshall's claim that the "policy is directed not against any country or doctrine, but against hunger, poverty, desperation and chaos."[8] The Western zones had diverged from the Soviet zone, particularly in the realm of German agency, reparations, and surveillance, and diplomatic relationships were strained at best along the border. Shipments of grain and agriculture from the east per the Potsdam Agreement dried up, even if the flow of refugees didn't. Plans to further integrate the Bizone continued though, demonstrated by the creation of the *Zonenbeirat* (Zonal Advisory Council) by June 11, 1947.[9] The process by which the Bizone was realized was incremental and included debates over how or even if to include the French zone. French claims on the Rhineland and Saar continued into 1947 and 1948, complicating efforts to produce broad coordination between the zones; this was mirrored by continual and increasingly overt obstruction by the Soviets.[10] In a December 1947 report on the "Big Four Parley" at a Council of Foreign Ministers meeting in London, George Marshall argued that talks were stalling due, in large part, to Soviet actions in the East:

> In the Eastern zone of Germany the Soviet Union has been taking reparations from current production and has also, under, [*sic*] the guise of reparation, seized vast holdings and formed them into a gigantic trust embracing a substantial part of the industry in that zone. This has resulted in a type of

monopolistic strangle-hold over the economic and political life of Eastern Germany which makes that region little more than a dependent province of the Soviet Union. . . . Acceptance of their claims for reparations from current production from the Western zones would extend that strangle-hold over the future economic life of all Germany. . . . A remarkable illustration of the Soviet position in this matter was their carping criticism of the economic procedure in our zones, which we freely publish for the world to read, while virtually in the same breath blandly refusing to provide any data at all concerning their zone.[11]

Setting up the former Allies' discord as an economic issue reflected British (and to a lesser extent American) insistence that recovery and stability in Europe required a functioning German economy, discounting the social and cultural upheaval wrought by continued occupation, shortages, and stilted rebuilding. The Soviets' unwillingness to integrate their zone at all—economically or otherwise—allowed the United States and the United Kingdom to steadily implement policies moving toward explicit unification while insisting they were simply rebuilding and following wartime agreements. Of course, it was more involved than that, not to say economic policy or necessity was uncomplicated. The editors of the *Westkultur-Verlag*, in the forward to the 1947 compilation *The Great Necessity* [*Die große Not*], explicitly connected economics, politics, and cultural self-reflection (as well as, it was hoped, rehabilitation):

> But we, the Germans of 1946, come out of this great misery only when we become clear about their causes; at last we reflect and change fundamentally. . . . Slowly and in spite of the great material misery, the intellectual confusion, the terrible impoverishment and the spreading vice, there are noticeably renewed forces everywhere, which clear away the rubble not only of the war, not only the rubble in the ruins, but also the rubble from our moral complacency, arrogance and superficiality. Slowly, the German people are recovering from their shock and despite wretched external living conditions, despite hunger and cold, things are progressing, because we want and must hope.[12]

Even in the title of the compilation, the editors acknowledged a nuanced, complicated situation. *Not*, which can mean emergency, necessity, and poverty/indigency, reflecting how intertwined economic, political, and social processes were. The control exacted by the Soviet Union in its zone, even in terms of economic activity and production, partially shaped the ways in which Germans navigated postwar conditions as well as the expectations of the occupier. It also shifted how postwar collective memory was understood and articulated, both within and outside Germany.

In September 1947, the Lübeck City Senate minutes included a report that the mayor had "suggested the organization of a special week of the economic and cultural kind with reference to the North in Lübeck in Summer 1948."[13] Considering the complex political and social conditions engulfing Lübeck and the rest of Germany in 1947 and 1948, the proposal of a cultural festival with distinctly economic facets is striking. What followed were months and years of debate and discussions about how "*Lübecker Woche*," ultimately called "*Nordische Tage* [Nordic Days]," should look, who the constituencies were, and who should attend. The foundational question, often explicitly considered in municipal minutes and in the press, was what the message of such an event should be, especially in the shadow of the Nazi regime and the denazification processes detailed in Chapter 5, which began upon the capitulation. In this way, *Nordische Tage* events were a strategy employed by local leaders to help explain—and even to investigate for themselves—what living in the postwar world entailed, what communities could be imagined, and how to best engage global society. It was also a return to a postwar playbook that had launched *Nordische Woche* decades earlier.

A main difference now was identity festivals of any kind could easily harken back to the Nazi era, especially one that referenced *Nordische Woche*, and could endanger Germany's perception of rehabilitation, whenever that would come to be.[14] Frau Senator Dr. Luise Klinsmann led the charge to mark Lübeck as a cultural and economic player in emergent West German politics, evident especially through her support for and leadership in mounting a series of events. The *Nordische Tage* planners encountered starts and stops, tabling discussions in light of uncertain political developments at the end of 1947 and into 1948, organization and logistical challenges related to diplomatic and business relationships outside of Germany, and Klinsmann's unflinching patronage.[15]

By 1948, the tensions between the Soviet and Western zones came to a head, when Stalin ordered the blockade of Western Berlin, interrupting the flows of goods and people into the Western enclave, following currency reform and unification in the Western zones. This reaction was not a surprise, as explicit Soviet policy was to undermine the Western Allies in their zones and construct a Germany wholly within the Soviet sphere of influence.[16] The Bizone became the Trizone when the French Zone joined the new currency of the combined Western zones, the *Deutschmark*, on June 1, 1948. Within weeks, Stalin further restricted access to Western Berlin, cutting off air routes and ground traffic. Eleven months of airlifts followed, spearheaded by American and British cargo planes, dropping supplies and information to the city. The airport at Blankensee, just outside Lübeck, served as a launching point for British deliveries, and the entire action provided a challenge to Soviet advances in central Europe.[17] The end of the blockade meant formalizing the divisions that had been steadily calcifying since capitulation, in the form of a mutual defense organization, the North Atlantic Treaty Organization (NATO) and the sense that German reunification would be incomplete for the foreseeable future. To that end, the Federal Republic of Germany (hereafter FRG), colloquially called West Germany or even the Bonn government, entered international politics on May 23, 1949. A new phase of the postwar period had begun.

THE CENTRALITY OF CHECKPOINTS

Contested resources—construction materials, capital, and the labor—to rebuild fused the goals of the Allies with the physical needs of the population. The focus on a *national* perspective did not always resonate with locals, especially if they felt they were being denied resources. This was definitely the case in Lübeck after World War II, as it had been following World War I. In both hyperinflationary Germany as well as in the postwar and foundational years of the FRG, Lübeckers focused on the economic sustainability of their city, seeing its vitality as an inherent part of their local identity, and they jealously pursued their access to financial resources and infrastructure.[18] The administrative centers in northwestern Germany, though, were Hamburg, Kiel, and Bremen, and both the Allies and Bonn focused on *them* as the keys to recovery.

Lübeck was little more than yet another midsized city needing rebuilding. It was located directly on the zonal boundary and the Baltic, a European crossroads with Scandinavian connections. As early as July 1947, the Lübeck Chamber of Commerce and Industry appealed to British officials to move the official border crossing closer to the city, in a district called Schlutup, from Herrnwyck.[19] Relations between the Western Allies and the Soviets had cooled considerably in the months after capitulation, but the border zone between Lübeck and Mecklenburg, though patrolled and controlled, still allowed for trade and a continuing flow of refugees and returning POWs from the east. The border zone itself was an ever-widening strip of land and was treated by both the occupiers and the later Bonn government as a "special" sector that had its own contingencies and pressures.[20] Appeals for help and consideration were buttressed by the estimate that, along the 1,329 kilometers of the inner border, 6.85 million people were impacted somehow.[21]

The German Democratic Republic (GDR, or East Germany) was formalized on October 7, 1949, and served as a counternarrative to emerging West German policy. In Lübeck, the Soviets were viewed as instigating the problems across the zonal boundary, endangering local traditional trading networks between Schleswig-Holstein, Lübeck, and Mecklenburg. Though the flow of people and material was sporadic, Lübeck benefited from having an official checkpoint on its eastern border at Herrnwyck, though the Soviets threatened to shut down the checkpoint as well as the entirety of the inner border. Between 1945 and 1952, crossing the border could be relatively easy depending on where one was. In the more rural north outside of Lübeck, it was a matter of crossing fields. As more and more people left the east, however, attention to the border zone increased on both sides. The Federal Border Defense (*Bundesgrenzschutz*) was established in 1951, with commandos located throughout Germany from Bavaria to the Baltic; these were constantly reordered and consolidated as the system developed in conjunction with American and British compatriots.[22]

Lübeckers grudgingly accepted their importance on the border being tied to connecting Hamburg to West Berlin; similarly, the centrality of a location to a border commando meant that, at least, the city would be on the government's financial radar. It was a tightrope. On one hand, the constant reminder and presence of Allied troops on the border maintained the feeling of slow-simmering conflict and potential war. On the other hand, the very presence of those troops brought economic resources. In May 1952, the inner border was sealed and further militarized coinciding with a realignment of border crossings. Lübeck's crossing was closed by September 1952, effectively cutting it off from the flow of trade and movement to the east in favor of a more direct route between Hamburg and Berlin. Concrete roads, even to the northern reaches of the region (especially the Priwall peninsula), became impassable due to the "construction of the zonal border," necessitating alternatives like a ferry service.[23] The rivalry with Hamburg was especially bitter, in that Lübeck had consistently "been losing" resources and even its "imperial city" status to Hamburg during the twentieth century.[24] The major exception was the establishment of the BGS training school in the St. Hubertus neighborhood of Lübeck, connecting Lübeck specifically with the federal apparatus managing border controls and training.[25]

For all intents and purposes, Lübeck and the Baltic coast of Schleswig-Holstein was bypassed in favor of connecting a major center of Allied control to the contested four-power city of Berlin. For nearly the next decade, Lübeck's mayor and municipal leaders bombarded Bonn, nearly pleading for the government to reopen the Lübeck crossing, arguing that Hamburg's gain was Lübeck's loss.[26] Resources were strained by the constant influx of refugees, former slave laborers, and returning German POWs, many of whom crossed the border into British-occupied Lübeck and remained in makeshift camps, former Luftwaffe barracks in the Priwall, and hastily constructed apartments throughout the city.[27] The locals saw the situation as filling Lübeck with problematic populations requiring care and shelter, locking the door, and throwing away the key, requiring appeals to Bundestag members and the Bonn government.[28] Attempts to mitigate the pressure took the form of aid packages to the zonal border regions stretching from Lübeck to Bavaria to the southern terminus at Hof, aimed at alleviating lost trade with the Soviet zone, dealing with the refugee problem, and subsidizing troubled sectors like farming and cultural institutions.[29]

WEST GERMANY EMERGENT AND THE UNEVEN ECONOMIC MIRACLE

Throughout the 1950s, building on the progress associated with the Marshall Plan, manufacturing revived in West Germany due to the deepening Cold War and global impacts of conflicts like the Korean War and war for independence in former colonies. After the immediate postwar period, but especially in the second half of the 1950s, West Germany experienced what was called the *Wirtschaftswunder*: the "economic miracle." At once both rooted in rapid economic improvements and Western propagandizing, the West German economy quickly strengthened and expanded. The myth was that it exploded all across the country and that every region and individual gained wealth and stability. The scholarship surrounding the 1950s-era so-called economic miracle of West Germany has historically been challenged by a sense of uniqueness and postwar political necessity. In *The Miracle Years* edited by Hanna Schissler, Lutz Niethammer argued that research regarding the emergence of the FRG had had "little success thus far in debunking the myth of the 1950s" and advocated for "microhistorical intervention[s]" to illuminate regional, social, and individual experiences of the time.[30] Especially following British occupation after World War II and the early days of the FRG, citizens and officials of Schleswig-Holstein in general and Lübeck in particular couched their position as one of economic and social quandary highlighting the divisions within the FRG and the unevenness of the much-lauded *Wirtschaftswunder*.

Efforts to shore up economic interests had concomitant effects on cultural and social identity, demonstrated by the imagery of "forgotten" cities and people, much like the "Rust Belt" cities in the United States in the later twentieth century. In a commemorative retrospective volume entitled *Lübeck—Aufbau aus dem Chaos* [Lübeck Rebuilt from Chaos] published in 1962, Hans Schönherr wrote about how Lübeck faced unique challenges in the wake of World War II, rebuilding from extensive bombing while navigating an influx of tens of thousands of refugees and a loss of attention and resources.[31] The *Lübecker Nachrichten* went so far as to call the cities of Schleswig-Holstein the "step-children [*Stiefkinder*] of the economic revival."[32] The frustration in Lübeck was summed up by Kurt Pohle in the *Lübecker Freie Presse* in

April 1956: "You cook in two pots in the confederation. The fat is loosened somewhere else—we eat watery soup in Schleswig-Holstein. A few globs of fat would have quite an invigorating effect."[33]

The discourse surrounding the experience of a unified West German identity was varied and recovery was uneven. The economic and social identity of Lübeck and Schleswig-Holstein more broadly was the inaccessibility of resources, particularly as part of the *Zonengrenzgebiet*. As with the post–World War I era, Lübeck struggled to find its place in a "new" Germany, following a cultural, military, and ethical cataclysm that dwarfed its predecessor. The landscape of a divided Germany, with Lübeck right on the border, meant that to access West German support, affluence, and society, the region had to advertise its importance and its commitment to the national project. Cultivating a distinctly *West* German identity was an ongoing process throughout the 1950s.

Local leaders, especially those who had survived the Nazi era and denazification proceedings, advocated for a multiday *Nordische Tage*, which connected economic revitalization and tourism with social and cultural rehabilitation. Some of this was political, inviting Scandinavian and West German dignitaries alike (such as the federal president), while sporting events, book displays, and exhibitions drew on new technologies like mass-produced film. If all of this sounds familiar, it was. By the time *Nordische Tage* opened in June 1953, the *Lübecker Nachrichten* (*LN*) ran a story about "The First 'Nordic Weeks' in Lübeck":

> That's how it was back then, more than thirty years ago: "The first 'Nordic Weeks' in Lübeck." The old Hanseatic city on the Trave as a "spiritual collection point ['*Unschlagplatz des Geistes*']" to Scandinavia. Many of the older Lübeckers remember the "Nordic Weeks" of past years, namely the first one, which with incomparable momentum and success founded a tradition that is now revived. The first "Nordic Week" was held in September 1921. It was a risk.[34]

Explicitly connecting the *Nordische Tage* of 1953 to the 1921 *Nordische Woche* served many needs. It immediately recalled a postwar (pre-Nazi) period wherein social, cultural, and economic norms were uncertain. It also presented a distinct narrative by which Lübeckers, separately from the nation-state though distinctly within its context, could participate in building identity, expressing shared values, and constructing a future. By virtue of skipping over the Nazi-era *Nordische Woche*, and even eliminating the role of the *Nordische Gesellschaft*, Lübeckers attempted to rehabilitate their economy, claims to a particular heritage, and their tendency to look North.

At the same time, though, the mobilization of the "Nordic" identity was problematic, even offensive. What did it mean to be "German" after the Nazis? After defeat and occupation? After division into the FRG and GDR?

As in the 1920s, Lübeckers returned to local identity tropes and norms first to reimagine their community, advocating as they had in the past for increased trade with Scandinavia, especially Denmark after the crossing closure in 1952, and the physical connection to the Baltic by way of the ferry.[35] They situated themselves as unique within the FRG, as the only major city directly on the border with East Germany (persistently still called the Soviet zone, even into the 1960s) but in a German region that increasingly felt cut off from recovery efforts, especially after checkpoint closed in May 1952.[36] Public discourse and news reporting emphasized the persistent circumstances that blocked even the perception of revitalization, and local and state leaders scrambled to alleviate not only public frustration but also financial pressure from an administrative standpoint.

NORDISCHE TAGE 1953

Confronted by crushing local needs as well the compulsion to prove stability and ideological commitment to the Western Allies, six years after discussions first began regarding an international festival in the city, Lübeck's cultural leaders led by Dr. Klinsmann promoted *Nordische Tage* as a way to improve business and foreign relations in the city and inspire tourism in a competitive (and limited) Western market in the shadow of an all-important global border. Contextualized by Lübeck's location within the "special border zone" and directly on the border with the emerging GDR, festival planners looked to the event as a way to solve several problems at once. The first *Nordische Tage* coincided with the border closures and the failed East German uprising following Josef Stalin's death, in 1953. It and two subsequent *Nordische Tage* exhibitions were seen as a way to show off the city and its potential as well as address the very real economic emergencies that confronted it, such as the numbers of refugees still housed in Lübeck and stagnating trade from the region.

What is most clear from planning notes and material ephemera is a narrative of destruction, rehabilitation, and reconnection. *Nordische Tage* was clearly planned and executed by city leaders for the benefit of Lübeck businesses, leaders, and potential guests, but there wasn't the same tone of the city's populace being all that active in putting the events together that there had been in 1921. This was a top-down event designed to showcase the postwar Lübeck, still rebuilding but more than ready to reach across the Baltic and resume friendships. At the same time, city leaders intended Lübeck to become more than a destination for a one-off event. Evidence of this was reported on November 15, 1952, in the *Lübecker Nachrichten*, which detailed a "Nordic meeting [*Nordisches Treffen*]," where Bürgermeister Otto

Passarge met the newest Swedish consul in Hamburg, Nils-Eric Ekblad, and "suggested a large Nordic meeting in Lübeck in the coming year, which was broadly determined to have strong mutual interest."[37] Four days later, the *LN* reported that the Lübeck Senate had "decided to carry out the planned 'Nordic Days in Lübeck' as a permanent institution for the first time in the coming year in the first half of June."[38] That *Nordische Tage* was envisioned as a permanent event only highlights the importance the Lübeck Senate and other city leaders placed on Lübeck-Scandinavian relations and connections in the effort to reorient German culture after Nazism, especially to potential foreign visitors.[39]

Most evident in editorials from Lübeck's newspapers, ambiguous acknowledgment of past mistakes and the guilt associated with the most recent world war—though the actual crimes are never listed and Jews are never mentioned by name—reflected a sort of non-apology while attempting to speed up the reintegration timeline. This was especially clear in the *Lübecker Freie Presse* (*LFP*), essentially the newspaper of the SPD, which heralded not only the events of the festival but also lauded the city planners, which were led by the SPD at the time. The theme of the 1953 *Nordische Tage* was "*Lübeck dankt dem Norden*": "Lübeck thanks the North."[40] The editorial, written by general *LFP* editor Albrecht Zießler, stated:

> Lübeck not only feels obligated but also deeply motivated to thank the North. This thanks is no coincidence. It has been proven that Scandinavian intervention saved our city from great damage caused by the war, and in the harsh postwar years it received support from the north, which was neither to be expected nor to be morally earned. . . . We have to be clear: to pronounce the word "forgotten" as an invitation is not up to us. But through our attitude, through practical work and true democratism [*Demokratentum*], in our country and beyond our borders, we can cause it to somehow pick itself up.[41]

More than anything, this editorial, echoed by other press in 1953, was that West Germans recognized they had had "dark years" and had little standing to advocate for repaired friendships and relationships, yet there was no clear statement that truly took responsibility for the Holocaust; the vague references to "unfortunate times" were as far as it went.[42]

In this, *Nordische Tage* 1953 was more about making it okay to celebrate "Nordic" heritage in Germany, to rescue it from the taint of Nazi excesses. This reflected the broader West German approach to the Nazi past and the crimes of the Holocaust more generally, papering over a real accounting for what the Nazis had done to the Jews in particular in favor of the language of reconciliation and appealing to foreign countries' goodwill and forgiveness. There was also a prevalent language of the victimhood of everyday Germans—the "bystanders"—who had suffered bombings (though the Allies were not mentioned by name) and hardship in the postwar years. The 1942 Palm Sunday bombing was front and center in a variety of publications, from newspaper reports and op-eds to the program itself to retrospectives commemorating the decade.

On the final page of the welcoming booklet, which described prominent features and buildings in Lübeck, Passarge noted,

> Still standing are the 7 towers of Lübeck. Although the fire of war took the golden peaks to 5 towers, St. Marien looks far into the land as a landmark and symbol. The Hanseatic city of Lübeck cordially invites you to the Nordic Days.[43]

It was an odd juxtaposition, the spirit of celebration and thanks balanced by the constant references to the Palm Sunday 1942 bombing. Even in materials that looked back and recalled *Nordische Tage*, especially the *Lübecker Nachrichten*'s 1962 retrospective *Lübeck—Aufbau aus dem Chaos,* opened with two chapters on the Palm Sunday bombing and the immediate aftermath, detailing the often stymied or uneven efforts to rebuild and return to normalcy.

Still, the conscious connection of the festival to the opening of the Trelleborg-Travemünde Ferry solidified a path forward, but it is clear the past hadn't been truly reckoned with in any self-reflective way and West German policy in the 1950s did not help. This was especially evident in the invitation extended to Carl-Jacob Burckhardt to be the keynote speaker; though it was largely unknown at the time, Burckhardt's questionable ties to the Nazi regime as a major leader of the International Committee of the Red Cross highlights the contentiousness of the Nazi past in the postwar period.[44] Passarge, in his invitation letter to Burckhardt in January 1953, explained that

> in Lübeck the custom had arisen to deepen the cultural relations and also to discuss economic issues with the Scandinavian countries every year as part of a "Nordic Week." Unfortunately, National Socialism discredited this valuable custom through its well-known propagandistic methods. . . . Lübeck now feels that the time has come to resume, in the established forms, to exchange views with the other Peoples of the North.[45]

He also emphasized Lübeck's self-appointed role as the "gateway to the north [*Tor zum Norden*]."[46]

Burckhardt waffled on the invitation, citing a full travel schedule, a lack of time to prepare remarks, and ignorance of Scandinavian cultures, entreating planners to "have a speaker more familiar with Nordic matters."[47] Early reports in Lübeck papers had indicated Burckhardt's involvement, though it is unclear if they were merely reporting his invitation or his commitment to the project. He finally declined by the end of March 1953, for that year's festival and all subsequent ones, citing standing trips to the United States.[48] Ultimately, event planners secured Odd Nansen, Norwegian architect and former prisoner of Sachsenhausen, as keynote speaker. In terms of optics, this emphasized the humanitarian work Nansen had engaged in before and during the war, especially relating to Jewish refugees fleeing the Nazi state and later in Czechoslovakia. Nansen's inclusion lent some credibility to the deferential tone to "the north," but the circuitous path it took to get him there demonstrated the ambivalence with which Germans navigated relationships with their past and with Scandinavia.

Nordische Tage had other cringe-worthy moments. In the same June 10 edition of the *LFP* as Zießler's op-ed, the authorless article "The Hansestadt Lübeck Invites You [*Die Hansestadt Lübeck lädt ein*]" insisted that "Lübeck has always been a hospitable city. It has always been a pleasure to the people of Lübeck to show guests the beauty of their city, the witnesses of their great historical past."[49] Again, this completely ignored the way Jews, in particular, had been treated in the city even well before the Nazi period, clearly privileging Scandinavian and western European visitors as they had in the 1920s. It narrowed the spaces within which Jews, black Germans, "easterners," and later immigrant groups occupied, and clearly held them outside the dominant identity. Lübeck was looking North, as it presumably always had.

Lübeck rolled out the red carpet to its guests, from foreign dignitaries to the performers who showcased traditional and more modern examples of Nordic-German music. Meals were held in Lübeck's most famous restaurants, and table assignments were carefully crafted to foment discussion. Unlike the 1921 *Nordische Woche*, less emphasis was put on ensuring wide participation from townspeople; it was much more about Lübeck being an international meeting place. Fireworks, launched at Travemünde, signified the celebratory feeling planners wished to foster for their guests. At the same time, though, this was to give exposure to German fireworks companies who had been limited to domestic trade following the war. The advertising brochure for Moog-Nicolaus pyrotechnics firm explicitly talked about its clientele before World War II (Portugal, Greece, Tripoli, and even the 1936 Olympiad) as compared to afterward (largely in Hamburg and carnival celebrations in Cologne).[50]

At the end of it all, city leaders heralded a successful festival and immediately set to planning the next one. The day after *Nordische Tage* ended, members of the planning committee debriefed, producing a critical examination of how the event was planned, how to fix it, and the feedback from the foreign guests. This document emphasized that the festival was really aimed outside Germany, as the Bürgermeister and others differentiated "honored guests [*Ehrengäste*]" from the "other guests [*übrigen Gästen*]."[51] Further distinction was made between guests from Scandinavia and those from Lübeck, suggesting that local festival goers should bear at least some of the costs of their food and excursions. This event was more about diplomacy and courting elites than a popularly attended event for everyone in the city, even if advertising alerted the citizenry that an important event was being hosted.

The immediate postmortem notes from the committee highlighted the desire to provide relaxation to the guests, to avoid the "dreaded German animal seriousness" and overplanning, especially to inspire guests to shop in the city.[52] *Nordische Tage* was an ongoing investment in outward-facing promotion and in regional diplomacy. It is difficult to ascertain how Lübeckers themselves consumed or considered *Nordische Tage*, if they even did, as it doesn't appear this was for *them*. The report to Hermann Ehlers, then-president of the Bundestag, indicated that approximately sixty "prominent" visitors and sixty members of the foreign press attended, clearly placing Lübeck as host but not necessarily participant. Some of this may have been due to the allotted budget—*Nordische Tage* cost somewhere between 50,000 and 55,000 Deutschmarks—and a call was made to double the budget for the following year.[53] The bigger budget could have of course widened the scope of the festival beyond an official capacity, including the public more fully and allowing for more affiliated performances and events.

Schönherr's look back on the event rated a dedicated chapter, but he actually spent little time on *Nordische Tage 1953* itself. Rather, he talked about all the background context, the international issues, the economic ambivalence of the early 1950s, and Lübeck's circumstances. In this way, while the 1953 event paved the way for two more *Nordische Tage*, it failed to really resonate locally as a defining moment of the early 1950s as Lübeck—and West Germany more broadly—left the postwar period behind and settled into a Cold War milieu. After the splash of the first postwar *Nordische Tage*, less attention was paid to enticing Scandinavian visitors and the public to consider Lübeck as a viable and preferred partner. The focus shifted more intensely to situating Lübeck vis-à-vis the rest of West Germany, integrating it and its unique connection to the Baltic into the emergent state.

NORDISCHE TAGE 1954

The planning for the second postwar *Nordische Tage* began in earnest in October 1953, forming a standing committee to plan the event; Passarge called for representatives from political and social groups to attend the first planning meeting, held at the town hall on November 30.[54] Dr. Klinsmann again was the backbone of the committee, and she also represented institutional memory in the reasons for mounting *Nordische Tage* in the first place; it had been partially her brainchild, in consultation with Dr. Kalkbrenner, who had been most instrumental in planning the 1921 *Nordische Woche*.

Planning for *Nordische Tage* built on the framework established the year before, utilizing the design for the program (and its format) and the way the festival was organized as a template. This cut down on the need to build from the ground up, but it also ran the organizers into trouble, particularly with graphic artists such as the prolific Herbert Müller-Fried, who threatened to bring suit against the city for modifying his design for the 1954 festival.[55] Overall, branding *Nordische Tage* with a common template from year to year indicated an attempt to consistently connect the breadth of the festival to the city, even if the overarching theme changed. Costs associated with commissioning new designs for each festival meant added time and funds; it would also conceptually detach the event from the previous one. If anything, what Klinsmann in particular hoped was to establish a recurrent cultural event separate from any individual office, personality, or current political climate. It was an example of remaking a locally sanctioned institution that could operate on a variety of levels, simultaneously reaching across the Baltic as well as teaching locals how to mobilize features of Lübeck identity in the postwar context, marking out the parameters of acceptable discourse and identifying what could be rescued after the Nazis.

And yet, Kalkbrenner (representing the *Deutsche Auslandsgesellschaft,* founded in 1949 along with Heinrich Jessen) was emblematic of both problematic continuity and unresolved history of local Lübeck identity.[56] Both Kalkbrenner and Jessen had been important members of the *Nordische Gesellschaft*, remaining in leadership after 1933. Their participation or at least input in *Nordische Tage*, along with now-Senator Ernst Timm, only seems to show the efforts to smooth over the wrongs of the past, possibly indicating their own personal rehabilitation along with the ideology—or at least identity—they espoused. Correspondence addressed to the *Nordische Gesellschaft* in 1955, corrected to reference the *Deutsche Auslandsgesellschaft*, shows that the connotations regarding the festival and organization still existed well into the postwar period; the intellectual predecessor could not be easily erased.[57]

One of the first things Bürgermeister Passarge did to plan *Nordische Tage* 1954 was contact Carl-Jacob Burckhardt, again requesting that he come give the keynote talk. In his request, he highlighted the success of the 1953 event while indicating the president of the FRG, Dr. Heuss, was likely to attend.[58] At the same time, Passarge wrote to Heuss, indicating that Burckhardt was likely to attend, having to cancel the previous year due to a trip to the United States.[59] Passarge's pursuit of securing Burckhardt as a speaker, or even just an attendee, again came up short, despite the fact that the descriptive commemorative booklet indicated his attendance. Ultimately ending up with Swedish historian Dr. Torvald Höjer and President Heuss, *Nordische Tage*

1954 blended the elite focus of the previous year with a few public-facing activities, notably President Heuss's public address on the Marktplatz.

In some ways, the tone of the 1954 festival was different from that of 1953. The year 1953 was viewed as the foundational and/or building year, and once the planners could claim success there was less need to blitz the press in Germany and outside of it regarding the "why." Even though economics had been one of the dominant topics in 1953, the 1954 festival looked less to fostering or maintaining links to Scandinavia (and acknowledging the immediate postwar investments in Germany) and more to connecting Lübeck and its door to "the North" with Bonn and West Germany. Opening on June 2 and running through June 4, it featured roundtable discussions, performances of classic German music as well as a "new Lübeck Dance of Death [*Lübecker Totentanz*]," and the Bundespräsident's speech on the Marktplatz. The opening ceremonies at the *Stadttheater* featured *Finlandia* by Sibelius and the prelude to *Der Meistersinger von Nürnberg* by Wagner, which framed the keynote for the entire event: Torvald Höjer's speech entitled "Historical Relations between the North and Germany: Facts and Problems, Observed by a Swede."[60]

The three days of the festival again, as in 1953, included cultural performances that highlighted Scandinavian and German artists and performers, with a special eye on situating Lübeck as a bridge or middle ground in the region. Drawing on famous compositions of the past, Walter Kraft, organist at St. Mary's among other things, debuted a new composition based on the early modern mural and musical work *Lübecker Totentanz*. The original work and the organ upon which it had historically been played was completely lost in the 1942 air raid, and the replacement organ was an important cultural move forward.[61] Alongside this program, Ingmar Bergmann hosted viewing and discussion of "Nordic" film on Breitestraße.[62] The thing that featured most, however, was food. Luncheons and evening meals, hosted by the Ratskeller and the Schiffersgesellschaft, provided less structured time for guests to interact—though the table assignments were again choreographed ahead of time. In this way, exchange was the name of game, even if it was more cultural than material.

The overarching theme for the 1954 *Nordische Tage* was not as explicit as it had been the year before, though Hans Schönherr remarked that the subject of the festival was tourism.[63] The *LFP* as in 1953 produced an issue in both German and Swedish dedicated to welcoming guests to Lübeck. Senator Paul Bromme framed the official line regarding *Nordische Tage*, stating that the event was about "acquir[ing] trust" and establishing personal relationships, despite a packed schedule.[64] In that same issue, tucked among short reports and classified ads, was an announcement calling "For Unity in Freedom [*Für Einheit in Freiheit!*]," commemorating the victims of June 17 uprising in

East Berlin; this commemoration became a yearly national holiday in West Germany until reunification in 1990.[65] Engendering trust in Scandinavian countries meant being solidly committed to the Western vision of European connectedness and openly deriding authoritarianism of any ideological stripe.

Despite these positive or even pollyannish overtures, public discourse focused on Lübeck's disconnection from the rest of West Germany, from trade with West Berlin, and its inability to fully recover, mobilizing imagery of being forgotten and overlooked, overshadowed by larger urban centers such as Hamburg or even seats of government like Kiel. Much of the backdrop for planning *Nordische Tage* 1954 involved official delegations to Bonn to request aid packages to deal with the ongoing issues of refugees (both from the Soviet east and former forced laborers) as well as more logistical issues associated with the special border zone. In a transcript abstract from a February 15, 1954, Lübeck Senate meeting, the city inspector related efforts of the Lübecker delegation to Bonn on behalf of the "refugee city [*Fluchtlingsstadt*]" and promoting the upcoming *Nordische Tage* to Scandinavian and German dignitaries.[66]

Nordische Tage 1954 incurred a cost of almost 70,000 DM, definitely an increase from the initial requisition of 50,000 DM.[67] The fact that the city would commit such a sum to a relatively short event, especially as officials were pleading for aid from the federal government, shows how useful local leaders felt the exposure and press was. Promoting Lübeck as a destination—one that attracted the general public as well as diplomats and intellectuals from across Europe—only reinforced the pleas to Bonn. How could the republic ignore a city that filled a niche that even neighboring Hamburg or Kiel could not? The additional fact that President Heuss attended and gave a public speech lent some legitimacy to the Lübeck city council's position; throughout his tenure as president, he enjoyed relative popularity and electoral support, garnering 71 percent approval in January 1953 survey.[68] The border only made Lübeck's position all the more important, but it was also about formulating what Lübeck could bring to the Federal Republic in exchange for aid, not simply an ongoing, entrenched crisis with no end in sight. Situating Lübeck as the site for important intellectual and scientific exchange, including "difficult conversations" made the city more than a recipient of ongoing help; it made it a unique and even preferred destination, not an eviscerated backwater. At the same time, the connections being forged made Lübeck less dependent on budget lines in Bonn.

Mounting a festival that was both recognizable as well as interesting from year to year was difficult. As early as June 8, only four days after *Nordische Tage* closed in 1954, one of the city's senior administrators, Herr Schweisfurth, suggested turning to having an event every two or even three years.[69] Part of the reasoning, he argued, was that despite the benefits, the business community in Lübeck showed little interest in *Nordische Tage*; the question, then, was financial sustainability. Additionally, he stated, refocusing the festival on Scandinavia, rather than highlighting German dignitaries (even those as popular as President Heuss) would ensure a further stream of support from the North.[70] Since much had been made of *Nordische Tage* as an economic venture from the time it was first conceived, the lack of concrete returns or even enthusiasm made it a hard sell as an annual event.

This was further complicated by the suspicion openly expressed by Scandinavian newspapers, particularly in Sweden and Denmark, regarding the connection or at least the roots in Nazism that *Nordische Tage* seemed to gloss over. On June 11, the *Berlingske Tidende*, at the time one of the most-circulated papers in Denmark, reported on the "Nazi irony" of the festival, noting that a meeting of the right-wing *Deutscher Block* was set for Lübeck at the end of the month.[71] The persistent connection between Nazism and the postwar *Nordische Tage*, despite planners' insistence on their cultural and economic motivations, rang a bit hollow when contextualized by the ongoing, even overt, realities of former Nazis' political activities. Reinforcing this facet of *Nordische Tage* was Waldemar Kraft's speech to attendees. Appearing as a federal minister appointed by Adenauer and chairman of the GB/BHE (the Refugees' Party), he touted Lübeck's importance as "an outpost of the free world" alongside the Iron Curtain while alluding to Lübeck's unique burden of a swollen expellee population; he was also a former member of the SS.[72] If nothing else, this reinforced the failure of denazification, and *Nordische Tage* allowed observers to point out West Germany's inconsistent handling of the Nazi past.

Cultural returns were hard to quantify, and though Dr. Klinsmann was a valuable asset, her support for the event could only go so far, especially in terms of financial accountability. In many ways, *Nordische Tage* was Dr. Klinsmann's event, and her vision was necessary to secure not only a budget but also attention. There was danger in this, in that *Nordische Tage*'s ongoing value was intrinsically tied to Klinsmann's career and influence, rather than truly becoming an institution that helped shape Lübeck's foreign and domestic relations. National discussions about festivals that were cultural or artistic, such as *Kieler Woche*, drew analysis about the types of events the federal government wanted to—or even should—fund.[73]

By early 1955, the decision had been made to postpone an official *Nordische Tage* for a year in favor of the 1955 traveling "World of the Woman" [*Welt der Frau*] exhibition, which featured a three-day "Nordic Women's Congress" in mid-May.[74] It also allowed other festivals, especially the *Deutsch-Nordische Sängerfest* [German-Nordic Songfest] and *Deutsch-Nordische Frauentagung* [German-Nordic Women's Conference] to "maintain the German-Nordic connection."[75] However, included in the 1955 city senate budget were funds—100,000 DM worth—for "Cultivation [*Pflege*] of Hanseatic-Nordic Relations."[76] Arguments in January 1956 were made to transfer these funds, if they hadn't fully been used, forward for the next fiscal year. Despite the discussions of fiscal responsibility and the ways cultural or local festivals fit within official programming contexts, the Lübeck City Senate had clearly made connections with Scandinavia a *local* priority, if a contentious one.

THE LAST *NORDISCHE TAGE*

After the break in 1955, Luise Klinsmann was focused on mounting the largest festival to that point. She stolidly supported holding *Nordische Tage* in 1956 despite warnings of overspending, little return, and the fear of "Nazi echoes."[77] This iteration of *Nordische Tage* was more sweeping and aimed at explicitly replicating the 1921 *Nordische Woche*. In the commemorative booklet produced by city leaders (a distinct publication from the program of events), the Bürgermeister remarked that

> while "Nordic Days 1954" sought to clarify the historical and political foundations of mutual relations, 'Nordic Days 1956' now seeks to shed light on what has been done among our peoples in the past fifteen years in order to gain experience for a winning future.[78]

In this way, all of the *Nordische Tage* events could be considered as a scaffolding process, each building on the previous events to craft not only an approach but a dominant perspective. Klinsmann herself reiterated this in her speech to open the book exhibit on August 31, when she argued that the foundational idea had always been "to get to know and understand" each other, and that meeting this goal required the participation of all kinds of artists, teachers, and writers.[79]

Much of the programming was still aimed at elites and operated on an official or diplomatic level, such as the roundtable discussion focused on the question, "What has happened in the last ten years for an understanding and rapprochement between our people and what else could be done?" and the speeches given by state and federal ministers.[80] Continued emphasis was put on dialogue, which continued in scheduled meals around town, again in the Ratskeller and Schiffersgesellschaft. Fostering interaction in this way speaks to the earnest desire many Lübeck leaders had to shore up relationships with Scandinavian countries and maintain official channels outside the purview of the federal government but with its support. The keynote speech, given by Professor Hal Koch, tackled the topic of "Adult Education as a Political Problem of our Time," wherein he linked the project of global democracy to active and ongoing education for a knowledgeable populace, particularly to avoid compromising identity and nationality the way the Nazis had.[81]

The Finnish National Ballet performed *Scaramouche* by Sibelius and Delibes's *Coppelia*, while a variety of sporting events, a book exhibit, and a film festival provided possible venues to include the general public. Capping off the event, as in 1954, was an address on the Marktplatz by President Heuss. Once again, the 1954 *Lübecker Totentanz* was performed at Marienkirche, making the pageant a new classic in Lübeck that contextualized a historic view of the past in the new postwar normal, embodied by the remains of melted bells that had smashed to the floor during the Palm Sunday bombing left as a memorial in the restored church. Many of the events from previous *Nordische Tage* continued, though on a grander scale and aimed at a more varied audience than the 1953 event which had been firmly lodged in elite circles.

By the time President Heuss stepped into the Marktplatz, Lübeck had hosted three days of varied events, many for the benefit of Scandinavian guests. In his closing remarks, Heuss recalled spending time with Thomas Mann, who had died the previous year, and acknowledged his contested legacy, as well as that of the term "Nordic."[82] That legacy, in so many ways, echoed in the other points he made, such as the divided reality Germans faced, the physical changes to the landscape along the border and "no-man's land" on the beaches of Travemünde, Lübeck's own marginalized existence in the twentieth century, and the unknown future. Before urging the crowd to sing the third verse of the *Deutschlandlied*, Heuss heralded the task and the responsibility of free speech and compromise; even as he referenced the broader community surrounding the Baltic Sea, he intimated it extended to the other Germany, who despite "absurd political separation" could still foster "spiritual connection."[83] Heuss touched on all the broad themes of all three *Nordische Tage* in his closing remarks—and ended up being the final word to occur during such an event.

LEAVING NORDISCHE TAGE BEHIND

The years following the 1956 *Nordische Tage* were years of continual reintegration, a connection between western European nations, and calcification of the Cold War. For Lübeck, the end of the 1950s brought cautious optimism. The towers of *Marienkirche* were rebuilt (utilizing funds raised from Bonn and guests at the 1956 events) and discussions about reopening a border crossing in Lübeck culminated with a checkpoint at Schlutup in March 1960. The fact that plans for further *Nordische Tage* during this period broke down is perhaps coincidental, but at least part of the stimulative effect the festival was supposed to have was picked up by the resumption of the flow of goods and people across the inner border directly from Lübeck. Still, the perception that Schleswig-Holstein and Lübeck in particular "missed out" on the economic miracle years of the 1950s persisted, especially as it related to refugees.

Economic stabilization by 1960 despite political distress, particularly related to trade with regional partners, the GDR, and protectionism for particular industries in Lübeck meant that local leaders could focus on "spooning the fat" back home, whether it was through new infrastructure and trade or rebuilding the city center, which was finally completed in 1986. Indeed, a working group designated to explore *Nordische Tage* 1961 found that "the Federal Press Office made it clear that it was basically willing to participate in the costs of such events, if Hansestadt Lübeck could decide to go beyond the hitherto purely cultural character of such events."[84] The federal government's view that *Nordische Tage* was purely cultural demonstrated the ongoing disconnect between Schleswig-Holstein and Bonn. It also highlighted how embedded economic or political outcomes were within cultural activities. President Heuss, who had been supportive of *Nordische Tage*, was no longer in office after 1959, succeeded by Heinrich Lübke. The SPD's overt support for *Nordische Tage* reported in the Lübeck Senate minutes, and the CDU's reticence to issue such a statement, could also explain the shift in the federal government's attitude toward the event, indicative of how politicized these cultural events always were. The next proposed *Nordische Tage* was pushed back, first from 1960 to 1961, to 1962, to 1963, to indefinitely suspended.[85]

Though *Nordische Tage* was never again held, there were of course other cultural and folk events in Lübeck and across Germany, but they didn't have the expansive ambition to essentially fix German-Scandinavian relations. By the 1960s, and in the wake of the Berlin Crisis and Berlin Wall, locally international relationships seemed more normalized, especially as the global community faced other, seemingly more pressing issues, such as anti-imperial conflicts, debates over nuclear power and weapons, and civil rights broadly defined. This isn't to say that Lübeck's issues were separate from any of these, but they certainly reframed the issues the city faced. The immediate postwar generation of politicians began to retire or die, including the venerable Dr. Klinsmann. Though the inner border continued to feature prominently in local and national debates, by the 1960s reunification seemed impossible. Economically, there were attempts to target specific sectors, such as the fishing industry and port in Lübeck.[86] This was less about protecting *German* resources, at least to locals; seafaring and fishing were hallmarks of Lübeck's industrial life dating back to the Hanseatic period, and it represented continuing survival and a way to remain relevant in an evolving technological and manufacturing climate.

In many ways, all three *Nordische Tage* were successful, especially the events from 1956. Its legacy was connected to the way Otto Passarge was remembered long after his retirement from politics, the festivals not only heralded as his idea following the war but the ongoing efforts to rebuild the city and integrate thousands of refugees.[87] The discussions about the problematic legacy of persistent Nordicism were important, even if they weren't interrogated fully enough. The networks established during the 1950s allowed for strengthening the physical connections across the Baltic, especially ferry lines, and Lübeck and Travemünde maintained their position as a doorway north. The community was not single-minded, but it had been reimagined over the course of a decade and incorporated into a modern nation-state.

NOTES

1. Julia E. Johnsen, "Preface," in *The Dilemma of Postwar Germany*, ed. Julia E. Johnsen, The Refence Shelf Vol. 20, No. 3 (New York: H.W. Wilson Company, 1948), n.p.
2. Michel de Certeau, *The Practice of Everyday Life*, 30.
3. *Denkschrift über das Ostgrenzgebiet der Bundesrepublik*, 4. HAL, 04.01 HA 1688: Ostgrenzgebiet.
4. Winston Churchill, "The Sinews of Peace," Westminster College, Fulton, MO, March 5, 1946. Accessed 1 February 2019, https://winstonchurchill.org/resources/speeches/1946–1963-elder-statesman/the-sinews-of-peace/. This speech is often referred to as the "Iron Curtain Speech," marking the intellectual beginnings of the Cold War.
5. James F. Byrnes, "United States Policy in Germany," in *The Dilemma of Postwar Germany*, ed. Julia E. Johnsen (New York: H.W. Wilson Co., 1948), 13–16. Byrnes gave this speech in Stuttgart on September 6, 1946, ostensibly to both quell fear in Germany that the United States would pursue the draconian Morgenthau Plan and put the Soviet Union on notice regarding its economic and increasingly political administration of its zone.
6. Alan Bullock, "The German Elections," *The Spectator*, 25 October 1946, 6.
7. George C. Marshall, "Marshall Plan" Speech, 5 June 1947, accessed February 1, 2019, http://www.oecd.org/general/themarshallplanspeechatharvarduniversity5june1947.htm.
8. Ibid.
9. Called by Sir Brian Robertson, Military Governor of the British Zone, the Zonenbeirat met over the course of several years, reflecting the political parties in the emerging Germany. See Annelies Dorendor, *Der Zonenbeirat der Britisch besetzten Zone: ein Rückblick auf seine Tätigkeit* (Göttingen: Schwartz, 1953).
10. This was also against the backdrop of failed Rhenish separatist movements, identified in Bullock's *Spectator* article highlighting the Rhineland People's Party.

These efforts ultimately failed, and Bullock expressed surprise at this development in the wake of the 1946 Berlin elections.

11. George C. Marshall, "Report on Big Four Parley," in *The Dilemma of Postwar Germany*, ed. Julia E. Johnsen (New York: H.W. Wilson Co., 1948), 256–257.

12. *Die große Not: Sammelbroschüre 1946/1947* (Meisenheim: Westkultur-Verlag, 1947), 4. University of Wisconsin Digital Collections, The History Collection. Accessed 11 March 2019. http://digital.library.wisc.edu/1711.dl/History.DieGrosseNot

13. *Auszug aus der Niederschrift über die Sitzung es Senats der Hansestadt Lübeck am Mittwoch, dem 24. September 1947.* HAL, 04.01 HA 1143: Planung einer "Lübecker-Woche" zum kulturellen und wirtschaftlichen Austauch mit dem Ausland.

14. As previous chapters have shown, there had been an explicitly Nazified *Nordische Woche* in Hamburg in 1938; this event was left out of discussions in the press of the history of the event and the reasons for staging such a wide-ranging festival.

15. *Auszug aus den Niederschrift über die Sitzung des Senats der Hansestadt Lübeck am Freitag, dem 9. Januar 1948.* HAL, 04.01 HA 1143. See also the memo from the Oberstadtdirektor to Lübeck Industrie- und Handelskammer and Handwerkskammer, 18 January 1948. HAL, 04.01 HA 1143.

16. Roger G. Miller, *To Save a City: The Berlin Airlift, 1948–1949* (College Station, TX: Texas A&M University Press, 2000), 12.

17. *Auftrag Luftbrücke: der Himmel über Berlin, 1948–1949* (Berlin: Nicolai, 1998). This book was a retrospective about a commemorative traveling exhibit regarding the collective memory and material history of the Berlin Airlift.

18. This not only included efforts to rebuild architecture and roads and retooling the city's drainage system, but also ongoing efforts to maintain and sustain the now-necessary Priwall ferry, which existed essentially as an island cut off by the zonal border with Mecklenburg and now was the only way to sustain refugees and citizens living there. Besprechungspunkte für die Aussprache zwischen Abgeordneten des Deutschen Bundestages und dem Senat, 1954. HAL, 04.01 HAL 1688, #46.

19. Letter from *Industrie- und Handelskammer zu Lübeck* to HQ Military Government KRO H. G. Sullivan, 14 July 1947. HAL, 04.01 HA 0154.

20. In the GDR, the border zone or *Sperrgebiet* [restricted zone] varied between 3 and 5 kilometers wide; once the inner border was sealed and increasingly patrolled and mechanized, special permits to live or work in the zone had to be obtained. In the FRG, this zone was more about pleas for aid, tax incentives, and monitoring checkpoint controls. There was some debate over who controlled the closure or maintenance of checkpoints; such debates were politicized and usually were spun to serve either German state's ideological positions.

21. *Denkschrift über das Ostgrenzgebiet der Bundesrepublik*, 3. HAL, 04.01 HA 1688: Ostgrenzgebiet.

22. Lübeck's commando was, over the course of several years, consolidated with *Bundesgrenzschutz West* in Kassel, leaving a smaller contingent to patrol Lübeck's boundaries. See telegram to Stadtpräsident Niendorf and Bürgermeister Passarge, 18 June 1951. HAL, 04.01 HA 0152: Bundesgrenzschutz.

23. Besprechungspunkte für die Aussprache zwischen Abgeordneten des Deutschen Bundestages und dem Senat, no date [c. 1954]. HAL, 04.01 HA 1688.

24. This included Hitler's decision in 1937 to strip the city of its independent-city status and briefly make it part of Hamburg's territory, the Greater Hamburg Act.

25. "Lübeck 10 Jahre Standort des Bündesgrenzschützes," *Lübecker Nachrichten*. 23 April 1961, 7. HAL, 04.01 HA 0153: Bundesgrenzschutz.

26. See for example Letter from EB Daniell to Otto Passarge, 24 July 1954. HAL, 04.01 HA 0154. This competition with Hamburg was especially bitter, in that Lübeck had consistently "been losing" resources and status to Hamburg during the twentieth century, compounded by Hitler's decision in 1937 to strip the city of its independent-city status and briefly make it part of Hamburg's territory.

27. Hans Schönherr, *Lübeck—Aufbau auf dem Chaos*, 47.

28. This is especially clear in a letter sent to Bundestag members by the Lübeck mayor, 20 January 1954, where he claimed "50% population increase compared to 1939," "long-term unemployment," and "a loss of Lübeck's hinterland." HAL, 04.01 HA 1688.

29. Auszug aus der Zeitung "Das Parlament": Das Förderungsprogramm für die Gebiete an der Sowjetzonengrenze. 15 July 1953. HAL, 04.01 HA 1688, #19.

30. Lutz Niethammer, "'Normalization' in the West: Traces of Memory Leading Back Into the 1950s," in *The Miracle Years: A Cultural History of West Germany, 1949–1968*, ed. Hanna Schissler (Princeton: Princeton University Press, 2001), 237, 238.

31. Hans Schönherr, *Lübeck—Aufbau auf dem Chaos*, 1. This theme permeated the book published by the major local paper, showing triumphs and challenges in the twenty years after the war.

32. "Von Lübeck bis Hof" *Lübecker Nachrichten*, June 20, 1952. 2.

33. "Keine Kredite mehr für Lübeck?" *Lübecker Freie Presse,* 6 April 1956.

34. "Die ersten 'Nordischen Wochen' in Lübeck," *Lübecker Nachrichten*, 10 June 1953. HAL, 04.01 HA 1151: Nordische Tage 1953-Zeitungsschnitte.

35. Memo from Innere Verwaltung Zentralamt to Finanzverwaltung-Kämmereiamt, 28 February 1953. HAL, 04.01 HA 1150: Nordische Tage 1953-Finanzangelegenheiten. In this memo, the occasion of *Nordische Tage* was connected to the establishment of the Tellesborg-Travemünde ferry, likely incorporated as the TT-Line in 1962 in Lübeck.

36. Schönherr, *Lübeck—Aufbau aus dem Chaos*, 50. Schönherr talked specifically about how Lübeck, with the closure of the checkpoint was cut off from its "natural hinterland" of Mecklenburg by the Soviet Union, fracturing historic relationships and preventing reunification.

37. "Nordisches Treffen in Lübeck," *Lübecker Nachrichten*, 15 November 1952. HAL, 04.01 HA 1151: Nordische Tage 1953-Zeitungsschnitte.

38. "'Nordische Tage' in Lübeck," *Lübecker Nachrichten*, 19 November 1952. HAL, 04.01 HA 1151. The paper reported that the event was explicitly to coincide with the opening of the Trelleborg-Travemünde ferry and "should serve the cultural exchange with the Nordic Countries."

39. “Lübeck als Tagungsort,” *Lübecker Nachrichten*, 7 April 1948. Clipping in HAL, 04.01 HA 1143.

40. Albrecht Zießler, “In Lübeck Willkommen,” *Lübecker Freie Presse*, 10 June 1953. HAL, 04.01 HA 1151.

41. Ibid.

42. See Philipp Gassert and Alan E. Steinweis, eds., *Coping with the Nazi Past: West German Debates on Nazism and Generational Conflict, 1955–1975* (New York: Berghahn Books, 2007) and Nicolas Berg, *The Holocaust and the West German Historians: Historical Interpretation and Autobiographical Memory,* George L. Mosse Series in Modern European Cultural and Intellectual History (Madison: University of Wisconsin Press, 2015).

43. Otto Passarge, *Lübeck Dankt*, May 1953. HAL, 04.01 HA 1148: Nordische Tage 1953: Durchführung.

44. See Livia Rothkirchen, *The Jews of Bohemia and Moravia: Facing the Holocaust,* Comprehensive History of the Holocaust (Lincoln: University of Nebraska Press, 2012).

45. Otto Passarge to Carl-Jacob Burckhardt, 10 January 1953. HAL, 04.01 HA 1148.

46. Ibid.

47. Carl-Jacob Burckhardt to Otto Passarge, 30 January 1953. HAL, 04. 01 HA 1148.

48. Carl-Jacob Burckhard to Otto Passarge, 26 March 1953. HAL, 04.01 HA 1148.

49. “Die Hansestadt Lübeck lädt ein,” *Lübecker Freie Presse,* 10 June 1953. HAL, 04.01 HA1151.

50. Back cover of Pyrotechnische Fabrik Hans Moog-H. Nicolaus. HAL, 04.01 HA 1149: Nordische Tage 1953-Gestaltung eines Feuerwerk in Travemünde.

51. Kritische Betrachtung zu den “Nordischen Tagen 1953,” 13 June 1953. HAL, 04.01 HA1148.

52. Ibid.

53. Memo from Armin Korn to Dr. Luise Klinsmann, 30 July 1953, 1. HAL, 04.01 HA 1148.

54. Series of memos from Passarge to SPD and others, 25 November 1953. HAL, 04.01 HA 1152: Nordische Tage 1954-Durchführung.

55. Letter to Kultusverwaltung from Herbert Müller-Fried, 3 June 1954. HAL, 04.01 HA 1152. Müller-Fried was active throughout the postwar period into the 1990s, designing well-known logos across Lübeck and participating in local cultural exhibitions, such as those mounted by the Overbeck-Gesellschaft, an artistic society meant to foster experimentation in the arts. See www.overbeck-gesellchaft.de.

56. The *Deutsche Auslandsgesellschaft*, roughly translated as the German Foreign Society, sought to (re)install and strengthen trade and cultural relationships between Germany (though more specifically Lübeck) and northern countries, particularly in Scandinavia. In many ways, this newest organization was simply more of the same for Kalkbrenner, who had been undertaking such efforts since the years following World War II. The organization was to be a more permanent operation that yearly (or even sporadic) events, such as *Nordische Woche* and *Nordische Tage*, echoed. At the same

time, however, Kalkbrenner and his contemporary Heinrich Jessen, who also led the *Deutsche Auslandsgesellschaft*, had been active in the *Nordische Gesellschaft* all through the Nazi years. Kalkbrenner's "honorary citizenship" was revoked by Lübeck in 2015 after decades of a fraught legacy. The *Deutsche Auslandsgesellschaft* still operates today, widening its mission to eastern Baltic states as well as Scandinavia after 1989. See https://www.deutausges.de/ueber-uns/geschichte.html for their own framing of their history.

57. Postcard to *Nordische Gesellschaft* from Dr. Hild, 28 September 1955. HAL, 04.01 HA 1158.

58. Letter from Otto Passarge to Carl-Jacob Burckhardt, 5 December 1953. HAL, 04.01 HA 1152.

59. Letter from Otto Passarge to Theodor Heuss, 5 December 1953. HAL, 04.01 HA 1152.

60. Eröffnungsfeier program, 1. HAL, 04.01 HA 1152.

61. The original organ of Marienkirche had been played, according to history by both Johann Sebastian Bach and the legendary organist Dietrich Buxtehude. The *Lübecker Totentanz* of the early modern period was recreated, notably in the 1926 parade for the 700th anniversary of the city of Lübeck, and had been connected to the fallout of the Black Death. In the postwar period, the *Totentanz* was explicitly connected to the RAF bombing, commemorated by Alfred Mahlau's stained glass windows constructed between 1954 and 1955.

62. Nordische Tage 1954 in Lübeck Program. HAL, 04.01 HA 1152.

63. Schönherr, *Lübeck Aufbau auf dem Chaos*, 54.

64. Paul Bromme, "Unser Gruss an den Norden," *Lübecker Freie Presse*, 2 June 1954, 1. HAL, 04.01 HA 1155: Nordische Tage 1954-Pressemitteilungen und Reden.

65. "Für Einheit in Freiheit!," *LFP*, 2 June 1954, 3.

66. Auszug aus der Niederschrift über die Sitzung des Senats der Hansestadt Lübeck, 15 February 1954. HAL, 04.01 HA 1688.

67. "Aufstellung der Ausgabegruppen 'Nordische Tage 1954' einschließlich der Gegenüberstellung zu N. T. 1953." HAL, 04.01 HA 1154: Nordische Tage 1954-Finanzangelegenheit.

68. Elizabeth Noelle and Erich Peter Neumann, eds, *The Germans: Public Opinion Polls, 1947–1966* (Bonn: Verlag für Demoskopie, 1967), 235. A survey of 2000 Germans in the FRG, including West Berlin but excluding the Saarland, revealed that in January of 1953 71 percent of the sample viewed Heuss positively ("liked him very much," "liked him," or "liked him quite well."). Additionally, in the same month, 41 percent sample believed that he exerted just the right amount of political influence; a further 21 percent felt he should exert more.

69. Kritische Betrachtung zu den "Nordischen Tagen 1954," 1. HAL, 04.01 HA 1154.

70. Ibid., 2.

71. "Nazi-Ironie," *Berlingske Tidende*, 11 June 1954. German translation and transcription of article in the file. HAL, 04.01 HA 1155.

72. "Bundesminister Kraft zu den Nordischen Tage," *Lübecker Nachrichten*, 2 June 1954. HAL, 04.01 HA 1155. Kraft's legacy was complicated, in that questions

arose about his enthusiasm for the SS, which he joined in 1933. His leadership of the GB/BHE—to which Ernst Timm also belonged in the early 1950s—situated him to the right of the CDU in politics. He later joined the CDU in 1956, a move also mirrored by Timm. For further reading regarding Kraft, his role and legacy in West Germany, and the GB/BHE, see Stephen L. Fisher, *The Minor Parties of the Federal Republic of Germany: Toward a Comparative Theory of Minor Parties* (The Hague: Martinus Nijhoff, 1974); Hans-Peter Schwarz, *Konrad Adenauer: A German Politician and Statesman in a Period of War, Revolution and Reconstruction. Vol. II: The Statesman, 1952–1967.* Trans. Louise Wilmot (Providence: Berghahn Books, 1997); Michael L. Hughes, "Just Desserts: Virtue, Agency, and Property in Mid-Twentieth Century Germany," in *Two Cultures of Rights: The Quest for Inclusion and Participation in Modern America and Germany*, ed. Manfred Berg and Martin H. Geyer (Washington, DC: German Historical Institute, 2002), 167–188; Ian Connor, *Refugees and Expellees in Post-War Germany* (Manchester: Manchester University Press, 2007), especially Chapter 5; Svea Regine Feldhoff, "Walter Kraft" in *Neues Lübecker Lebensläufe*, ed. Alken Bruns (Neumünster: Wachholz, 2009), 351–356; and Pascal Maeder, *Forging a New Heimat: Expellees in Post-War West Germany and Canada*, Transkulturelle Perspektiven 10 (Göttingen: V&R Unipress, 2011), especially chapter IV.

73. "Kultur darf kein Geld kosten," *Die Welt*, 2 July 1954. HAL, 04.01 HA 1155.

74. "Großer Frauenkongress in Lübeck: Ausstellung in acht Hallen am Holstentor—Nordische Gäste," *Lübecker Nachrichten*, 23 February 1955. HAL, 04.01 HA 1703—Verschiedene Ausstellungen und Museen. The exhibition was organized largely by the State Association of Schleswig-Holstein Housewives, part of the larger umbrella organization German Housewives Association led at the time by Fini Pfannes.

75. Memo to Nordwestdeutschen Rundfunk from Städt. Amtsrat, 2 May 1955. HAL, 04.01 HA 1152.

76. Jetziger Haushaltsplan, 4 January 1956. HAL, 04.01 HA 1166: Nordische Tage 1956-Finanzangelegenheiten.

77. Additionally, debates in the press, both in Germany and outside of it, warned of "Nazi echoes" in the 1956 *Nordische Tage*; columns such as "Deutsche Dummheiten" by "Dagens Nyheter" (likely a pen-name) on Sept. 10, 1956 got picked up by a variety of outlets. HAL, 04.01 HA 1172: Nordische Tage 1956-ausländische Presseberichte. Interestingly, the phrase "Nazi leaven" was used repeated by this author.

78. Nordische Tage 1956 Commemorative Booklet, 1. HAL, 04.01 HA 1167: Nordische Tage 1956-Programme, Fotos.

79. Luise Klinsmann, "Ansprache zur Eröffnung der Buchausstellung im Rahmen der Nordischen Tage 1956," 1. HAL, 04.01 HA 1168: Nordische Tage 1956-Reden und Wortprotokoll.

80. Nordische Tage 1956 Program. HAL, 04.01 HA 1156: Nordische Tage 1956-Programmgestaltung and 04.01 Hauptamt 1167.

81. Noridsche Tage 1956 Commemorative Booklet. HAL, 04.01 HA 1167. Hal Koch, who had been imprisoned by the Nazis during the war, was also associated

with the concept of "deliberative democracy," as a way to prevent a tyranny of the majority.

82. Theodor Heuss, "Der Sinn der Nordischen Tage," 2–3. HAL, 04.01 HA 1168.

83. Ibid., 4. It is worth noting that from May 1952 the third verse of the *Deutschlandlied* was the official anthem of West Germany; the first two verses were "official but unsung" until reunification in 1990 when only the third verse was made the official anthem.

84. Auszug aus der Niederschrift über die Sitzung des Senats der Hansestadt Lübeck, 9 November 1960. HAL 04.01 HA 1174.

85. See, for example, "1962 keine Nordische Tage," *Lübecker Morgen*, 8 November 1961 and "Die Nordsichen Tage erst im Jahr 1963," *Lübecker Nachrichten*, 8 November 1961. HAL, 04.01 HA 1174. Incidentally, the *LN* cited the need for elections in March 1962 as part of the reason for postponing the event until the following year.

86. Verwaltung für Handel, Schiffahrt, and Gewerbe to Bürgermeister Wartemann, 24 January 1968. HAL, 04.01 HA 1690.

87. Hans-Henning Freitag, "Otto Passarge," in *Neue Lübecker Lebensläufe*, ed. Alken Bruns (Neumünster: Wachholz, 2009), 482–484.

Conclusion

Identities over Time

Lübeck is today a thriving city, with numerous improvement projects ranging from an Ikea on the former Dänischburg site of Villeroy and Boch to continued historical preservation spearheaded by the Possehl Foundation to the 2015 opening of the European Hanseatic Museum. Since reunification, remnants of the inner border have been reduced to a small museum in Schlutup and a historic marker on the Priwall where the road to Mecklenburg had been blocked. The German Greenway, a bike path spanning the old border reinforcements from the Baltic to Hof has utilized twenty-first-century tourism to reimagine the contested spaces of the Cold War and keep it in collective memory. Pieces of the twentieth century litter Lübeck; it is likely visitors who see these remnants experience them differently than native inhabitants, but the echoes of the past can be louder than expected. The memorial on the Marktplatz to the four Lübeck Martyrs, *Abendsmusik* in *Marienkirche*, and subtle references to the city's connections north and east combine with a twenty-first-century cosmopolitanism in an age of refugee crises, political upheaval, a pandemic, climate crisis, and a resurgent mainstreaming right-wing. Renewed interest in and persistent identification with Hanseatic history presents a continuity in collective memory even as the population is diverse and international.

In the time I've spent in Lübeck, I find few references to a unique past that is painful, optimistic, and pessimistic all at once. The physical objects that survived the war—the wood-carved miniature *Innenstadt* now housed in the *Holstentor*, the melted bells of *Marienkirche*, and cobblestone streets—are mixed with new reminders of a past that is not all that distant: the *Stolpersteine* throughout the city, memorials to victims of Nazi aggression that have melted into collective memory, and festivals that have exclusive facets to them. It all is part of the past, but that past is consistently reevaluated in terms of meaning and memory in the present. The focus on a series of related festivals stretching from the end of World War I to the Cold War provides an opportunity to do a "close reading" of each festival through its remaining documentation while also considering changing background circumstances. Elements from *Nordische Woche* in 1921 helped seed an identity group that evolved alongside polarized politics and, then, one-party rule. That party mounted its own version of the previous festival, though it was removed from its original context and served a particular political purpose on the way to global war and genocide. Returning to the "beginning" (though 1921 of course wasn't really the beginning) for a "new" *Nordische Tage*, set against new social and cultural forces in the wake of catastrophic war was an interesting choice for city leaders, and they mobilized similar arguments as they had thirty years earlier. That warrants investigation, especially when we consider what had happened in those three decades.

The goal of this book has been to highlight how the everyday and mundane, like local parades and celebrations, currency and collectibles, and place and space reveal important insights about how identity can become framed and then weaponized over time. By thinking theoretically or conceptually about these objects and events, we can focus on the contexts that produced them in a variety of ways. It also allows us to think creatively about how time periods are connected to each other. In this case, analyzing how the Weimar Republic gave way to Nazism and then emerged as two Germanys after the war has revealed surprising elements of continuity and complexity. The ways that nationalism and local identity developed in Lübeck and in Germany more broadly were social and cultural, drawing on contemporary circumstances and public discussions that we likely recognize today. The primacy of economic concerns and discourse, for example, contextualizes the reasons for *Nordische Woche* and *Nordische Tage*, but there was more to it than simply trying to resuscitate markets. The trope that financial promises led to a general acceptance of Nazi ideology can't be ignored, but it's also not that simple. It can be easy to dismiss the power of economic arguments (especially if they are mobilized to foment disinformation), but they are indeed powerful.

Perhaps this is meant to be a warning, a reminder to people who look at the interwar and post–World War II periods as ancient history. Perhaps it's a model to apply when it's easy to detach local festival from broader trends, patterns, and meaning. More than anything, this book has sought to identify the things that lodge in people's minds about home while ominously allowing us—whomever that is—to pretend we don't know and can't see oppression and prejudice that doesn't directly impact us. We all participate in constructions of identity and what "we" are; who and what constitute the groups we belong to is something that requires reflection and critical analysis. That

Lübeckers returned in the 1950s to an event first proposed and mounted in the 1920s speaks to something about the ways in which Nordic identity and language are embedded in the imagined community of the city, who they are connected to, and what needs to be interrogated in the future.

When presented with economic and social challenges, municipal and business leaders tended to focus heavily on potential economic benefits first. This is not to say that cultural or social identity was not important or even a close second; rather, Lübeckers were pretty willing to construct and accept exclusionary norms and law in pursuit of economic ends, even security. This resonates, I would argue, in 2022 even as it did as a motivation for revolution in the eighteenth century; economic arguments are intensely cultural, drawing on social norms, societal fears, and structural inequities. This is especially clear in Lübeck following both world wars; in both periods, Lübeckers found themselves caught in economic, political, and cultural turmoil. Reminisces of the "Turnip Winter" in 1916–1917 extended beyond armistice, especially as economic instability deepened in the early 1920s. Similarly, official discussions regarding the supply of potatoes in November 1945—and how to avoid a "*Hungerkastrophe*"—show not only logistical concerns but also cultural resonance for Lübeckers with long memories.[1] While certainly not excusing individual Lübeckers' inaction toward or even enthusiastic endorsement of the persecution of Jews and others during the Nazi regime, it illustrates how Nazism consumed Germany, infecting every aspect of life it could in subtle as well as overt ways. The ongoing and evolving construction of in-groups was and is a constant process—who is an insider and why, as well as who remains *outside* the community—and that makes it an important element to analyze.

NOTE

1. Memo to Oberpräsidenten der Provinz Schleswig-Holstein from Oberbürgermeister of Kiel, 14 November 1945. Hansestadt Archiv Lübeck [HAL] 04.01 Hauptamt [HA] 0183: "Ergänzungen des Zentralamts zu den Monatsberichten über die 'Deutsche Moral.'"

Bibliography

DIGITAL AND MANUSCRIPT SOURCES

Altonaer Museum für Kultur und Kulturgeschichte
Archiv der Kulturgeschichte, Notgeld Collection
Of. 127, 128, 138
Archdiocese of Hamburg.
Lübeck Martyrer.
Canadian Military Headquarters Digital Collection
Historical Section, Report. 174.
Hansestadt Archiv Lübeck, Lübeck, Germany
1.2 Neues Senats-Akten 639, 1660, 2462, 2468, 2473
Handelskammer zu Lübeck 144, 145, 146, 275
04. 01 Hauptamt 0152, 0153, 0154, 0592, 0596, 0597, 1127, 1143, 1148, 1149, 1150, 1151, 1152, 1154, 1155, 1156, 1158, 1166, 1167, 1168, 1172, 1174, 1673, 1688, 1690, 1703
Nachrichtenamt 117, 283
NSA 05.02: Nordische Gesellschaft papers
Nordische Woche Collection
Polizeiamt 3769
Schul- und Kulturverwaltung 699
Hoover Institute, Stanford, CA
Deutsch Kongress-Zentrale collection, Nordische Woche 1938
Imperial War Museum
Royal Air Force Bombing Command, 1942–1945
Initiative Stolpersteine für Lübeck
Library of Congress Digital Collection
Enactments and Approved Papers of the Control Council and Coordinating Committee for Germany for the Year 1945, Vol. I.
Newberry Library, Chicago, IL

Ben Hecht Papers (Midwest MS Hecht)
Notgeld Collection
Stadtarchiv Kiel
Kiel 1921–1928 (6075)
Kieler Notgeld 1917–1954 collection (36065)
Nordische Messe (6898)
Struan Robertson, *A History of Jews in Hamburg*
The University Museum, Southern Illinois University Edwardsville, Edwardsville IL
Harrington Notgeld Collection
University of North Carolina-Wilmington
Ralph Brauer Papers
Friedrich Brauer Papers (MS 060)
University of Wisconsin Digital Collections
The History Collection

PRINTED PRIMARY SOURCES

Åbo Handelskammer. *Åbo-Turku Suomi-Finnland: Das Heft wurde von der Åbo Handelskammer für die Nordische Woche in Lübeck herausgegeben.* Åbo, Finland: Åbo Drucherei und Zeitungs Aktiengesellschaft, 1921.

Avenstrup, A. Eskil. *Der Norden Lacht: Humor des Nordens.* Berlin: Wilhelm Limpert-Verlag, 1938.

Baltzer, Johann, F. Bruns and H. Rahtgens, eds. *Die Bau- und Kunstdenkmäler der freien und Hansestadt Lübeck, Bd 4.* Lübeck: H. G. Rahtgens, 1928.

Clauß, Ludwig Ferdinand. *Die Nordische Seele.* Berlin: J. F. Lehmann, 1932.

Der Norden

Der Nordische Rundschau

Der Notgeld-Schein-Werfer: Organ für Alle Notgeld Angelegenheiten.

Der Notgeldmarkt Hannover.

Deutsch, Gotthard. *The Jewish Encyclopedia.* Vol. 8. New York: Funk and Wagnalls, 1904.

Domes, Fred J., editor. *Die Schicksalsgemeinschaft der Ostsee.* Berlin: Gerhard Stalling, Verlagsbuchhandlung/Nordischen Gesellschaft, 1935.

Dorendor, Annalies. *Der Zonenbereit der Britischen besetzten Zone: ein Rückblick auf seine Tätigkeit.* Göttingen: Schwartz, 1953.

Engelmann, Victor. *Einiges über Notgeld.* Kiel: Verlag von Victor Engelmann, 1921.

Funkenberg, Alexander. *Haus und Hof im Nordischen Raum.* Lübeck: C. Kabitzsch/ Nordische Gesellschaft, 1937.

Goebbels, Josef. *The Goebbels Diaries, 1939–1941.* Translated by Fred Taylor. New York: G. P. Putnam's Sons, 1983.

———. *The Goebbels Diaries, 1942–1943.* Translated by Louis P. Lochner. Garden City, NJ: Doubleday & Co., 1948.

Goldensohn, Leon. *The Nuremberg Interviews: An American Psychiatrist's Conversations with the Defendants and Witnesses.* Edited by Robert Gellately. New York: Alfred

A. Knopf, 2004.

Günther, Hans F. K. *Der Nordische Gedanke unter den Deutschen.* Munchen: J. F. Lehmann, 1925/1927.

———. *Rassenkunde des deutschen Volkes.* München: J. F. Lehmann-Verlag, 1922.

———. *The Racial Elements of European History.* London: Methuen & Co., 1927.

Joesten, Joachim. "The Nazis in Scandinavia." *Foreign Affairs.* Vol. 15, No. 4 (Jul. 1937): 720–728.

Johnsen, Julia E., ed. *The Dilemma of Postwar Germany.* New York: H.W. Wilson & Co., 1948.

Kaes, Anton, Martin Jay, and Edward Dimendberg, eds. *The Weimar Republic Sourcebook.* Berkeley: University of California Press, 1995.

Keller, Arnold, ed. *Das Notgeld: Zeitschrift für Notgeldkunde.* Munich: n.p., 1920–1922.

Kiss, George. "Political Geography into Geopolitics: Recent Trends in Germany." *Geographical Review.* Vol. 32, No. 4 (Oct. 1942): 632–645.

Kjellén, Rudolf. *Der Staat als Lebensform.* Leipzig: S. Hirzel, 1917.

Klinger, Werner. *Die Degenhardts.* Tobis Filmkunst, 1944.

Krüger, Alexander, ed. *Der historische Festzug anschließend der Festzug der Gewerbe und Innungen zur 700-Jahrfeier der Freien und Hansestadt Lübeck (6. Juni 1926).* Lübeck: Verlag Theodor Schubert, 1926.

Kruszewski, Charles. "International Affairs: Germany's *Lebensraum.*" *The American Political Science Review.* Vol. 34, No. 5 (Oct. 1940): 964–975.

Lübecker Volksbote.

Mahn, Heinz. *Festschrift zur Nordischen Woche in Lübeck, 1–11 September 1921.* Lübeck: H. G. Rahtgens Verlag, 1921.

Mann, Thomas. "Goethe und Tolstoi." *Deutsche Rundschau.* Band 190 (March 1922), 225–246.

———. *Goethe und Tolstoi.* Aachen: K. Speitzer, 1923.

Meyer, H., ed. *Nordische Messe in Kiel Messkatalog 1921.* Kiel: Nordische Messe in Kiel G.m.b.H, 1921.

Noakes, Jeremy and Geoffrey Pridham, eds. *Documents on Nazism, 1919–1945.* New York: Viking Press, 1975.

Noelle, Elizabeth and Erich Peter Neumann. *The Germans: Public Opinion Polls, 1947- 1966.* Verlag für Demoskopie, 1967.

Nordische Gesellschaft. *Führer durch die Nordische Woche in der Hansestadt Hamburg vom 15. bis 23. Oktober 1938.* Hamburg: Kontor der Nordischen Gesellschaft, 1938.

———. *Tag des Nordens.* Lübeck: H.G. Rahtgens, 1938. *Ostsee Rundschau*

Paul, Bengt, ed. *700-Jahrfeier der Reichsfreiheit Lübeck 3–6 Juni 1926, Programm-Buch und Katalog aller Ausstellungen.* Lübeck: Gebrüder Borchers G.m.b.H., 1926.

———. "Die Wirtschaft der nordischen Länder im Jahre 1924." *Das Jahr 1924 (Ostsee-Schriften, Heft* 2). Lübeck: Nordischer Verlag/Nordische Gesellschaft, 1925.

Pieth, Willy. *Lübish-nordische Ausstellung im oberen Chor der Katharinenkirche 1.-11. September.* Lübeck: Schmidt, 1921.

Rasse

Schönherr, Hans. *Lübeck-Aufbau aus dem Chaos: Die Hansestadt zwischen 1942 und 1962.* Lübeck: Lübecker Nachrichten, 1962.

Skowronnek, Karl. *Wie sammelt man Notgeld?* München: Verlag "Das Notgeld," n.d.

The Spectator.

Verein für Lübeckische Geschichte und Altertumskunde, ed. *Lübische Forschungen: Jahrhundertgabe des Vereins für Lübeckische Geschichte und Altertumskunde.* Lübeck: H. G. Rahtgens, 1921.

Volksspiel und Feier: Alphabetisches Suchbuch nebst Stoffsammlung für Brauch, Freizeit und Spiel. München, Hamburg, Berlin: Christian Kaiser Verlag; Hanseatische Verlagsanstalt; Theaterverlag Albert Langen/Georg Müller; 1936.

Wesergilde, ed. *Die Freie Hansestadt Bremen.* Bremen: Angelsachsenverlag, 1922.

SECONDARY BIBLIOGRAPHY

Abrams, Lynn. "From Control to Commercialization: the Triumph of Mass Entertainment in Germany 1900–1925?" *German History.* Vol. 8, No. 3 (2005): 278–293.

———. *Workers' Culture in Imperial Germany: Leisure and Recreation in the Rhineland and Westphalia.* London: Routledge, 1992.

Allen, William Sheridan. *The Nazi Seizure of Power: The Experience of a Single German Town, 1922–1945.* Brattleboro, VT: Echo Point Books, 1965, 1984, 2014.

Allport, Gordon W. *The Nature of Prejudice.* Cambridge, MA: Perseus Books, 1979.

Almgren, Birgitta, Jan Hecker-Stampehl, and Ernst Piper. "Alfred Rosenberg und die Nordische Gesellschaft: Der 'nordische Gedanke' in Theorie und Praxis." *NORDEUROPAforum.* Heft 2/2008, 7–51.

Aly, Götz. *Hitler's Beneficiaries: Plunder, Racial War, and the Nazi Welfare State.* London: Picador, 2007.

Anderson, Benedict. *Imagined Communities: Reflections on the Origins and Spread of Nationalism.* London: Verso, 1991.

Angrick, Andrej and Peter Klein. *Die "Endlösung" in Riga: Aubeutung und Vernichtung, 1941–1944.* Darmstadt: Wissenschaftliche Buchgesellschaft, 2006.

Applegate, Celia. *A Nation of Provincials: The German Idea of Heimat.* Berkeley: University of California Press, 1990.

Ault, Brian. "Joining the Nazi Party before 1930: Material Interests or Identity Politics?" *Social Science History.* Vol. 26, No. 2 (Summer 2002): 273–310.

Auslander, Leora. *Taste and Power: Furnishing Modern France.* Berkeley: University of California, 1998.

Baker, Patricia A. *The Archaeology of Medicine in the Greco-Roman World.* Cambridge: Cambridge University Press, 2013.

Bastek, Alexander. "Thomas Mann, Carl Georg Heise und die bildende Kunst in Lübeck." *Thomas Mann Jahrbuch* 26 (2013): 53–67.

Benedict, Susan, et al. "Children's 'Euthanasia' in Nazi Germany." *Journal of Pediatric Nursing.* Vol. 24, No. 6 (Dec. 2009): 506–516.

Berend, Ivan T. *History Derailed: Central and Eastern Europe in the Long Nineteenth Century.* Berkeley: University of California Press, 2003.

Berezin, Mabel. "The Festival State: Celebration and Community in Fascist Italy." *Journal of Modern European History.* Vol. 4, No. 1 (Mar. 2006): 60–74.

Berg, Manfred and Martin H. Geyer, eds. *Two Cultures of Rights: The Quest for Inclusion and Participation in Modern America and Germany.* Washington: German Historical Institute, 2002.

Berg, Nicolas. *The Holocaust and West German Historians: Historical Interpretation and Autobiographical Memory.* George L. Mosse Series in Modern European Cultural and Intelletual History. Madison: University of Wisconsin Press, 2015.

Bergen, Doris. *The Holocaust: A Concise History.* Lanham, MD: Rowman & Littlefield, 2009.

Bessel, Richard. *Germany 1945: From War to Peace.* New York: HarperPerennial, 2009.

Blackbourn, David. *History of Germany, 1780–1918: The Long Nineteenth Century.* Malden, MA: Blackwell Publishing, 2003.

Blickle, Peter. *Heimat: A Critical Theory of the German Idea of Homeland.* Rochester, NY: Camden House, 2004.

Boa, Elizabeth and Rachel Palfreyman. *Heimat: A German Dream: Regional Loyalties and National Identity in German Culture.* Oxford: Oxford University Press, 2000.

Bohn, Robert, ed. *Deutschland, Europa und der Norden: Ausgewählte Probleme der nord- europäischen Geschichte im 19. und 20. Jahrhundert.* Stuttgart: Franz Steiner Verlag, 1993.

Bonde, Hans. *Gymnastics and Politics: Niels Bukh and Male Aesthetics.* Copenhagen: Museum Tusculanum Press, 2006.

Bourdieu, Pierre. *Distinction: A Social Critique of the Judgement* [*sic*] *of Taste.* Trans. Richard Nice. Cambridge: Harvard University Press, 1984.

———. *Language and Symbolic Power.* Cambridge, MA: Harvard University Press, 1991.

———. "Social Space and Symbolic Space." In *Language and Symbolic Power.* Ed. J. Thompson. Cambridge: Harvard University Press, 1991. Reprinted in *Contemporary Sociological Theory.* Ed. Craig Calhoun et al. Oxford: Blackwell, 2002, 267–275.

Bramwell, Anna. *Blood and Soil: Richard Walther Darré and Hitler's "Green Party."* Abbotsbrook: Kensal Press, 1985.

Brandt, Nikolaj and Alec Due. "A Humourist in the Shadow of the Swastika." *Perspective.* SMK-National Gallery of Denmark. 2017. http://perspective.smk.dk/en/humourist-shadow-swastika.

Bresciani-Turroni, Costantino. *The Economics of Inflation: A Study of Currency Depreciation in Post-War Germany,* trans. Millicent E. Sayers. New York: Augustus M. Kelley, 1937, 1968.

Breuer, Stefan. *Die Nordische Bewegung in der Weimarer Republik.* Kultur- und Sozialwissenschaftliche Studien 18. Wiesbaden: Harrassowitz, 2018.

Browning, Christopher. *The Origins of the Final Solutions: The Evolution of Nazi Jewish Policy, September 1939-March 1942*. Comprehensive History of the Holocaust. Lincoln: University of Nebraska Press, 2007.

Brubaker, Rogers. *Citizenship and Nationhood in France and Germany*. Cambridge, MA: Harvard University Press, 1992.

Bruns, Alken, ed. *Lübecker Lebensläufe aus neun Jahrhunderten*. Neumünster: Wachholz, 1993.

———. *Neue Lübecker Lebensläufe*. Neumünster: Wachholz, 2009.

Burleigh, Michael and Wolfgang Wipperman. *The Racial State: Germany 1933–1945*. Cambridge: Cambridge University Press, 1991.

Buruma, Ian. *Year Zero: A History of 1945*. New York: Penguin, 2013.

Carrier, James. "Reconciling Commodities and Personal Relations in Industrial Society." *Theory and Society*. Vol. 19, No. 5 (Oct. 1990): 579–598.

Carrier, James and Josiah McHeyman. "Consumption and Political Economy." *The Journal of the Royal Anthropological Institute*. Vol. 3, No. 2 (June 1997): 355–373.

Chase, Jefferson. "Remembering the 'Forgotten Victims' of Nazi 'Euthanasia' Murders." *Deutsche Welle*. 26 January 2017.

Childers, Thomas. *The Nazi Voter: The Social Foundations of Fascism in Germany, 1919–1933*. Chapel Hill: University of North Carolina Press, 1983, 2010.

Confino, Alon. *The Nation as a Local Metaphor: Württemberg, Imperial Germany, and National Memory, 1871–1918*. Chapel Hill: University of North Carolina Press, 1997.

Connor, Ian. *Refugees and Expellees in Post-War Germany*. Manchester: Manchester University Press, 2007.

Dahl, Hans Fredrik. *Quisling: A Study in Treachery*. Translated by Anne-Marie Stanton-Ife. Cambridge: Cambridge University Press, 1999.

Daunton, Martin and Matthew Hilton, eds. *The Politics of Consumption: Material Culture and Citizenship in Europe and America*. London: Berg, 2001.

De Certeau, Michel. *The Practice of Everyday Life*. Translated by Steve Rendall. Berkley: University of California Press, 1984.

DeGrazia, Victoria and Ellen Furlough, eds. *The Sex of Things: Gender and Consumption in Historical Perspective*. Berkeley: University of California Press, 1996.

Dennis, David B. *Inhumanities: Nazi Interpretations of Western Culture*. Cambridge: Cambridge University Press, 2012.

Deutsche Technikmuseum Berlin, ed. *Auftrag Luftbrücke: Der Himmel über Berlin, 1948–1949*. Berlin: Nicolai, 1998.

Duranti, Marco. "Utopia, Nostalgia and World War at the 1939–40 New York World's Fair." *Journal of Contemporary History*. Vol. 41, No. 4 (Oct. 2006): 663–683.

Durkheim, Emile. *The Rules of Sociological Method and Selected Texts on Sociology and its Method*. Ed. Steven Lukes. Trans. W. D. Halls. New York: The Free Press, 1982.

Eksteins, Modris. *Rites of Spring: The Great War and Birth of the Modern Age*. New York: Houghten Mifflin & Company, 1989.

Eley, Geoff and Jan Palmowski, eds. *Citizenship and National Identity in Twentieth-Century Germany*. Stanford: Stanford University Press, 2008.

Enns, Abram. *Kunst und Bürgertum: Die Kontroversen Zwanziger Jahre in Lübeck*. Hamburg: Hans Christians Verlag, 1978.

Erzegailis, Andrew. *The Holocaust in Latvia, 1941–1944: The Missing Center*. Riga: Historical Institute of Riga, 1996.

Evans, Richard J. *The Third Reich in History and Memory*. Oxford: Oxford University Press, 2015.

Feldman, Gerald. *The Great Disorder: Politics, Economics, and Society in the German Inflation, 1914–1924*. New York: Oxford University Press, 1993.

Fergusson, Adam. *When Money Dies: The Nightmare of the Weimar Hyperinflation*. New York: PublicAffairs, 1975, 2010.

Field, Geoffry G. "Nordic Racism." *Journal of the History of Ideas*. Vol. 38, No. 3 (Jul.-Sep. 1977): 523–540.

Fischer, Stephen L. *The Minor Parties of the Federal Republic of Germany: Toward a Comparative Theory of Minor Parties*. The Hague: Martinus Nijhoff, 1974.

Frick, Carole Collier. *Dressing Renaissance Florence: Families, Fortunes, and Fine Clothing*. Baltimore: Johns Hopkins University Press, 2005.

Friedlander, Henry. *The Origins of Nazi Genocide: From Euthanasia to the Final Solution*. Chapel Hill: University of North Carolina Press, 1995.

Friedrich, Karin, ed. *Festive Culture in Germany and Europe from the Sixteenth to the Twentieth Century*. Lewiston, NY: The Edwin Mellon Press, 2000.

Fritz, Stephen. *Endkampf: Civilians, Soldiers, and the Death of the Third Reich*. Lexington: University of Kentucky, 2004.

Fritzsche, Peter. *Germans into Nazis*. Cambridge, MA: Harvard University Press, 1998.

———. *Life and Death in the Third Reich*. Cambridge, MA: Belknap Press, 2008.

Führer, Karl Christian. "Contradicting Nazi Propaganda: Classified Advertisements as Documents of Jewish Life in Nazi Germany, 1933–1938." *Media History*. Vol. 18, No. 1 (2012): 65–76.

Fulbrook, Mary and Martin Swales, eds. *Representing the German Nation: History and Identity in Twentieth-Century Germany*. Manchester: Manchester University Press, 2000.

Fussell, Paul. *The Great War and Modern Memory*. Oxford: Oxford University Press, 2000.

Gassert, Philipp and Alan E. Steinweis. *Coping with the Nazi Past: West German Debates on Nazism and Generational Conflict, 1955–1975*. New York: Berghahn Books, 2007.

Gay, Peter. *Weimar Culture: The Outsider as Insider*. New York: Harper & Row Publishers, 1968.

Gellately, Robert. *Stalin's Curse: Battling for Communism in War and Cold War*. Oxford: Oxford University Press, 2013.

Giddens, Anthony, ed. *Emile Durkheim: Selected Writings*. Cambridge: Cambridge University Press, 1972.

Glassie, Henry. *Material Culture*. Bloomington, IN: Indian University Press, 1999.

———. "Meaningful Things and Appropriate Myths: The Artifact's Place in American Studies." In *Material Life in America, 1600–1850*. Ed. Robert St. George. Boston: Northeastern University Press, 1977, 62–92.

Gordon, Peter and John P. McCormick, eds. *Weimar Thought: A Contested Legacy*. Princeton: Princeton University Press, 2013.

Graham, Frank D. *Exchange, Prices, and Production in Hyper-inflation: Germany, 1920-1923*. New York: Russell & Russell, 1930, reprinted 1967.

Graham-Dixon, Francis. *The Allied Occupation of Germany: The Refugee Crisis, Denazification, and the Path to Reconstruction*. London: I.B. Tauris, 2013.

Gray, Richard T. *About Face: German Physiognomic Thought from Lavater to Auschwitz*. Detroit: Wayne State University Press, 2004.

Grayling, A.C. *Among the Dead Cities: The History and Moral Legacy of the WWII Bombing of Civilians in Germany and Japan*. New York: Walker & Co./Bloomsbury, 2007.

Green, Abigail. *Fatherlands: State-Building and Nationhood in Nineteenth-Century Germany*. Cambridge: Cambridge University Press, 2001.

Greenhagh, Paul. *Ephemeral Vistas: A History of the* Expositions Universelles, *Great Exhibitions, and World's Fairs, 1851–1939*. Manchester: University of Manchester Press, 1988.

Grenville, J.A.S. *The Jews and Germans of Hamburg: The Destruction of a Civilization, 1790- 1945*. New York: Routledge, 2012.

Grill, Johnpeter Horst. "The Nazi Party's Rural Propaganda Before 1928." *Central European History*. Vol. 15, No. 2 (June 1982): 149–185.

Hagen, Joshua. "Parades, Public Space, and Propaganda: The Nazi Culture Parades of Munich." *Geografiska Annaler:Series B, Human Geography*. Vol. 90, No. 4 (2008): 349–367.

Hansen, Steffen Stummann. "The Wandering Congress: The Sixth Nordic Archaeological Meeting in Denmark 1937." *Acta Archaeologica*. Vol. 74, No. 1 (Oct. 2003): 293–305.

Hare, J. Laurence. *Excavating Nations: Archaeology, Museums, and the German-Danish Border*. Toronto: University of Toronto Press, 2015.

Hauptfleisch, Temple, et al., eds, *Festivalising!: Theatrical Events, Politics and Culture*. Amsterdam: Rodopi, 2007.

Hewitson, Mark. *Nationalism in Germany, 1848–1866: Revolutionary Nation*. New York: Palgrave MacMillan, 2010.

Hilberg, Raul. *Perpetrators, Victims, Bystanders: The Jewish Catastrophe, 1933–1945*. New York: HarperPerennial, 1993.

Hoerle, W. Scott. *Hans Friedrich Blunck: Poet and Nazi Collaborator, 1888–1961*. Studies in Modern German Literature, Vol. 97. Bern: Peter Lang, 2004.

Holtfrerich, Carl-Ludwig. *The German Inflation, 1914–1923: Causes and Effects in International Perspective*. New York: Walter de Gruyter, 1986.

Hutton, Christopher. *Race and the Third Reich: Linguistics, Racial Anthropology and Genetics in the Dialectic of Volk*. Cambridge: Polity Press, 2005.

Jacobsen, Hans-Adolf. *Nationalsozialistische Außenpolitik, 1933–1938*. Frankfurt am Main: Alfred Metzner Verlag, 1968.

Jarausch, Konrad. *After Hitler: Recivilizing Germans, 1945–1995*. Oxford: Oxford University Press, 2006.

Jarausch, Konrad H. and Michael Geyer. *Shattered Past: Reconstructing German Histories*. Princeton: Princeton University Press, 2003.

Johnson, Eric A. and Karl-Heinz Reuband. *What We Knew: Terror, Mass Murder, and Everyday Life in Nazi Germany. An Oral History*. New York: Basic Books, 2006.

Jones, Jill. "Eradicating Nazism from the British Zone of Germany: Early Policy and Practice." *German History*. Vol. 8, No. 2 (1990): 145–162.

Judt, Tony. *Postwar: A History of Europe since 1945*. New York: Penguin, 2005.

Kaes, Anton. *Shell Shock Cinema: Weimar Culture and the Wounds of War*. Princeton: Princeton University Press, 2009.

Kammen, Carol. *On Doing Local History*. Third Edition. Lanham, MD: Rowman & Littlefield, 2014.

Kaplan, Marion. *Between Dignity and Despair: Jewish Life in Nazi Germany*. Oxford: Oxford University Press, 1999.

Kershaw, Ian. *The End: Hitler's Germany, 1944–1945*. New York: Penguin, 2011.

———. *The Global Age: Europe 1950–2017*. New York: Penguin, 2018.

———. *The Nazi Dictatorship: Problems and Perspectives of Interpretation*. London: Bloomsbury, 2015.

———. *To Hell and Back: Europe 1914–1949*. New York: Penguin, 2016.

Knappet, Carl. *Thinking Through Material Culture: An Interdisciplinary Perspective*. Philadelphia: University of Pennsylvania Press, 2005.

Koelb, Clayton, ed. *Thomas Mann's "Goethe and Tolstoy:" Notes and Sources*. Trans. Alcyone Scott and Clayton Koelb. Tuscaloosa, AL: University of Alabama Press, 1984.

Krüger, Peter. "A Rainy Day, April 16, 1922: The Rapallo Treaty and the Cloudy Perspective for German Foreign Policy." In *Genoa, Rapallo, and European Reconstruction in 1922*. Ed. Carole Fink and Axel Frohn. Cambridge: Cambridge University Press, 2002.

Kühne, Thomas. *Belonging and Genocide: Hitler's Community, 1918–1945*. New Haven: Yale University Press, 2010.

LaCapra, Dominick. *Emile Durkheim: Sociologist and Philosopher*. Critical Studies in the Humanities, Revised Edition. Ithaca: Cornell University Press, 2001.

Laursen, Karsten and Jørgen Pedersen. *The German Inflation 1918–1923*. Amsterdam: North-Holland Publishing Company, 1964.

Lifton, Robert Jay. *The Nazi Doctors: Medical Killing and the Psychology of Genocide*. New York: Basic Books, 1986.

Lindemann, Mary and Jared Poley, eds. *Money in the German-Speaking Lands*. Spektrum. New York: Berghahn Books, 2017.

Lipp, Christine. *Frauen in der Lübecker Geschichte: Lübecker Frauenportraits im Laufe der Jahrhunderte-Katalog zur Wanderausstellung*. 2005.

Loeber, Matthias. *Völkische Bewegung zwsichen Weser und Ems: Richard von Hoff und die Nordische Gesellschaft in Bremen und Nordwestdeutschland*. Frankfurt am Main: Peter Lang, 2016.

Loock, Hans-Dietrich. *Quisling, Rosenberg, und Terboven: Zur Vorgeschichte und Geschichte der Nationalsozialistischen Revolution in Norwegen.* Stuttgart: Deutsche Verlags-Anstalt, 1970.

Lowe, Keith. *Savage Continent: Europe in the Aftermath of World War II.* New York: St. Martin's Press, 2012.

Lundbak, Henrik. *Danish Unity: A Political Party between Fascism and Resistance, 1936–1947.* Copenhagen: Museum Tusculanum Press/University of Copenhagen, 2003.

Lutzhöft, Hans-Jürgen. *Der Nordische Gedanke in Deutschland, 1920–1940.* Kieler Historischen Studien. Stuttgart: Ernst Klett Verlag, 1971.

MacMillian, Margaret. *Paris 1919: Six Months that Changed the World.* New York: Random House, 2001.

Maeder, Pascal. *Forging a New Heimat: Expellees in Post-War West Germany and Canada.* Transkulturelle Perspektiven 10. Göttingen: V&R Unipress, 2011.

Mariager, Rasmus. "'British Leadership Is Experienced, Cool-Headed and Predictable': Anglo-Danish Relations and the United States from the End of the Second World War to the Cold War." *Scandinavian Journal of History.* Vol. 37, No. 2 (May 2012): 246–260.

Markus, Hazel and Paula Nurius. "Possible Selves." *American Psychologist.* Vol. 41 (Sept. 1986): 954–969.

Matthäus, Jürgen and Mark Roseman. *Jewish Responses to Persecution, Vol. 1: 1933–1938.* Lanham, MD: Altamira Press, 2010.

Mazower, Mark. *Dark Continent: Europe's Twentieth Century.* New York: Vintage Books, 1998.

McDonough, Giles. *After the Reich: The Brutal History of the Allied Occupation.* Cambridge, MA: Basic Books, 2009.

McElligott, Anthony. *Contested City: Municipal Politics and the Rise of Nazism in Altona, 1917–1937.* Ann Arbor: University of Michigan Press, 1998.

Mehl, Manfred. *Deutsche Serienscheine von 1918–1922. Band 1 & 2.* Regenstauf: H. Gietl Verlag & Publikationsservice G.m.b.H, 1998.

Miller, Daniel. *Stuff.* Cambridge: Polity, 2010.

———, ed. *Why Some Things Matter.* Chicago: University of Chicago Press, 1998.

Miller, Roger G. *To Save a City: The Berlin Airlift, 1948–1949.* College Station, TX: Texas A&M University Press, 2000.

Mommsen, Hans. *The Rise and Fall of Weimar Democracy.* Chapel Hill: University of North Carolina Press, 1998.

Morris-Reich, Amos. "Race, Ideas, and Ideals: A Comparison of Frank Boas and Hans F. K. Günther." *History of European Ideas.* Vol. 32, No. 3 (Sept. 2006): 313–332.

Mosse, George L. *The Crisis of German Ideology: Intellectual Origins of the Third Reich.* Reprint Edition. New York: H. Fertig, 1964, 1998.

———. *Nazi Culture: Intellectual, Cultural, and Social Life in the Third Reich.* Madison: University of Wisconsin Press, 2003.

Nicosia, Francis and David Scrase, eds. *Jewish Life in Nazi Germany: Dilemmas and Responses.* Vermont Studies on Nazi Germany and the Holocaust. New York: Berghahn Books, 2010.

Nielsen, Niels Kayser. "The Cult of the Nordic Superman – Between the Pre-modern and Modern." *The Sports Historian*. Vol. 19, No. 1 (May 1999): 61–80.

Oberkrome, Willi. *"Deutsche Heimat:" Nationale Konzeption und regionale Praxis von Naturschutz, Landschaftsgestaltung und Kulturpolitik in Westfalen-Lippe und Thüringen(1900–1960)*. Paderborn: Verlag Ferdinand Schöningh GmbH, 2004.

Paret, Peter. *Art as History: Episodes in the Culture and Politics of Nineteenth-Century Germany*. Princeton, NJ: Princeton University Press, 1988.

———. *German Encounters with Modernism, 1840–1945*. Cambridge: Cambridge University Press, 2001.

Paul, Gerhard and Miriam Gillis-Carlebach. *Manora und Hakenkreuz: zur Geschichte der Juden in und aus Schleswig-Holstein, Lübeck, und Altona, 1918–1998*. Neumünster: Wachholz, 1998.

Paxton, Robert O. and Julie Hessler. *Europe in the Twentieth Century*. Boston: Wadsworth, 2005.

Pearce, Susan M. *Museums, Objects, and Collections: A Cultural Study*. Washington, DC: Smithsonian Institution Press, 1992.

Peer, Shanny. *France on Display: Peasants, Provincials, and Folklore in the 1937 Paris World's Fair*. Albany: State University of New York Press, 1998.

Peters, Olaf, Ruth Heftrig, and Barbara Schellewald, eds. *Kunstgeschichte im "Dritten Reich": Theorien, Methoden, Praktiken*. Berlin: Akademie Verlag GmbH, 2008.

Petropoulos, Jonathan. *Art as Politics in the Third Reich*. Chapel Hill: University of North Carolina Press, 1999.

Peukert, Detlev K. *Inside Nazi Germany: Conformity, Oppression, and Racism in Everyday Life*. New Haven: Yale University Press, 1989.

———. *The Weimar Republic: The Crisis of Classical Modernity*. New York: Hill and Wang, 1987.

Poliakov, Leon. *The Aryan Myth: A History of Racist and Nationalist Ideas in Europe*. Trans. Edmund Howard. New York: Basic Books, 1974.

Prown, Jules David. "Mind in Matter: An Introduction to Material Culture Theory and Method." *Winterthur Portfolio*. Vol. 17, No. 1 (Spring 1982): 1–19.

Reimer, Robert C., ed. *Cultural History through a National Socialist Lens: Essays on the Cinema of the Third Reich*. Rochester, NY: Camden House, 2000.

Retallack, James. *Saxony in German History: Culture, Society, and Politics, 1830–1933*. Ann Arbor: University of Michigan Press, 2000.

Rothkirchen, Livia. *The Jews of Bohemia and Moravia: Facing the Holocaust*. Comprehensive History of the Holocaust. Lincoln: University of Nebraska Press, 2012.

Ryback, Timothy W. *Hitler's Private Library: The Books That Shaped His Life*. New York: Knopf, 2008.

Rydell, Robert W. *All the World's a Fair: Visions of Empire at American International Expositions, 1876–1916*. Chicago: University of Chicago Press, 1987.

Sarti, Rafaella. *Europe at Home: Family and Material Culture, 1500–1800*. New Haven: Yale University Press, 2004.

Saunders, Nicholas J., ed. *Matters of Conflict: Material Culture, Memory, and the First World War*. London: Routledge, 2004.

Schissler, Hanna, ed. *The Miracle Years: A Cultural History of West Germany, 1949–1968*. Princeton: Princeton University Press, 2001.

Schulze, Hagen. *The Course of German Nationalism: From Frederick the Great to Bismarck, 1763–1867*. Cambridge: Cambridge University Press, 1991.

Schwartz, Hans-Peter. *Konrad Adenauer: A German Politician and Statesman in a Period of War, Revolution and Reconstruction. Vol. II: The Statesman, 1952-1967*. Translated by Louise Wilmot. Providence: Berghahn Books, 1997.

Serpe, Richard and Sheldon Stryker. "Commitment, Identity Salience, and Role Behavior." In *Personality, Roles, and Social Behavior*. Ed. William Ickes and Eric S. Knowles. New York: Springer-Verlag, 1982.

Shirer, William L. *The Challenge of Scandinavia: Norway, Sweden, Denmark, and Finland in our Time*. New York: Little, Brown, 1955.

———. *The Rise and Fall of the Third Reich: A History of Nazi Germany*. New York: Simon and Schuster, 1959, 1990.

Smith, Woodruff D. "Friedrich Ratzel and the Origins of *Lebensraum*." *German Studies Review*. Vol. 3, No. 1 (Feb. 1980): 51–68.

Sperber, Jonathan. "Festivals of National Unity in the German Revolution of 1848–1849." *Past and Present* 136 (Aug. 1992): 114–138.

Steigmann-Gall, Richard. *The Holy Reich: Nazi Conceptions of Christianity, 1919–1945*. Cambridge: Cambridge University Press, 2003.

Stocking, George W., ed. *Objects and Others: Museums and Material Culture*. History of Anthropology, Vol. 3. Madison: University of Wisconsin Press, 1988.

Taylor, Frederick. *Exorcising Hitler: The Occupation and Denazification of Germany*. New York: Bloomsbury, 2011.

Tenorio-Trillo, Mauricio. *Mexico at the World's Fairs: Crafting a Modern Nation*. Berkeley: University of California Press, 1996.

Thaler, Peter. "A Tale of Three Communities: National Identification in the German-Danish Borderlands." *Scandinavian Journal of History*. Vol. 32, No. 2 (June 2007): 141–166.

———. *Of Mind and Matter: The Duality of National Identity in the German-Danish Borderlands*. West Lafayette, IN: Purdue University Press, 2009.

Thomas, Nicholas. *Entangled Objects: Exchange, Material Culture, and Colonialism in the Pacific*. Cambridge, MA: Harvard University Press, 1991.

Tooze, J. Adam. *Wages of Destruction: The Making and Breaking of the Nazi Economy*. New York: Viking, 2007.

Tunander, Ola. "Swedish-German Geopolitics for a New Century: Rudolf Kjellen's 'The State as a Living Organism'." *Review of International Studies*. Vol. 27, No. 3 (July 2001): 451–463.

Van Ginderachter, Maarten and Marnix Beyen, eds. *Nationhood from Below: Europe in the Long Nineteenth Century*. London: Palgrave Macmillan, 2012.

Vinen, Richard. *A History in Fragments: Europe in the Twentieth Century*. London: Da Capo Press, 2002.

Ward, Janet. *Weimar Surfaces: Urban Visual Culture in 1920s Germany*. Berkeley: University of California Press, 2001.

Weitz, Eric D. *Weimar Germany: Promise and Tragedy*. Princeton: Princeton University Press, 2007.

Widdig, Bernd. *Culture and Inflation in Weimar Germany*. Berkeley: University of California Press, 2001.

Winter, Jay. *Sites of Memory, Sites of Mourning: The Great War in European Cultural History*. Cambridge: Cambridge University Press, 1998.

Winter, Jay, ed. *The Legacy of the Great War: Ninety Years On*. Columbia, MO: University of Missouri Press, 2009.

Wohl, Robert. *The Generation of 1914*. Cambridge, MA: Harvard University Press, 1979.

Zatlin, Jonathan R. *The Currency of Socialism: Money and Political Culture in East Germany*. Washington, DC: Cambridge University Press, 2007.

Index

About the Author

Erika L. Briesacher is an associate professor of history at Worcester State University in Worcester, MA. Her work on emergency money and identity construction is included in *Money in the German-Speaking Lands* (2017, pb 2022), and she currently has a second book project under contract, entitled *Make Me a Mask: Material/Culture of a Pandemic* analyzing the material culture of facemasks during the current Coronavirus pandemic.